ELECTRONIC
and
EXPERIMENTAL
music

ELECTRONIC and EXPERIMENTAL music

THOMAS B. HOLMES

CHARLES SCRIBNER'S SONS • NEW YORK

This book is dedicated to my wife, Laurie, and to my daughter, Shaina.

It is also dedicated to John Cage, without whose influence I would never have become interested in electronic and experimental music.

Copyright © 1985 Thomas B. Holmes

Library of Congress Cataloging in Publication Data
Holmes, Thomas B.
  Electronic and experimental music.
  Discography: p.
  Bibliography: p.
  Includes Index.
  1. Electronic music—History and criticism.
I. Title.
ML1380.H64 1985   789.9'9'09   84-26715
ISBN 0-684-18135-5
ISBN 0-684-18395-1 (pbk.)

1 3 5 7 9 11 13 15 17 19 V/C 20 18 16 14 12 10 8 6 4 2

Printed in the United States of America.

Contents

Preface

hile I was growing up during the 1950s and 60s in the suburbs of Detroit, Michigan, I somehow became interested in this thing called electronic music. To this day, I am not sure what prompted my interest in it, but there was an implied strangeness about it that appealed to my budding sense of nonconformity. By the age of ten, I had also become pretty good at driving my parents mad by pounding on the pump-organ at our summer cabin and by acting out science fiction stories using a battery-powered tape recorder that my father had given me. By the time I was in high school, I had begun my search for the true meaning of "avant-garde music" (a term I picked up while reading *High Fidelity* magazine). The only resources I possessed to learn about the music were liner notes on record covers. I began to collect recordings of anything that could be construed as being the least bit electronic or experimental, from the music of Edgard Varèse to the strange behavior of "psychedelic" rock bands. It was only through pure perseverance that I learned all I did about the field and finally became a part of the artistic world of electronic music as a composer, performer, and writer.

I have always thought that something I desperately needed back then was a kind of guidebook to the field of electronic and experimental music, a book that would explain where it all came from, how it worked, and who was doing what. Now I have written it, and I hope it will help everyone who is now in the state of confusion I was in for so long.

Electronic and Experimental Music is intended to accomplish a number of things. For the composer, it serves as a guide to the aesthetic ideas that have been used in electronic music, as well as a primer on the basic technical principles and approaches used to make the music. For the listener, it provides a history of the field, some background on the various aesthetic developments in experimental music and rock music, and a who's who of composers, groups, and their records. The book includes a listing of mail-order outlets for electronic-music recordings, a glossary of musical and technical terms, a bibliography of publications and books of note, and a listing of the manufacturers of equipment.

I hope that this book will serve as an enjoyable guide to the world of electronic music for the listener, the fan, the composer, the performer, and anyone else who is interested in the future of music.

Acknowledgments

S pecial thanks are due to a number of people who helped make the writing of this book a little easier: Michael Pietsch at Scribners for support and sound advice; William R. Maginnis, Jr., for his splendid accounts and photos of the San Francisco Tape Music Center; and John Cage, Robert Ashley, and David Behrman for conversation; Gordon Mumma, Pauline Oliveros, Ruth White, Lejaren Hiller, Ilhan Mimaroglu, Harald Bode, and Herbert Deutsch for invaluable information and contacts; Mimi Johnson and Barbara Mayfield of Performing Artservices for a sustained level of miracles and tolerance; Robert Eliason, Curator of Musical Instruments at the Henry Ford Museum; and the staff of the Holyoke Public Library in Holyoke, Massachusetts, who now know a little more about one of Holyoke's favorite sons, Thaddeus Cahill. Laurie Holmes took the photo of me.

1

ELECTRONIC MUSIC: WHAT IT IS, HOW IT IS MADE

a
DEFINITION

The term *electronic music* is somewhat misleading because it implies that it is a form of music different from, say, "classical music" or "rock music." This designation dates back to when the production of sounds through electronic means was quite novel, and the term stuck even after the field became quite diverse. During the 1950s and 1960s many composers began to use electronic devices to produce music, and it was during this era that the term *electronic music* began to acquire its avant-garde connotations—a flavor it retains to this day in the minds of most music enthusiasts.

To be fair, the term *electronic music* is really generic and should have no special meaning other than the fact that a certain class of devices is used to produce the sounds. In this sense, it would bear no greater implication than do the terms *piano music* or *guitar music*. Nevertheless, the term *electronic music* has come to suggest something different and new, implying futuristic concepts and a radical approach.

TYPES OF ELECTRONIC MUSIC

In speaking of types of electronic music, I refer to the methods used to create sounds, not to the form of the music itself (such as pop, classical, rock, experimental, or jazz). We will examine forms of music later; let us begin with a closer look at the three broad types of electronic music: purely electronic music, electroacoustic music, and tape composition.

Purely Electronic Music

Purely electronic music is that made up only of sounds created through electrical synthesis, without the use of traditional instruments or of sounds found in nature. Sound is produced by air-pressure waves, which cause the eardrum to vibrate. These vibrations are converted by auditory nerves into impulses that the brain recognizes as sounds. If the wave vibrates in a regular pattern, then it is perceived as a pitched sound, such as those used in music; if the wave does not vibrate in a regular pattern, then it is perceived as unpitched sound or noise. Purely electronic music is created through the synthesis of sound waves.

Purely electronic music can be produced through either analog or digital synthesis. The difference between the two forms merely lies in the way electricity is controlled. In analog synthesis, composers work with continuous electrical current that represents analogous auditory sound waves. The sound begins as an electric current (alternating current, or AC). The vibrating pattern of the current can be controlled by the composer to create regular or irregular patterns of current. This current is then fed to a loudspeaker system, which converts the electrical oscillations into air-pressure waves that can be detected by the ear. The resulting sound waves vibrate at the same rate as the electrical waves produced by the synthesizer. The vibrations of the electric current are controlled through triggering devices like rotating dials and piano-style keyboards.

Instead of working directly with the control of continuous electric current, a digital-computer synthesizer represents sound waves as binary information, coded into a series of "on" and "off" electrical pulses. This bit-stream represents sounds much the same way a computer can be used to represent numbers or letters of the alphabet. There are codes used by the computer to represent different pitches of sound. These sounds can be triggered by using a computer keyboard or a specially adapted piano-style keyboard. In order to make the sound patterns audible, the computer must convert the codes into an analog form of electrical current that can be used to operate a loudspeaker. This is done through what is called a digital-to-analog converter. Once the digital codes are converted into continuous electric current and fed to a speaker system, they sound the same as sounds produced through conventional analog means. Digital synthesis provides distinct advantages over analog systems because a greater variety of waveforms can be invented by the composer, and they can be recorded and manipulated in ways that are more complex than previously available on analog systems.

The music synthesizer is a device designed to generate purely electronic sounds by analog or digital means. Until the recent availability of computer processors for music systems, all synthesizers were analog in nature. The term *synthesizer* refers to the process of constructing sounds using electronic, or synthetic, means.

Digital music is naturally associated with computers. There are three general approaches that can be taken. First, the computer can be used to generate sounds directly. In this case, after a composer has entered the desired sequence of numeric codes, the digital output is converted to an analog electric current (through a digital-to-analog converter) that is connected to amplifiers and loudspeakers. This early form of computer music was first performed in the 1950s on large central computers that were normally designed for other data-processing tasks. We have recently seen the development of computer systems designed specifically for music, many of them affordable to the home user. The second use of computers is to trigger audio output from analog synthesizers. In this case, the computer provides what the synthesizer does not have: memory to store specific program instructions in order to repeat given passages and supplement real-time performance. Finally, just as digital output can be converted into analog waveforms for audio reproduction, sounds in an analog form can be converted to digital patterns for further processing and manipulation. Such input to a computer might include sounds on magnetic tape or even real-time, natural sounds fed through a microphone.

Electroacoustic Music

Electroacoustic music is any that uses electronics to amplify or alter natural or ambient sounds. "Natural sounds" include such things as environmental noise, the human voice, mechanical sounds, and the sounds of acoustic musical instruments. Since the entire spectrum of worldly sounds comprises the source material for such music, many artists have used this approach in many different ways. The term *electroacoustic* is most commonly associated with music that is oriented toward live performance or at least with music that is created without an abundance of postproduction editing and mixing. Often it is based on the amplification of small sounds, sounds that, when made louder and mixed with others, exhibit highly unusual qualities and textures. The sounds can also be modified or processed using standard electronic effects to enhance the result. This form of electroacoustic music is very popular with modern composers and has been used with great effect to amplify and modify such sounds as alpha brain waves, voices, machines, traffic noise, subways, crowds, emanations from the stratosphere, and other available sources that could be perceived as interesting.

Another branch of electroacoustic music uses the sounds of traditional music instruments as source material. The acoustic sound of an instrument is either amplified in a special way and mixed with other audio effects, or the sound is piped into an electronic device that modifies and alters the original sound. In its simplest form, this involves devices like electric pianos and guitars. The experimental music composer uses this approach to create new sound textures through the altering of the sounds of a familiar instrument. The piano, for example, exhibits some completely unexpected sound qualities when the wires are scraped with a microphone or the resonating of the sounding board is amplified to create a thunderous drone. By adding some filtering of the frequencies, a little reverberation, or some modulation of the incoming signal, a composer can completely transform such material.

Tape Composition

The third type of electronic music, tape composition, really incorporates elements of the first two. The sources of sound used in tape composition are the same as those of purely electronic and

electroacoustic music. Tape composition, though, is a postper-
formance activity in which sounds that have been recorded are
sculpted and edited into a final form that fulfills the desires of the
composer.

In formal tape composition, sounds are collected on tape
from whatever sources the composer chooses. Then, back in the
studio with razor blade and splicing tape in hand, the composer
organizes and mixes the tapes, using all of the resources of the
studio to enhance and further modify the sounds. This method of
composition can be likened to the process of making a movie, in
which location shots are taken, brought back to the studio, and
then edited into the desired sequence. During the editing and
postproduction process, the effect of the film will be heightened
through specific shot selection, pacing the duration of the takes,
and the cumulative effects of montage—the meaningful sequencing
of given shots to elicit a specific idea, mood, or feeling. The postproduction process of moviemaking may also involve the addition
of special effects to the location shots, such as dissolves, super-
impositions, and special film-processing techniques like negative
or sepia-tone imagery.

In tape composition the "location shots" are the sounds that
have been recorded ahead of time. Tape editing also involves the
selection of the desired sounds from the recorded body of material
and the creation of a specific sound sequence or montage. Special
effects are produced by electronic modulation; filtering; the mixing
and superimposing of sounds; or tape manipulation, such as varying the tape speed to raise or lower the pitch or adjust the duration
of a sequence, using feedback as a sound source, playing sounds
in reverse, creating repeating loops of tape, adding echo effects,
rerecording source material for additional use, multiple-tracking
(sound on sound, sound with sound), mixing the same sound source
over multiple tracks, tape delays, manipulation of the way in which
a sound begins and ends by the use of splicing techniques, and
simple volume control during rerecording and mixing.

When the magnetic tape recorder first became available during the late 1940s, several French technicians and composers, headed
by Pierre Schaeffer, were the first to dabble in tape composition
as an abstract form of composition. They called their work *musique
concrète* ("concrete music"), a term that has been used in various
ways ever since. In its purest state, musique concrète is music that
is composed using classic tape-manipulation techniques, such as
those just described. Originally it was highly structured and controlled, and maintained an air of classical composition and form
that would evoke specific responses from the listener. As a classic

studio art, musique concrète was limited by the number of aural tricks and effects in its bag, and after a time it simply became old hat. Today, tape composition techniques are as vital and important as they ever were, but they are used with more subtlety and with other resources of the studio, including real-time performance instruments.

Two

PRINCIPLES
of
ELECTRONIC
MUSIC

It is nearly impossible to discuss electronic music without

some understanding of how it is created. It is an art that

effectively marries technology and human imagination.

While the goal of designers is to devise electronic musical

instruments that require no prior technical expertise to

operate, the fact remains that most systems require some

understanding on the part of the user in order to make them work. In this section, I will discuss a few technical terms and processes in order to make it easier for the reader to understand the discussions of electronic music in the rest of the book.

THE COMPONENTS OF SOUND

The science of musical acoustics developed during the latter half of the nineteenth century in tandem with general discoveries in the field of electricity. Hermann von Helmholtz was largely responsible for this work; in 1862 he published his landmark paper "Sensations of Tone." In this work, Helmholtz demonstrated that musical sound could be analyzed according to a few basic physiological principles. Using combinations of tuning forks to illustrate his point, he showed that the quality (or timbre) of a tone was reliant on the intensity, order, and number of harmonics (overt ones and partials) present in the note. A single musical note was not so simple after all; Helmholtz showed that it actually consists of a base, or fundamental, tone accompanied by related vibrations (harmonics) above the pitch of the fundamental, which create timbre, or tone color. Timbre is what makes the sound of a violin distinguishable from the sound of a piano, even though both instruments might be playing the same note. Every instrument exhibits its own unique mixture of harmonics. This theory suggested that sound could be analyzed by its component parts.

John Cage was the first composer to dramatize the relationship between the physics of sound and the creation of music. In 1937, while giving a talk to an arts society in Seattle, he clearly stated that music could be defined through an understanding and manipulation of four basic functions: the timbre, frequency, amplitude, and duration of sounds. In the 1950s he added one more function to the list—the "morphology" or envelope of the sound, otherwise known as the attack and decay characteristics of a sound, or "how the sound begins, goes on, and dies away." It was by no accident that when Cage first proposed these ideas in 1937, he also related them directly to the potentials of using electronic musical devices to broaden our sound spectrum and create a new kind of music. The special nature of "electrical instruments" was that they could provide total control over the principal components of sound. In perhaps his most prophetic statement, Cage said in 1937, "I believe that the use of noise to make music will continue and increase until we reach a music produced through the aid of electrical instruments which will make available for musical purposes any and all sounds that can be heard."

Cage was by no means working in aesthetic isolation. He had the benefit of knowing and working with other new-music prophets like Edgard Varèse, Henry Cowell, Charles Ives, and Arnold Schoenberg. But in analyzing sound according to the five basic parameters—timbre, frequency, duration, amplitude, and envelope—Cage defined the common denominators by which all sound can be described. He also took a controversial step in applying these principles to an aesthetic understanding and appreciation of music; he claimed that since all sounds are composed of the same primary parts and since music is sound, then it must follow that all sounds can be defined as being musical. (We will explore this issue later.)

Following is a brief explanation of the components of sound as defined by Cage.

Frequency   Frequency is the pitch of a sound. In a more scientific sense, it is the number of vibrations per second that, when in the audible range, are detected as a certain pitch. In electronic music, this pitch becomes audible as an expression of the alternating electrical current that is used to vibrate the cone of a loudspeaker at a certain rate per second.

Amplitude   Amplitude is the loudness of a sound. In electronic music, loudness or volume is determined and controlled through the application of AC voltage. Amplitude is expressed through a loudspeaker and is the function of how far the speaker cone is moved back and forth from its neutral position. This varies from frequency, which determines how fast the speaker cone vibrates, but not how powerfully it does so.

Timbre   The nature or quality of a sound, sometimes known as tone color, is its timbre. All sound waves are complex and contain more than just one simple frequency or fundamental tone. These additional wave structures are called such things as partials, harmonics, and transients. If one pitch, or fundamental, predominates, then the sound can be related to a note on the musical scale. When there is more competition for dominance or there are very complex sets of overtones present, a sound may take on highly dense and unusual characteristics. Timbre is what distinguishes the sounds of different musical instruments playing the same note. It is a function that can be controlled or shaped by the electronic-music composer.

Duration   The length of time that a sound is audible is its duration. An acoustic instrument that is played through the physical action of mechanical devices—the hammers of a piano, for example—has inherent limitations in terms of duration. Electronic instruments introduce the ability to sustain a sound indefinitely, making duration a key element in composition. Duration is closely allied with the principles of the sound envelope.

Envelope   The attack and decay characteristics of a sound—the way it changes as it begins and ends—make up its envelope. This is actually a function of amplitude. Attack refers to the time it takes for a sound to end after it reaches maximum loudness. In electronic music, the envelope of a sound wave can be systematically controlled, a fact that allows the composer to use attack and decay characteristics in shaping the character of a sound.

WAVEFORMS

Sound waves can be represented graphically according to their varying frequency and amplitude functions. Sound waves have two basic characteristics, pitch and loudness. In electronic music, pitch is referred to as frequency and is defined by the number of vibrations that occur each second (also known as hertz, or Hz). The loudness of a sound is referred to as the amplitude of the wave and, in a diagram of a wave, is represented by the height of the wave. While most of the sounds we hear in electronic music are combinations of multiple waves or are specially treated for added tone color, it is possible to catalog a few basic waveforms, or waveshapes, for starting purposes. Electronic music synthesizers often come with audio oscillators (a sound-producing device that will be described in the next chapter) capable of generating any one of these waves in an approximately pure form.

Sine wave   The sine is the simplest type of wave. Theoretically, it should contain no harmonics or overtones. Although some liken the sound of a sine wave to that of a flute, even the flute has more body and depth than that of a pure sine tone. The sine is a thin, precise tone, similar to a whistle.

Triangle wave   A triangle wave is a fundamental sine-type wave but with a number of harmonics added. The sound is somewhat like that of a sine wave, but with more body and depth and a more hollow sound, like that of a flute, trumpet, or musical saw.

BASIC AUDIO WAVEFORMS

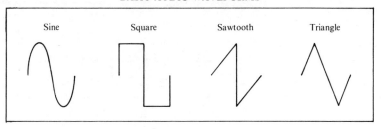

Sine   Square   Sawtooth   Triangle

Sawtooth wave   The sawtooth is more complex than the triangle wave and contains twice as many harmonics as a simple sine wave. This wave has a very full sound, much like that of a reed instrument such as a saxophone.

Pulse wave   The pulse wave is a sharp, angular wave exhibiting the same number of overtones as a triangle wave but the grittiness and reedy feel of a sawtooth. Graphically, the wave jumps instantly from the lowest point of its waveshape to the highest, the resulting diagram having no angles or curves. Because of this visual depiction, the pulse is often called a square or rectangular wave. A pulse wave has a sound that is somewhat like the combined sounds of a flute and an oboe.

All of the waveforms just described have predictable structures that exhibit strict amplitude relationships between the harmonics and their fundamentals. The result is a set of harmonious building blocks that offer the composer a controllable means to create music from electrical signals.

Another basic source of electronic sound, one that does not exhibit the structural rigidness of sine, triangle, sawtooth, or pulse waves, is called white noise. In the simplest sense, white noise is to those four basic waveforms what the color gray is to the primary colors: it is a combination of all of them, with no particular element dominating the mix. White noise occurs when all frequency and amplitude characteristics of a sound occur at random within a wide audio spectrum. In other words, it is a continuous dense hiss. Author and synthesist Allen Strange defines white noise more precisely as containing all audible frequencies between 18 Hz and 22,000 Hz. A somewhat refined form of white noise is called pink noise, which Strange defines as containing all frequencies between 18 Hz and 1,000 Hz. It can be filtered and refined to sound like such things as the wind or the ocean. It is a rich source of background sound and texture for the composer of electronic music.

Three

ELEMENTARY TECHNIQUES for MAKING ELECTRONIC MUSIC

Now that we have a basic understanding of the primary

components of sound, I would like to introduce a few basic

principles and terms used in the production of electronic

music. These terms are generally associated with the kinds

of analog synthesizers that have been in use since the mid-

1960s, and they should be useful in understanding some

of the terminology found in the music of today.

VOLTAGE CONTROL

Robert Moog was the first synthesizer designer to popularize the technique of voltage control in analog electronic musical instruments. Prior to 1964, when he first demonstrated his equipment, the sound of a synthesizer was controlled directly through the manual adjustment of dials that would affect the AC output of a device. This method was difficult to control because each separate component of a system, from the multiple oscillators to filters and other special devices, required precise manual adjustments to duplicate any given effect. In a voltage-controlled device, a small amount of current is applied to the control input of a given component to modify the output signal. This voltage signal is preset, precise, and quick, and can be activated by such easy-to-use voltage-control components as the synthesizer keyboard, thus making the analog synthesizer much easier to control. What the keyboard is actually doing is sending a voltage signal of a particular amount to the sound-generating oscillator of the synthesizer and telling it to produce a note of a certain pitch. The modern analog synthesizer is designed as a modular device with self-contained components to generate, modify, mix, and present sounds. By making each of these components voltage-controlled, Robert Moog was one of the people who made systems that were easier to play and manipulate.

VOLTAGE-CONTROLLED OSCILLATORS

The primary component of an analog synthesizer is an audio oscillator, a device that electrically creates a sound signal. It simply generates an alternating current in the frequency range that is audible to the human ear, from approximately 20 Hz to 20,000 Hz. This alternating current is used to drive the cone of a loudspeaker and create vibrations in the air of a given frequency or pitch. Some oscillators may actually reach frequencies above and below hearing range, say, from 1 Hz to 22,000 Hz. These extended ranges are used to expand the control voltages that are available to change one wave when combining it with another as a control input.

Oscillators used in analog synthesizers are voltage-controlled, meaning that the frequency (or pitch) of the unit is determined by the variable voltage, which affects the alternating current of the device. Modern synthesizer oscillators usually provide a selectable range of waveforms for use by the composer, generally including the four basic types described earlier—sine, triangle, sawtooth, and pulse. Voltage-controlled oscillators, or VCOs, may be tuned or manipulated manually through the use of a voltage dial or automatically through the use of a voltage-control device.

VOLTAGE-CONTROL DEVICES

In addition to the number and range of oscillators available on a synthesizer, a primary design feature is the type of voltage-control devices available. Voltage-control devices use DC voltage signals to control other electrical components of the instrument. They can also be used to manipulate the output of a voltage-controlled amplifier (VCA) or filter bank.

Voltage-control devices are perhaps the most important design feature to examine when evaluating a synthesizer. These devices are the means through which the player can play the instrument. A system is usually judged by such things as the range and action of the keyboard and the availability of other special controls for activating sound—all of them voltage-control devices.

Common sources of voltage control for a synthesizer are described below.

Keyboard   The keyboard connected to a synthesizer is actually a device that selects a given voltage for the control of other synthesizer components. Each key represents a different amount of voltage. Some synthesizers allow the player to adjust the pitch range of the keyboard by raising or lowering the voltage range of the device. Keyboards are typically used to drive the sound-generating oscillators of the instrument, and in some instruments the keyboard can also be used to trigger activity in the VCA and filters. Another common feature of keyboards is a separate control—usually in the form of a rotary dial—for "bending" notes (increasing or decreasing slightly their pitch) that are being played by the keys.

Synthesizer keyboards can also be made pressure-sensitive to the touch in order to duplicate the feel of actual piano keyboard action. This innovation greatly improves the expressiveness of the keyboard when used by a piano-trained performer.

The earliest voltage-controlled synthesizers could only play one note at a time and so were called monophonic synthesizers. These are still available, although duophonic (two notes) and polyphonic (three or more notes) keyboards predominate in today's market.

Ribbon controller   A ribbon controller is a monophonic device for the linear control of voltage. It is used by sliding a finger up and down a slender metallic ribbon to cause changes in pitch. The device is typically used to create glissando and wavering effects with unbroken chains of rising or falling notes.

Sequencer   A sequencer produces a repeated sequence of DC control voltages that are fed into a VCO. The sequencer may receive its control voltage pattern from a keyboard, ribbon controller, or other voltage-control source. The sequencer is typically used to provide steady rhythms and harmonic lines that can be repeated while other sounds are generated simultaneously. This technique is often used in rock music and is strongly illustrated in the steady, trancelike rhythms that characterize the music of such groups as Tangerine Dream and Kraftwerk.

A variety of other devices are used to control voltages in a synthesizer. Among these are joysticks, foot pedals, dials, push buttons, and touch-sensitive panels. All of these have in common the end result of providing better control over the creation and modification of sound in a synthesizer.

ADDITIVE SYNTHESIS AND MIXING

When playing a synthesizer, one may choose to use the preset sounds that the instrument is designed to provide automatically, or one may begin to create new types of sounds through the mixing and modification of the basic sounds that are provided. The remarkable versatility of a synthesizer becomes apparent when one begins to invent—or synthesize—unique sounds. The word *synthesis* refers to the ability to use the fundamental building blocks of sound that are provided by an instrument to create new sounds.

The simplest form of sound synthesis is the combination of two or more sine waves into a more complex waveform. This process is called additive synthesis and can be used to create colorful sounds by building up layers of many individual sounds. Each wave source can be treated and varied independently. The result is often difficult to reproduce later and is largely determined through a trial-and-error process.

Prior to the development of modern synthesizers, most electronic-music composers used additive synthesis as one of their primary techniques. They would simply line up a bank of individual audio oscillators and play them at the same time or mix the sounds on tape. The results were some of the most haunting resonances committed to tape during the 1950s.

SUBTRACTIVE SYNTHESIS OR FILTERING

Just as waveforms can be constructed by the addition of one form to another, so too can waveforms be altered through the systematic elimination of certain parts of the sound (overtones, and fundamental frequency). This practice is commonly achieved through sound filtering. This general approach to sound modification is called subtractive synthesis.

A familiar example of a filter is the sound "equalizer" available for stereo systems. This device permits the listener to filter out various bands of frequency, usually for the purpose of eliminating noise in the high ranges and adjusting bass and treble to more closely match the acoustic requirements of a given space. In a more novel way, equalizers are sometimes used to filter out the voice of a performer on a record in order to leave only the instruments playing.

Synthesizers and electronic-music studios generally exercise much greater control and manipulation of filtering than does the equalizer. Various types of filtering are available, and the filter bank of a synthesizer can actually be voltage-controlled so that a keyboard, sequencer, or other trigger device can be used to automatically generate results. Common types of filters are described below.

Band-pass filter   A band-pass filter allows only those sounds between specified high- and low-frequency cutoff points to be heard.

Band-reject filter   A band-reject filter only allows those sounds above or below specified high- and low-frequency cutoff points to be heard.

Low-pass filter   A low-pass filter only permits frequencies below a specified cutoff point to be passed.

High-pass filter   A high-pass filter only permits frequencies above a specified cutoff point to be passed.

Filters may be manually controlled and adjusted, or controlled through a device like a keyboard if they incorporate a control-input port to accept the voltage-control signals.

MODULATION OF WAVEFORMS

One of the most familiar, but least understood, terms in electronic music, is *modulation*. In a generic sense, the word seems to imply any method that can be used to electronically alter a given wave-form or sound. If used that way, the term can describe every technique discussed in this chapter. Technically, *modulation* refers to specific techniques available to the composer, which fall within two basic categories, amplitude modulation (AM) and frequency modulation (FM). The acronyms *AM* and *FM* are most familiar when used to describe bands on the radio, and although the radio process is related technically to the modulation techniques used in electronic musical instruments, there is no need to compare the two for the sake of this discussion.

Amplitude Modulation (AM)   Amplitude modulation is the use of a control voltage to alter (or modulate) the loudness of another signal. This is done by feeding a voltage signal to the input of a VCA on a synthesizer. The sound that is being modulated is called the carrier signal. When a subaudio signal is used to mod-ulate a given sound wave, the result is a slow, undulating effect called tremolo, which consists in the volume of the sound becoming alternately loud and soft but without changing the pitch. The loud-ness rises and falls around a central amplitude.

All types of voltage waveshapes can be used as control sig-nals. Using a sine wave to modulate the carrier will cause the loudness to rise and fall very gradually. A triangle wave will effect a gradual rise in loudness that sharply turns down and gradually falls, only to switch directions again very sharply. The use of a pulse wave as an amplitude-modulating signal will eliminate the various gradients between loud and soft, and cause the carrier to instantly be one or the other.

The envelope of a sound, as noted, refers to the loudness of a sound as it begins and ends. The beginning of a sound, or the attack, may be slow and gradual as it becomes louder or abrupt if it begins at peak loudness. The end of a sound, or the decay, may also be gradual or sudden. A note played on the piano, for example, begins with a sharp attack but may be made to end quickly or slowly, depending on whether the sustaining pedal of the instrument is depressed. Notes played on wind instruments, such as the saxophone or flute, typically begin and end sharply. Electronic musical instruments offer the unique ability to vary and control the envelope characteristics of a sound. The envelope gen-erator and the VCA are voltage-control devices used to control automatically the loudness of a sound as it begins and ends. This technique can be used, for example, to change the attack char-acteristics of all sounds activated by the keyboard. Rather than having abrupt, instantaneous attacks, like the notes played on a piano, the sounds can be made to have slowly rising attacks of increasing volume.

When the control signal is a waveform in the audio range, the changes in loudness become much more difficult to perceive because of their rapidity, and the resultant effect is the creation of audible "sidebands" of the carrier signal. Sidebands are the partials or harmonics that make up part of a total sound but do not dominate it. They add tone color or body to the sound. Sidebands are mathematically related to the carrier: the upper sidebands are equal to the sum of the carrier and control frequencies, while the lower sidebands are equal to the difference between them. When sidebands become audible, the carrier signal remains the dominant of the signals. Ring modulation is a form of AM in which special circuitry suppresses the carrier signal and reproduces the sidebands only.

Frequency Modulation (FM)   Frequency modulation is the use of a control voltage to alter the frequency (pitch) of the sound. This is done by feeding a voltage signal to the input of a VCO on a synthesizer. A subaudio control voltage will produce a vibrato effect, which is an undulation of pitch around the central carrier tone. (This should not be confused with tremolo, which is an undulation in loudness.) As in amplitude modulation, when the control voltage is in the audible frequency range, the resultant signal contains sidebands to the carrier wave. The complexity and harmonics of FM sidebands are much more intricate and rich than those produced by AM. Unlike AM, FM sidebands may actually dominate the carrier tone.

MODULATION OF LIVE SOUNDS

Electronically generated sound may be combined with live sound to provide a broader range of aural textures and to create an interactive performance situation that can include the participation of people who may be playing nonelectronic instruments or contraptions. A simple microphone can be used to "transduce" any audible sound into an electrical signal that can be mixed or processed electronically. Special mikes can be used to amplify the sounds of woodwind and brass instruments if conventional miking will not do, and magnetic pickups—which convert the vibrations of strings into electrical signals—are used with electric guitars to amplify their sounds.

Many fundamental techniques for handling live sounds are

available. Following are some basic ways to use miked sounds or sounds obtained through some other sort of pickup. The possibilities are limitless.

Amplification of Sounds   The microphone and amplifier provide the opportunity to amplify all types of sounds, especially those that may otherwise be impossible to hear. Normal mikes, contact mikes, or phono cartridges may be used to do this. John Cage and David Tudor used this technique in *Cartridge Music* (1960) to amplify such familiar musical instruments as slinkies, toothpicks, waste paper baskets, piano wires, and whatever else was in the studio at the time. The performance of this piece, which can be done in real-time, has nothing to do with the playing of any traditional instruments but has everything to do with artistic decisions being made impulsively by performers engaged in adjusting volume controls and attaching microphones to various objects to hear what they sound like. Robert Ashley used a microphone to amplify the barely audible sounds produced by the vocal cavity when a person speaks (movements of the tongue, parting of the lips, breathing, and the like) to help shape the characterizations of two people speaking in *Automatic Writing* (1979). The technique has also been widely used to amplify the sounds of musical instruments and to introduce some new sounds in the process, such as the scraping of a piano wire or the resonance of the surface of a gong. The use of amplified sounds naturally leads to other electronic-music techniques in the electroacoustic domain, such as feedback, modulation, and tape manipulation.

Feedback   Composer Robert Ashley calls feedback the most fundamental effect of electronic music. It is not only a natural effect that is available whenever a microphone or audio pickup is used; it also introduces the use of sustained sounds, which is one of electronic music's inherent attributes. While it is certainly one of the most familiar and easily obtainable effects using a microphone, it is one of the most delicate and difficult to control.

Most people associate feedback with errors in audio engineering, not to be treated with any more respect than the feedback that sometimes occurs in a gymnasium when someone tries to use a public address system. Used creatively, feedback is a wonderfully rich and effective expressive device. Ashley himself is famous for his piece *The Wolfman* (1964), in which the level of amplification is set very high and at the point of feedback for the given audio space. The performer delivers a set of vocal patterns while keeping his mouth in very close proximity to the microphone. As Ashley describes the effect, the vocal cavity actually becomes a miniature version of the room itself, and through movements of the mouth the performer can create controlled feedback situations that are amplified in the room.

Another experimental composer who has used the principles of feedback and resonance to great effect is Gordon Mumma. In 1967 he devised a piece for his French horn in which special circuitry of his own design—contained in something called a "cybersonic console" worn on his belt—monitors and responds interactively to the sounds of the horn in the performance space. Inside the cybersonic console are eight electronically resonant circuits that automatically tune themselves to the resonances of the performance space during the first few minutes of the piece. The acoustical properties of the room cause and shape distortions in the circuits as the horn is played, and the unit acts as a complex feedback device that generates electronic sounds as the console attempts to rebalance itself in response to this activity. The result is something akin to feedback broadcast over loudspeakers. The "hornist" can work interactively with the console circuitry by learning which horn sounds are likely to stimulate the electronics.

Feedback is often used in electronic music that amplifies sounds but is most familiar to people in the context of rock music. Jimi Hendrix was a master of guitar feedback, and through amplification adjustments and the physical manipulation of the guitar relative to the audio monitors, he became as adept at playing feedback as he did at playing notes and chords. Through the influence and inspiration of Hendrix, the use of feedback and distortion by rock musicians has become a well cultivated art and supports an entire industry that produces interesting effect units to be used with guitars and other rock instruments.

Echo and Reverberation   Echo and reverberation should not be confused. Echo is the periodic repetition of the same sound signal with an accompanying decay pattern that decreases the loudness of the signal with each repetition. This is traditionally achieved through the use of a tape recorder in which the output of the playback head is fed back directly into the record head of the same machine. As the signal is played back, it is rerecorded and played over and over again, each time losing some of its original brilliance and amplitude. The time between the periodic repeats is dependent on the distance that the tape has to travel between the record and playback heads. Many tape echo units are available that use a tape loop and adjustable playback heads to produce variable echo effects using live or recorded input. Digital echo units are also available but are most costly and not as prevalent.

Unlike echo, reverberation does not involve the periodic repetition of a given sound. "Reverb" adds resonance and depth to a sound, much as singing in the bathroom or shouting in a large auditorium does. In a sense, reverb is really a sound with many echoes that are spaced so closely that they do not become distinct or separate from the original sound. The way to achieve a reverb effect is quite different from that used to achieve echo. The traditional method for producing reverb is simply to run the sound signal through a metal spring to create further vibrations of the sound, resulting in a degree of reverberation that can be controlled by the musician through amplification. This altered version of the signal can then be mixed with the original sound to produce the desired reverb effect. Reverb has been a very popular method of distorting sound since the 1950s and has been used by experimental composers as well as rock musicians to achieve interesting colorations.

Amplitude and Frequency Modulation   Just as purely electronic sounds can be modulated through AM and FM techniques, the input from a microphone or pickup can be processed using other electronic devices. This can be done by patching the microphone or pickup input into a synthesizer so that the resultant signal can be treated just like any other waveform being produced within the machine. The range of processing effects is as endless as the capabilities of the synthesizers themselves.

Examples of the modulation of live sounds abound, no matter which field of music you look at. Karlheinz Stockhausen has been as influential as anyone in the processing of live instrumental music. His portfolio of sonic works from the mid-1960s introduced the "microphonist" as a performing member of his ensemble. In *Mikrophonie I* (1964), the only instrument was a tam-tam that was miked by two individuals while three others altered the sounds through amplification and filtering. Stockhausen then expanded this idea in 1965 with the more elaborate *Mikrophonie II*. In this piece, the raw music is provided by a choir and organ, which are picked up by microphones and then processed using ring modulation, amplitude adjustments, and mixing. Ring modulation is also used in his beautiful piano work *Mantra* (1970). In this piece, two pianos are amplified and processed using sine-wave ring modulation, and the result is amplified and projected by loudspeakers.

In some other, more familiar idioms, such as jazz and rock music, modulation of live sounds is common. Ring modulators became quite common in jazz even before workable portable synthesizers became common. Herbie Hancock was one of the early users of these with the electric piano, and other musicians, such as trumpeter Don Ellis, began listing ring modulators as one of their instruments in the late 1960s. In rock, of course, the use of an endless array of effects devices has been common since the 1960s and includes such contraptions as wah-wah pedals (foot-operated variable high-pass filters), fuzz boxes (for sound distortion), flangers (for producing time-delay filtering effects), chorus devices and harmonizers (for producing additional sidebands to guitar, bass, and keyboard sounds), bass boosters, sustainers, and many more. We will look at some examples in chapter 9.

Tape Effects   We have already looked at echo effects, which are really a tape-delay process. Tape recorders can also be used in live performance to manipulate sound in other ways. The degenerating effect that occurs when the same sound is recorded over and over was used dramatically by Alvin Lucier in *I Am Sitting in a Room* (1970). In this piece, a short text statement by the composer is read and recorded on tape. The tape is then played back, and the amplified sound is rerecorded on another tape recorder. Each time the next generation of the passage is played back it is rerecorded. The sound naturally begins to lose portions of its clarity and quality with each successive recording, until eventually the entire passage is reduced to a pulsating, undulating drone of distortion.

An equally compelling piece that uses tape recorders in the performance situation is *Mugic* (1973), by Charles Amirkhanian. In this case, a single reel of magnetic tape is threaded through the recording and playback heads of three tape recorders sitting in a row. Spoken words are recorded on tape machine 1 and played back on machines 2 and 3 for broadcast over loudspeakers. The inherent tape-delay effect is compounded by the fact that the performer continues to speak while the microphone picks up the sound being broadcast over the speakers. The acoustic resonance of the room is also amplified over the microphone and develops into a broader and broader range of noisy harmonics with each successive pass of the tape.

Until recently knowledge needed to make electronic music was extensive and forbidding to the novice. But with the introduction of digital musical instruments and computer controls, modern instruments have been simplified so that the composer can get down to the creative business of making music. Still, a little technical knowledge is not a bad thing, and the techniques and processes described in this chapter should assist the artist in better understanding what is happening in the instrument. With this increased knowledge, the composer may be able to do things he could not have conceived of before.

2

A HISTORY OF ELECTRONIC MUSIC TECHNOLOGY

The technology of electronic music has a long and intriguing history. Rudimentary experiments in the electrical production of sound were taking place before the invention of the light bulb. The principles of electricity were hardly understood until the late 1800s, and it is interesting to note that experiments in acoustics were often cited to demonstate the oscillatory nature of electric waves. The German physicist Hermann Helmholtz, a prominent scientist of the late 1800s, illustrated many of his theories regarding electromagnetic wave action by using tuning forks and musical sound demonstrations.

The development of electronic-music equipment can be described in terms of three eras. Everything prior to the introduction of the modern tape recorder in 1948 is designated the early years. This period witnessed not only the fundamental experiments made with electrical sound prior to 1900 but also the first popular age of electronic music, which witnessed the invention of such instruments as the telharmonium of Thaddeus Cahill (1900), the theremin by Leon Theremin (1920), the Sphärophon of Jörg Mager (1924), the ondes martenot of Maurice Martenot (1928), the Trautonium (1930), and numerous others. Because no convenient form of sound recording had been introduced to allow editing and manipulation of the music, all of these instruments were designed for live performance.

The studio age began with the introduction of the tape recorder in the late 1940s. This was a dream come true for the visionary composers who had been hoping for a means for storing and manipulating sounds electronically, and it brought all of the electronic musical instruments then in use (especially the ondes martenot, theremin, and Trautonium) into the recording studio, where they could be applied more creatively. The use of microphones also invited the incorporation of natural sounds into music. The design of recording studios and the invention of still more electronic effects and processing devices greatly expanded the possibilities of the music. During the 1950s and 1960s, electronic-music equipment was so expensive to own and operate that only large organizations or institutions could afford to sponsor studios. In the

United States, such studios usually belonged to universities or to recording companies that specialized in producing special effects music for movies. In many other countries, studios were subsidized by governments as part of a nationalized radio broadcasting system.

The synthesizer era is the last of the three periods in the history of electronic music. All current developments in electronic music, both analog and digital, can be traced to the invention of the voltage-controlled synthesizer by Robert Moog in 1964. Moog and his contemporaries revolutionized the design of synthesizing equipment by employing the latest in integrated circuitry to produce an entirely self-contained electronic music machine. The modern synthesizer, unlike those invented before Moog's, is not just a tone generator: it also provides the means to process, modulate, mix, and amplify any conceivable sound. In putting such potential in the hands of one person, the modern synthesizer not only eliminates the need for a traditional recording studio but invites the creation of electronic music outside of the institutionalized environment. This change has become even more apparent as the cost of equipment has gone down and such equipment has been made available to anyone who wants it. The future of electronic music will see equipment spreading from the hands of trained musicians to those who have a musical imagination but little or no formal musical knowledge. This will be the next musical revolution: the possibility for anyone to produce personal music using inexpensive, sophisticated, but easy-to-use music systems.

the
EARLY
YEARS

Some of the earliest devices that produced sounds elec-

trically were the results of experimental accidents that re-

mained largely misunderstood by their inventors. In 1837,

for example, one Dr. C. G. Page of Salem, Massachusetts,

reported in the *American Journal of Science* that he had

discovered a way of generating a "distinct ringing sound"

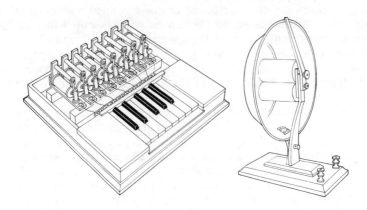

The Musical Telegraph, the first electronic music instrument. The device employed an octave of single-tone telegraph transmitters activated by a small keyboard and amplified through an upended washbasin equipped with paired electromagnets to produce sonic vibrations. (From David A. Hounshell, "Two Paths to the Telephone." Copyright 1980 by Scientific American Inc. All rights reserved.)

by toying with the action of horseshoe magnets and a spiral of copper wire with its ends connected to a zinc-lead battery. He called the result "galvanic music," and although he was at a loss to explain the phenomenon, he had stumbled on a way of producing fairly pure electronic sounds. Related experiments were conducted by others, but no one seemed successful in applying this discovery to the design of an instrument.

The first actual electronic musical instrument was invented in 1874 by an American, Elisha Gray. Gray is best known for his contention with Alexander Graham Bell to patent the design of the original telephone in 1876. Professionally he was involved in the field of communications. He obtained his first telegraph patent in 1867 and was employed by the Western Electric Company as a supervisor.

In early 1874, Gray discovered that his young nephew had connected some curious electrical circuits involving batteries and a vibrating metal reed to a bathtub, and this produced an audible hum when the circuits were opened and closed. In essence, Gray's nephew had inadvertently devised a primitive method for transmitting vibratory currents created by the spring-loaded metal reed. Gray reproduced the experiment in his lab and began exploring a number of practical applications of the effect. One of these was the invention of a small keyboard device equipped with enough single-tone "transmitters" to play an octave. He called this the "musical telegraph" and took the instrument on tour with him to England in August and September of 1874. He also produced a two-octave version late in the same year. The unit was polyphonic and predated the introduction of the first practical electric organ by sixty-one years.

Any significance that this invention might have had to the world of music was nullified when Gray dropped further research into the musical applications of his discovery in order to pursue related efforts to invent a multiplexer for the telegraph (a device that would allow the telegraph to carry several signals at once). In 1885 a German, Ernst Lorenz, developed an elaboration of the sound-generating circuit demonstrated by Gray, and investigated ways of controlling the envelope of the sound. Although this device was patented, it apparently never enjoyed any practical use outside of the laboratory.

The "Singing Arc" of the English physicist William Duddell became a familiar novelty around the turn of the century. Duddell was trying to devise a way of eliminating the annoying whining sound that emanated from carbon-arc streetlights. In 1899 he learned that he could actually control the irregular piercing tones that were produced through the use of a secondary circuit system connected to the direct current of the arc. This secondary circuit was used to modulate and control the oscillations of the arc. Duddell later attached a simple keyboard to his primitive voltage-controlling device and took his show on the road. His device was a very crude version of FM using a controlling circuit

THADDEUS CAHILL AND THE TELHARMONIUM

The haphazard experiments of Page, Gray, and Duddell all pale next to the work of Thaddeus Cahill (1867–1934). Cahill was a spirited American inventor who had the technical know-how, creative genius, and marketing foresight to complete what can only be described as the most ambitious electronic-music project ever conceived. Not only was he working against great technological odds (his first telharmonium preceded the general availability of vacuum tubes by fifteen years), but his unique idea to market live electronic music over a telephone network foreshadowed the concepts of radio broadcasting and cable television by decades. Cahill was the first man to possess a true vision of electronic music as well as the means and persistence to fulfill his dream. Among his achievements, he was the first to build an electronic music syn-

Dr. Thaddeus Cahill, 1906.

thesizer, one capable of several effects and sound-shaping; he used a polyphonic keyboard with touch-sensitive (dynamic) keys; he was the first to perfect the sound-generating technique of the rotating wheel element, later used by Laurens Hammond for his famous electronic organ; and he transmitted his electronic music "live" over the telephone wires.

On February 4, 1896, Cahill filed his first patent for a machine to produce what he described as "electrical music." He was twenty-nine at the time, but his original theories and plans for this device seem to date back to 1884, when he was a seventeen-year-old enrolled in the Conservatory of Music of the Oberlin Academy in Ohio. The science of musical acoustics was becoming better known at the time because of the pioneering work of Helmholtz. It appears that Cahill was sufficiently inspired by such work to dream up his electrical method for purifying musical sound and putting the power of a synthetic orchestra in the hands of a single performer. He first filed for a patent for the device on August 10, 1895, but finding the original design overly complicated and impractical, he assimilated its pertinent features into his well-conceived forty-five-page patent opus of 1896. In Cahill's own words, the "grand objects" of his invention were to "generate music electrically with tones of good quality and great power and with perfect musical expression, and to distribute music electrically generated by what we may term 'original electrical generation' from a central station to translating instruments located at different points." Cahill's plan was to build an electronic-music device and pipe live music to remote locations, an idea not unlike present-day Muzak systems in concept. This device could imitate the sounds of familiar orchestral instruments or use the unusual electronic sonorities that were unique to this device.

The patent he obtained in 1896 described his system in great detail. The instrument itself became known by two different names—the dynamophone and the telharmonium. Cahill seemed to prefer the second. The original patent described a device with electrical tone generating devices, dynamics-controlling devices for building and shaping individual tones, a keyboard for activating the tone-generating circuitry, and a speaker system for reproducing the sound.

The opening paragraph of his patent even uses the word *synthesizing* to describe the way the telharmonium would combine individual tones to create composite sounds, and we can credit Cahill with coining the term in this field.

The complexity of his early musical machine is surprising. The tone-generating mechanism of the first patent consisted of twelve "pitch shafts," or axles, on which were mounted a series of "rheotomes," or cogged metal wheels. These were, in essence, a series of elementary alternators that, when rotated rapidly by the turning of the pitch shafts, brought each cogged wheel into contact with a metal brush, which was part of an electrical circuit. The on-and-off contact of a cogged wheel with a brush created an electrical oscillation of a given frequency or tone.

Each of the twelve pitch shafts corresponded to one note of the chromatic scale. All of the shafts were rotated in unison by a single motor using an elaborate wheel and belt system, therefore maintaining a steady rate of rotation and keeping all of the shafts spinning at a constant pace. This design assured that all of the pitch shafts would remain in tune with one another unless, of course, there was some slippage in the belts. Cahill eliminated the latter possibility by later designing a direct-drive system using mechanical linkage.

To derive each of the twelve notes of the scale, Cahill had to cut the correct size and number of grooves in the surface of each rheotome. Each individual cogged wheel could produce a single pure sine tone, but Cahill's knowledge of the physics of tonal sound told him that he would need to add harmonics to each tone in order to create a full-bodied sound. He did this by employing multiple rheotomes for each note, each wheel representing one partial of the designated base frequency. The first partial was identified as the "ground tone," and to this he added as many as five more rheotomes to provide overtones for any given note of the scale.

Cahill set aside one rotating pitch shaft for each note of the twelve-tone scale. To add octaves of a single note, he simply added corresponding groups of rheotomes to the appropriate shafts. Each shaft, therefore, was designed to hold a series of rheotome groups, each corresponding to a different octave of the same note. The device described in this patent had seven octaves per note. The first five octaves each used six partials, while the sixth used four and the seventh only two. Cahill based this design on the fact that at higher frequencies, musical sounds have fewer overtones and so become purer. The original telharmonium design, then, included eighty-four notes or rheotome groups, corresponding to the eighty-four notes of a seven-octave piano. These notes employed 408 individual rheotomes to create all of the partials needed to create the tones.

The telharmonium used a specially designed keyboard that was sensitive to the degree of touch of the fingers. Every group of rheotome wheels—each representing one note of the scale—was connected to an individual key through an electromagnetic circuit. When depressed, each key served to close the rheotome-interrupted circuits, thus producing a tone. The keys were made touch-sensitive through the use of a coil in the circuit-closing action. The harder a key was depressed, the closer the proximity of the coil and the louder the resultant sound. Unlike the pipe organ, but very much like a piano, the telharmonium keyboard was sensitive to the amount of pressure applied by the fingers.

The tones being played were first combined in a "tone mixer" (transformer), where the individual components of the total sound could be controlled and balanced. Through creative mixing and filtering of the sound, Cahill was able to use the telharmonium to imitate common orchestral instruments like the oboe, cello, or French horn. The sound was then directed through ordinary telephone wires to "vibration-translating devices." These were no more than common telephone receivers equipped with large paper horns to provide amplification. This patent included his preferred design for an electromagnetic speaker outfitted with a wooden soundboard, but there is no evidence to show that he was ever successful in using this unique forerunner of the modern loudspeaker.

Cahill's design, therefore, was for a complete electronic-music synthesizer. In creating this instrument, he encountered all of the same basic technical problems faced by the designers of modern synthesizers: the method of tone generation, keeping the system in tune, purifying or modulating the tones, mixing and amplification, and the control of dynamic features for the shaping of sounds. Cahill was never able to build a telharmonium that precisely followed his original specifications, although we will see that he came very close despite financial and technical difficulties. In all, he built three of these devices, each somewhat more complicated than its predecessor.

The first telharmonium, a small prototype version, was built in Washington, D.C., in 1900. Cahill constructed this version purely for demonstration purposes, with the hope of gaining the financial backing that he needed to support full-scale production. This model contained only thirty-five rheotomes distributed over a single octave of twelve notes. This only allowed for two or three tone partials per note but was impressive enough to interest investors in his idea. His first transmissions of electronic music over the telephone wire occurred during 1900 and 1901. These attempts were limited to sending the sound from his laboratory in one part of Washington to his home and office in other parts of town. In 1902 he sent some of his live telharmonic music to the home of George Westinghouse, also in Washington, as well as to the office of a friend in Baltimore via leased telephone lines. Westinghouse was the magnate of the locomotive air-brake industry, and through his recommendation, Cahill was put in touch with his first financial benefactors. It was during this same time that the eminent British mathematician and physicist Lord Kelvin was taken on a tour of the Cahill lab and reportedly gave his blessing to the young inventor.

With financial support available, Cahill moved his lab in 1902 to larger facilities in Holyoke, Massachusetts. Cahill finally had adequate space in which to work, and he set to the task of building a much larger machine for commercial applications. By 1904, Thaddeus and his brothers, George and Arthur, had submitted articles of incorporation for the Cahill Telharmonium Company.

Two plans emerged for the marketing of telharmonic music. The first telephone-based distribution network was to take place in Boston under the auspices of the New England Electric Music Company, the head of which was one of Cahill's financial sponsors. This network would have included two thousand subscribers. The telharmonium was to be built in Holyoke and installed in Boston. A second machine was planned for use in New York City by the New York Electric Music Company. Construction went slowly, though, and by 1906, when the first large telharmonium was completed, the plans for Boston were abandoned and all efforts were focused on getting a unit ready for the New York site.

Working under pressure from his sponsors, Cahill completed his second telharmonium, which still did not live up to his original patent specifications. Even so, it was much larger and more functional than the prototype. He worked feverishly to complete an instrument for staging a demonstration of the device for the local Holyokers. At the same time, he was building the additional components needed to upgrade the Holyoke model for use by the New York Electric Music Company, all of this to be shipped to New York by mid-1906.

Cahill's second model used 145 rheotome/alternators instead of the intended 408. Because of this, five octaves were used instead of seven, and the machine lacked some upper tonal ranges. In spite of these limitations, though, the device was versatile and sophisticated. It included two of Cahill's touch-sensitive keyboards mounted one atop the other in pipe-organ fashion, and contained all the "stops" and "expression devices" needed to vary tone color, introduce vibrato effects, and control the crescendo or diminuendo of sounds. Other enhancements included the use of the more familiar alternator rotating element in place of the cogged rheotomes and a direct-drive mechanism for rotating pitch shafts instead of the original belt-and-pulley system. He subsequently updated his patent to reflect these improvements.

The Holyoke instrument was quite large and occupied the better part of the factory building it was located in. The 145 alternators were each attached to an eleven-inch section of a steel pitch shaft and divided into eight groups. This meant that each note (including six partials, for example) used almost six feet of shaft and that a shaft with five octaves measured almost 30 feet in length. The bed plate supporting all of this was comprised of 18-inch-thick steel girders mounted on brick supports and extending 60 feet. Nearly two thousand switches were required to connect the keyboard with the alternators and various electrical devices needed to synthesize and amplify the sounds. The entire instrument weighed about 200 tons. To the casual viewer, this device probably resembled a power plant more than anything, and it must have created quite a racket when it was operating. The musician himself was stationed in a small room in the same building and had a telephone receiver behind him so he could hear the music he was playing.

Playing the telharmonium was no small feat. In 1903, Cahill hired one Edwin Hall Pierce to master the instrument and to teach junior members of the staff. Pierce, a professional pianist and organist, persevered gallantly to overcome the many technical problems he faced. Not only was he surrounded by a jungle of wires in a small room, but he had to master two keyboards and become adept at using two levels of expression devices. The first level of "stops" opened or closed the many individual partials of a single note. The second level, controlled by the hands and feet, permitted the shaping of the attack and decay of the sounds.

The first public demonstrations of the telharmonium began on the weekend of March 16, 1906. The music was transmitted by telephone wire to the ballroom of the Hotel Hamilton, nearly a mile away. The sound was reproduced by a single telephone receiver equipped with a large paper horn and placed on a chair in the middle of the room. This is remarkably reminiscent of the "loudspeaker concerts" of electronic music that were prevalent during the 1950s and 1960s. What did this marvelous machine sound like? While no recordings of the telharmonium exist, we are lucky to have some published accounts of the events that took place. The most widely read of these was by Ray Stannard Baker and appeared in the popular *McClure's* magazine in July 1906. He described the music as consisting of "singularly clear, sweet, perfect tones" and was amazed that the "whir of machinery" from the Cabot Street plant could not be heard at all. The music must have consisted of penetrating sine and triangular waves, and perhaps had the depth and presence that is associated with the theremin. The music was of sufficient amplitude to pervade all parts of the ballroom without revealing the precise location of the sound source. Baker was very moved by the experience and further described the sound as being "pure music, conveying musical emotion without interference or diversion." An account appearing in *Electrical World* also mentioned that the tones were "remarkably pure and beautiful" and that the result sounded nothing like the more familiar mechanical means for reproducing sound, the phonograph and the telephone.

On this occasion, it seems that the musicians succeeded in

A musician, probably Edwin Hall Pierce, playing the Cahill telharmonium in Holyoke, Massachusetts, 1906. The music that was originated from this tiny room and generated by the massive telharmonium in an adjacent chamber and was transmitted nearly a mile by telephone wire to the Hotel Hamilton ballroom. The musician could hear the music from a single telephone receiver placed behind him. (Smithsonian Institution photo no. 77469.)

taming the telharmonium quite well. Their musical selections made generous use of vibrato effects, tone color, and various degrees of attack and decay. Among the pieces first played were Schumann's "Träumerei," Beethoven's Trio in C Major for Two Oboes and Cor Anglais, selections by Bach and Schubert, Stein's "Arkansas Traveler," and a rousing imitation of a fife-and-drum corps playing "Dixie." One of the novel features of the telharmonium was its ability to imitate familiar orchestral instruments. These concerts demonstrated this capability through the replication of oboes, flutes, French horns, bugles, and cellos.

After a number of well-received demonstrations, Cahill readied his equipment for the move to New York City during the summer of 1906. This included the partially completed instrument used for the Hotel Hamilton concerts as well as the additional equipment needed to bring the instrument up to fuller capacity. The equipment weighed over 200 tons and required over thirty flatcars when shipped to New York. The New York Electric Music Company occupied a new building in Manhattan at Thirty-ninth

The largest telharmonium built by Cahill was this one installed in "Telharmonic Hall" in New York in 1906. (Smithsonian Institution photo no. 77494.)

Street and Broadway, across the street from the original Metropolitan Opera House. The building was later dubbed Telharmonic Hall and consisted of a main floor with an auditorium. The telharmonium itself was located in the basement.

This final model of the telharmonium still used only 144 alternators instead of the 408 suggested in the original patent. Through the use of additional wiring and switches, Cahill devised a way to use each single alternator for more than one note of the scale. This meant that a ground tone for one note might also be used as a partial for another. This was probably an economic compromise on his part, but it seemed to add more body to the sounds being produced. This model also used only five octaves but included three keyboards that could be played simultaneously to represent different instrumental voices.

Concerts in New York began on September 26, 1906, and subscribers to the electronic-music service were actively recruited up and down Broadway. Technical problems began to arise in the practical matter of transmitting the music over telephone wires. Because of the massive amount of power needed to shoot the music through the telephone network, other telephone users began to complain that it was interfering with normal telephone traffic. Cahill's alternative was to run his own wires, but legal difficulties prevented this. Imperfections in the telharmonium itself also contributed to his headaches, and although Cahill worked relentlessly to solve such problems, the business fell apart, and the New York Electric Music Company officially ceased operation in 1911.

Had Thaddeus Cahill attempted to build his telharmonium twenty years later, he probably could have seen his research come to some fruitful conclusion. Unfortunately, none of that was to be, and the most ambitious achievement in the history of electronic music was soon forgotten. In spite of the fact that the mighty telharmonium was apparently sold as scrap, the principles underlying it still enjoy popular use in the Hammond organ that was developed in the late 1920s.

THE 1920s: THEREMIN, MARTENOT, AND OTHERS

With the arrival of the vacuum tube and radio electronics during the 1920s, many industrious individuals set to work on curious electronic musical devices. The musical climate of the time was

Telharmonic Hall in New York City, showing the telharmonist in the background. Telephone receiver loudspeakers were strategically hidden in hanging plants and behind potted flowers. (Smithsonian Institution photo no. 77493.)

one of radical experimentation and pioneering; composers like Edgard Varèse, Erik Satie, Arnold Schoenberg, Bela Bartok, and George Antheil were already calling for more freedom in music and a break from moribund European traditions. While they were inventing novel approaches to traditional composition with familiar instruments, they were also prescribing their needs for new and unusual electronic instruments to fully realize their intentions. In the midst of this activity appeared a number of interesting and important electrical devices for producing music.

Whereas Cahill's telharmonium derived its sound from the electromechanical action of spinning alternators, the vacuum tube allowed inventors of the 1920s to produce the first truly electronic devices that did not require moving elements to generate music. These devices possessed unique electronic voices of their own and were not designed to mimic traditional instruments. This change in approach signaled the beginning of the search for the ultimate electronic-music machine, a goal that continues to inspire designers today.

The Theremin

One of the earliest instruments to capture the fancy of audience and composers alike was the invention of Russian scientist Leon Theremin. Originally called the etherophone or thereminovox but later simply the theremin, this device was first built in Russia around 1920. Theremin applied for patents in Germany and America during 1924 and 1925, but it was not until 1927 that Westerners first heard public performances of the instrument. The theremin was distinguished by the sound of sweeping, monophonic sine waves and a performance technique that lent it to solo instrumental parts. Perhaps its strangest characteristic was that it was performed merely by waving the hands in the vicinity of two antennae. This mystifying technique not only baffled most onlookers but also added a high degree of theatricality to a performance.

The theremin operated on a principle of modulation called heterodyning, as did numerous other early electronic music instruments. This entailed mixing two signals that were nearly equal in frequency, with the combination of the two waves resulting in a third signal that was equal to the difference between the two original oscillations. The resulting sound is often referred to as the beat frequency. In the theremin, the radio-frequency oscillators that were used were above the human range of hearing, but the

A theremin enthusiast and player, Lucie Bigelow Rosen, in the music room of her New York home in the 1930s. (Smithsonian Institution photo no. 78040.)

difference between them was audible. One of the high-frequency oscillators was fixed, while the other could be altered by moving a hand in the vicinity of a vertical antenna about a foot tall. As the hand entered the electromagnetic field of this antenna, the frequency of the oscillator would vary and result in a corresponding change to the audible beat frequency or pitch. In addition to this pitch antenna, there was a secondary loop antenna (sometimes positioned horizontally) or foot pedal to control the loudness of the sound. The sound that was produced was very close to a pure sine wave but had enough sidebands to add depth to the tone. It had a range of five octaves. The sound was continuous unless the hand was moved in and out of the vicinity of the antenna. Special effects such as vibrato were easy to produce with simple movements of the hand.

Theremin designed many variations of his instrument, including keyboard-activated versions and "cello" models for playing bass parts. The instrument was essentially melodic in nature and for many years enjoyed great popularity. In 1929, RCA Victor was even licensed by Theremin to market a commercial version of his instrument to the public. The theremin remained a quaint novelty at recitals until the mid-1930s, and although ambitious composers such as Varèse, Joseph Schillinger, and Andrei Pashchenko wrote special music for it, public interest in the instrument faded. Theremin and others—particularly Martin Taubmann with his electronde in 1933—made several variations of the original device in order to improve on its fundamental design. These included key and foot controls to switch the sound on and off in a more conventional manner so as to avoid the continuous whining and glissando effects that were normally attributed to it. There has always remained a small following for the instrument, and it is interesting to note that Robert Moog began his business in electronic musical instruments with a transistorized version of the theremin in the early 1960s. Until the availability of voltage-controlled synthesizers, theremins found a place in some musical circles as a source of sound effects in movies (such as *The Day the Earth Stood Still*) or in popular music (note the Moog theremin operated by a slide control used in the Beach Boys' 1966 hit "Good Vibrations"). The noted jazz thereminist Youssef Yancy is probably the most skilled performer of the modern theremin.

Leon Theremin had two notable collaborations with composers during the 1930s. The first was with Henry Cowell, who in 1931 asked him to produce a special keyboard device that came to be known as the rhythmicon. This instrument permitted the

Leon Theremin (left) in a performance for two theremins and other instruments. (Smithsonian Institution photo no. 77461.)

automatic repetition of any note selected from its keyboard. The rhythms could be varied in pitch, duration, and tempo, and it was possible to play multiple notes and rhythms by depressing more than one key at a time. The effect of the rhythmicon was very much like that of modern sequencers used to program series of notes on synthesizers. Cowell used this device in a number of compositions during the 1930s. Edgard Varèse also contracted Theremin to construct two instruments to his precise specifications to be used in his piece *Ecuatorial* (1933–1934). The devices were to be keyboard-activated and were to have a pitch range that exceeded the high C on the normal piano by an octave and a fifth. There is no evidence that Theremin ever finished these instruments. By the time the score for *Ecuatorial* was published, Varèse had substituted two ondes martenots in place of the theremin contraptions, and that is the way the piece has always been performed.

Youseff Yancy playing a modern theremin. He is one of the only remaining virtuosos of the instrument. The model shown in this photo dates from 1967. (Photo by Raymond Ross Photography, New York.)

Jörg Mager and the Sphärophon

After the initial success of the theremin, activity in the design of electronic musical instruments began to liven up. The German Jörg Mager was the first inventor with a serious mind for music to try and invent an instrument that could expand the accepted tonal range of the chromatic scale. He was interested in microtonal music, which provides more divisions of notes than those found on the normal piano keyboard. To this end, he designed his instrument so that it could easily produce quarter tones. Called the Sphärophon, it was described in a pamphlet by Mager in 1924 and demonstrated to the public during 1925 and 1926. The device was monophonic, like the theremin, but was played from a keyboard and was not restricted to sweeping glissandi tones. To produce its sound, it used radio components and a beat-frequency principle similar to the theremin. Mager had great faith in the potential of quarter-tone music and built his keyboard for this purpose. Unfortunately, this idea was still a bit too futuristic for his contemporaries, and the Sphärophon sank into oblivion. The one shining moment for the device came in 1931, when Winifred Wagner commissioned Mager to produce electronic bell sounds for use in a Bayreuth production of the opera *Parsifal*. In 1935, Mager successfully redesigned the Sphärophon in order to produce a polyphonic instrument that could play any keyboard music using the conventional chromatic scale. This device was called the Partiturophon, but it failed to gain any popularity, in part because of the earlier appearance of the electric organ of Hammond. In any event, all of Mager's instruments were lost during World War II, and another pioneer in the field failed to gain wide recognition.

The Ondes Martenot

A more successful early electronic instrument was the ondes martenot, originally called the ondes musicales. This device was designed and invented by the French musician Maurice Martenot, who introduced it in 1928 as a soloist performing the premiere of Dimitri Levidis' Symphonic Poem for Solo Ondes Musicales and Orchestra, a piece written for the instrument. Martenot wanted to create an instrument that would be taken seriously and could, in fact, join the ranks of traditional symphonic instruments in use at the time. He did this by designing a device that looked at home in the orchestra and by providing a flexible range of controls that was unique at the time.

The ondes martenot resembles a small, upright keyboard device like a clavichord. Sounds are produced using the same heterodyning or beat-frequency methods employed by Theremin, but better controls were provided so that the performer could play traditional keyboard music. The device was purely monophonic and was therefore restricted to the playing of melodies, but Martenot used a method of triggering notes that enabled the musician to relate the tones to the chromatic scale. The pitch of a note was determined by the lateral movement of a finger ring that was attached to a metal ribbon. This ribbon, when moved, adjusted a variable capacitor that in turn changed the frequency of the tone over a seven-octave range. This was done using the index finger of the right hand. The ribbon was ingeniously superimposed over a keyboard, and movements of the ring corresponded to notes of the scale and gradations in between. The left hand controlled volume with a pressure-sensitive key. This was unique in that when fully released, the key would produce silence, and when depressed using increasing degrees of pressure, it would produce sounds of increasing loudness. A knee lever was also available for use in place of this volume key, thus freeing the performer to play the melody with the left hand. The left hand also controlled a small bank of expression keys that permitted selected filtering of the tones.

The fact that one could silence the sound of the ondes martenot by releasing the volume key allowed the performer to cover up the glissandi movements of the ribbon from note to note, thus eliminating the primary irritant associated with the theremin. The key also permitted the use of glissandi when desired, control over the attack of a tone, and the playing of microtonal gradations between the twelve notes of the scale. These features of the instrument were of primary concern to Maurice Martenot. He wanted to invent a device that would outlast the tentative novelty of the theremin and that would succeed in inspiring serious composers to write music for it. In his very first public performance of the instrument—Levidis' Symphonic Poem, mentioned above—Martenot and the composer successfully used both quarter tones and eighth tones in an otherwise purely conventional musical context.

A second version of the ondes martenot used an actual keyboard in place of the finger-ring ribbon controller. This instrument was also monophonic and would play the lowest note being keyed at any moment. Five- and seven-octave versions were available. An intriguing feature of these keyboards was the fact that any individual key could be jiggled laterally back and forth to produce minute fluctuations in pitch for vibrato effects.

The ondes martenot met with unprecedented success. Following the impressive debut of the device in Paris in 1928, Leopold Stokowski brought Martenot to the United States to perform the Levidis work with the Philadelphia Orchestra. This led to a tremendous flurry of composition for the device and the creation of a formalized training program and school for the instrument under the direction of Martenot in Paris. During the 1930s, well-known composers such as Darius Milhaud, Arthur Honegger, and Olivier Messiaen wrote serious music for the instrument. To date, more than three hundred composers have contributed to this repertoire, which includes no less than one hundred chamber works, fifty operas, one hundred symphonic works, numerous ballets, and over five hundred incidental scores for films and theater. Perhaps the best-known ondes martenot performer is Jeanne Loriod, who has dedicated her career to mastery of the instrument since the age of eighteen. She studied with Martenot himself, and recordings of her performances are commercially available.

Other Devices

The Trautonium of Dr. Friedrich Trautwein was developed between 1928 and 1930 in Germany. This instrument possessed some of the features of the ondes martenot, but used a neon-tube oscillator in place of the capacitance-grounding principle of heterodyning found in the theremin and ondes martenot. Tones were produced by adjusting the resistance of the tube via a finger ribbon that was similar in function to the one found on the ondes martenot. Because of the use of a neon-tube oscillator, the sound of the Trautonium was distinctly different from that of its predecessors. The monophonic sound consisted of a rich sawtooth waveform that could be selectively filtered by using controls on the unit. Although Trautwein himself was an engineer by profession, his primary sponsor was the director of the Berlin Hochschule für Musik, who had many connections with composers. Through his influence, German-born composer Paul Hindemith became enamored with the Trautonium and even learned how to play it. He composed the Concertino for Trautonium and String Orchestra in 1931. The instrument was surprisingly long-lived, and variations of it were in continuous use in media applications until the late 1960s. Trautwein himself invented a variation called the monochord, which was used in the Cologne electronic-music studio in the 1950s. Oskar Sala, a student of Hindemith who gained attention for his virtuosity on the original Trautonium, also worked with the inventor during the 1950s to create the Mixtur-Trautonium, an expanded version of the instrument that was designed for use in the recording studio.

Another of the many unusual electronic-music machines invented during this era was the Hellertion of Bruno Helberger and Peter Lertes. Again, the neon-tube method of generating oscillations was experimented with, and the instrument must have had a sound similar to the Trautonium. It was played by pressing a leather ribbon against a resistance plate that changed the pitch of the note being played. The use of the finger ribbon instead of an actual keyboard is reminiscent of both the ondes martenot and the Trautonium. The earliest version of the unit was developed around 1930 and featured one monophonic ribbon board. A later version demonstrated in 1936 had a surprising arrangement of four separate monophonic fingering ribbons so that four notes could be played simultaneously. This would certainly have been a trick for two hands but could have been accomplished with four hands. Like many other early electronic musical instruments, the Hellertion had a dim future and has not been heard from since.

*

The story of early electronic-music instruments certainly does not end with the few devices that have been discussed here. The history is rich with other experiments and dozens of additional instruments with those odd, pseudoscientific names. In addition to the inventors of the theremin, ondes martenot, telharmonium, Trautonium, and Hellertion, there were many others who attempted to perfect the basic designs of the better-known devices. They produced such instruments as the mellertion, dynaphone, emicon, melodium, oscillion, croix sonore, magnetton, and photophone. There were also polyphonic devices, such as the Warbo formant organ and the electrone, which were predecessors of modern electric organs.

As can be seen from this short history of the early years, electronic music was an active field during the first half of this century, and had a tremendous influence on some of our most experimental composers. During the 1920s and 1930s, for example, men like Varèse, Cage, Hindemith, Cowell, and Ernst Toch were already exploring the use of noisemaking devices and even manipulated phonograph records or radios in the performance of music. They waited eagerly for the invention of the right kind of electronic musical instrument, a device that could produce whatever sound they could imagine. Those who were still active during the 1960s began to realize that wish to the fullest, but even those primitive vacuum-tube instruments of the 1920s offered sounds that had never been heard before in music. The newness was all-important and greatly enriched the vocabulary of music; it was the lack of flexibility and variety that proved to be the downfall of the early instruments.

THE ELECTRONIC ORGAN

During the early 1930s, the family tree of electronic musical instruments developed a separate branch devoted to the design of electronic organs. Whereas devices like the theremin, ondes martenot, Trautonium, and Partiturophon were designed to create new types of sounds never heard before—and consequently new music to go along with them—most electronic organs were meant to replace traditional pipe organs. In this sense, they were strictly utilitarian. The goal of the typical electronic-organ designer was to produce a device that could mimic the sound of a wind-blown organ pipe but would occupy less space and cost less than a conventional church organ. Such devices were used to play traditional keyboard music and, with few exceptions, were not equipped with unusual expression features or anything particularly out of the ordinary. Over the years, the small electronic organ became a familiar instrument in the pop, jazz, and rock combo. In spite of the parochial application of the electronic organ, its history has many important connections to the development of the synthesizer.

The electronic organ that one normally associates with music stores also had its roots in the early years of electronic instruments. The tone-wheel principle that was perfected by Cahill in 1900 resurfaced in 1929 when the Chicagoan Laurens Hammond built his first electronic organ. Hammond had the advantage of using vacuum tubes, amplifiers, and loudspeakers to surmount some of the basic technical problems that had faced Cahill, but his method for generating the tones themselves was identical with that used in the telharmonium. This technique of the tone wheel is actually electromechanical, unlike the theremin and ondes martenot, but has proved to be a highly reliable method for producing harmonic tones. Although most electronic organs made today use entirely electronic means to produce sound, many of the older Hammonds can still be found in operation. Henry Ford was so impressed that he purchased the first available unit in 1935, when the Hammond organ was finally introduced.

Even though the Hammond organ was not the first electronic organ to hit the market (the Rangertone, for example, which also used an updated version of Cahill's tone-wheel principle, was introduced in 1931), it became very popular because of its excellent design. It was built to replicate the functions of a pipe organ and offered sliding tone filters to remove partials from the sound that resembled traditional organ stops in operation. (Many electronic organs still have stops that are labeled in feet as lengths of pipe, even though not an inch of pipe is used to create a sound.) The popularity of the Hammond organ led to its use in the pop-music field, where it became a staple of the bar-and-grill circuit and was supplanted only recently by the influx of inexpensive synthesizers and other organ devices.

The next generation of electronic organs began to explore totally electronic means to produce music through the use of vacuum-tube oscillators. In 1939 the Hammond organization introduced two additional models, the monophonic Solovox and the polyphonic Novachord. The Solovox was a soloing instrument that was customarily used in combination with a piano or other organ. The Novachord was a much more ambitious creation and possessed sophisticated attack and decay characteristics, tone-color controls, and a six-octave keyboard instead of the five-octave model associated with most other organs. Both of these devices were totally electronic and used twelve triode-tube oscillators to generate the

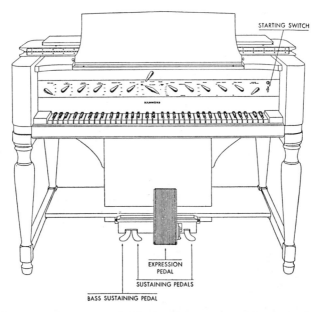

STARTING SWITCH

EXPRESSION
PEDAL

SUSTAINING PEDALS

BASS SUSTAINING PEDAL

The Hammond Novachord, introduced in 1939, was an entirely electronic organ that used triode-tube oscillators. It was extremely versatile but proved unreliable because of the large number of vacuum tubes it used.

upper octave of the keyboard. A complicated network of additional vacuum tubes was needed to divide these upper frequencies into oscillations of lower pitch for the other octaves. The instrument had numerous tone controls available to the performer, including "deep," "brilliant," and "full" tone controls; "normal" and "small" vibrato; and "strong" and "soft" bass and percussion. The combination of these variable switches made it possible to imitate accurately many instruments of the traditional orchestra, an unusual feat in those days and one that amazed many listeners. The Novachord was one of the few electronic organs that featured extraordinary timbre controls and that, in its way, was the forerunner of the modern synthesizer tuned with "presets" for orchestral effects. Unfortunately, Hammond's ambitious instrument had really overstepped the capabilities of technology in 1939, and because of the complex circuitry and the unstable nature of the hundred or so vacuum tubes he had to use, the device was not

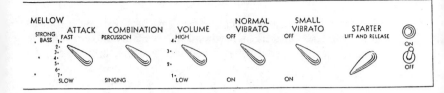

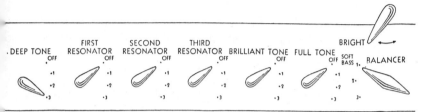

**Controls of the Hammond Novachord (1939). The instrument featured an un-
usually flexible set of tone controls and envelope-shaping capabilities.**

very reliable in performance and did not stay on the market very
long.

    Other "pipeless" organs using audio-frequency oscillators of
various types included one employing no less than seven hundred
vacuum tubes, produced by Edouard Coupleaux and Joseph Giv-
elet during the 1930s; the Clavioline by Selmer; the Electrone by
John Compton; and organs that were introduced by the Allen,
Baldwin, Connsonata, and Miller organ companies. In addition,
there appeared various devices using techniques such as vibratory
reeds combined with electromagnetic pickups (like the Orgatron,
invented by F. A. Hoschke in 1935, later sold by Wurlitzer) or
photoelectric means (like the Photona of Ivan Eremeef, 1935).

THE ELECTRIC PIANO

The first electric pianos were developed during the 1920s and 1930s,
and although the instruments themselves did not revolutionize music, the technology created was seminal to the development of
electronic music. The principle of the electric piano was that instead of having a soundboard, an otherwise conventional piano
would be equipped with electromagnetic pickups that would con-
vey the vibrations of the strings to an amplifier for broadcast over
a loudspeaker. The key-and-hammer action of the piano remained
the same; only the means of generating the sound differed. The

uniqueness of the electric piano was that the resultant amplified sound could be filtered or modulated in various ways to change its tone color. The performer could also exercise greater control over the duration of notes and the volume of the sound.

The practice of using electromagnetic pickups and amplification was soon applied to other types of plucked instruments with metal strings, particularly the electric guitar, which was first introduced in 1931 by the Electro String Company using designs by Adolph Rickenbacker. This has naturally led to the proliferation of guitars and effects that can be achieved with modern instruments of this type. A microphone pickup was also developed during the 1930s as a means of amplifying traditional wind instruments or string instruments that use nonmetallic strings. The invention of instruments using magnetic pickups or microphone amplification did not radically change the design of the musical instruments themselves or the type of music played on them. They offered an alternative means for electrifying acoustic vibrations but did not significantly inspire truly electronic music-synthesizing devices.

the
STUDIO
AGE

The next evolutionary period for electronic music followed

World War II. Interestingly enough, it was not the de-

velopment of a new and unique musical instrument that

inspired this new activity but the invention of the modern

tape recorder. When the tape recorder was used in com-

bination with microphones, magnetic pickups, and existing

electronic musical instruments, the entire realm of musical possibilities expanded dramatically. With the coming of the tape recorder came the creation of the recording studio and thus the
sudden confinement of electronic music to an institutional environment in which composers, like scientists, worked in isolation,
perfecting their formulas for splicing and mixing sounds and creating tape pieces that would later be aired over loudspeakers. Not
all composers permitted themselves to depart from the live performance of electronic music; this was particularly true in America,
where John Cage, David Tudor, Gordon Mumma, Robert Ashley,
and others continued to do their work in a live setting. Even for
those composers, the tape recorder became an essential piece of
equipment for both the creation and presentation of electronic
music. The studio age can be differentiated from the early years
of electronic music because of the fact that sounds could now be
easily recorded and manipulated. Up until this time, all electronic
musical instruments were designed for live-performance situations.
It was a time to collect these instruments for studio use, to make
improvements on them, and to gather together all of the miscellaneous pieces of technical equipment that could assist one in processing recorded sound.

The studio age began in 1948 in Paris and soon spread to
Germany, North and South America, Japan, and other countries.
The field of electronic music became increasingly technical, and
composers had to become familiar with the operation of machines
and the principles of acoustics that governed the electrical generation of sound. This dependence on the institutional studio lasted
until voltage-controlled synthesizers became portable and affordable around 1970. Even though the appearance of solid-state voltage-controlled synthesizers in the mid-1960s was initially confined
to studios, these same devices were the ones that inspired electronic-music composers and performers eventually to leave the
walls of the institution; I therefore intend to reserve my discussion
of devices like the Moogs and Buchlas to the next chapter.

THE TAPE RECORDER

The tape recorder was an outgrowth of efforts to record sound
that were originally focused on the technologies of cylinder and
disc recording, developed by Thomas Edison and Emile Berliner.
The first magnetic sound recorder was actually invented in 1898
by the Dane Valdemar Poulsen, but further technical development
of a device that was practical for commercial distribution did not

occur until the late 1940s. Following is a brief history of the development of sound recording.

1857, France. Irish-born E. Leon Scott invented the "phonautograph," a device capable of inscribing a visual record of sound being directed into a diaphragm. The device used a stylus to record sound on a disc of smoked paper. The phonautograph had one serious problem: although it could indeed inscribe representations of sound onto paper, it could not reproduce the sound in any way. Twenty years later, in 1877, French physicist Charles Cros added the concept of reversibility to Scott's idea so that one might play back the recorded sound. Cros called this device the paleophone but never succeeded in building a working model.

1876, United States. Edison successfully reproduced recorded sound for the first time. In 1877 he patented his first "talking machine." With this device, a recording of sound was made on a piece of tinfoil wrapped around a rotating brass drum. The recorder consisted of a membrane of parchment stretched over the end of a short brass cylinder. The membrane had attached to it a spring-mounted chisel needle that would vibrate as incoming sound caused the membrane to vibrate. The action of the needle on the piece of revolving tinfoil inscribed a mark that corresponded to the sound. The recording could be reproduced by rotating the cylinder again but with the needle resting in the existing cut groove. Edison called this device the "phonograph." Edison also tried wax cylinders as a recording medium. He envisioned the phonograph being used for such practical applications as dictation.

1887, United States. Emile Berliner introduced disc recording, solving some of the recording and reproducing problems associated with the cylinder recorder of Edison. His first discs consisted of glass that was coated with a thick fluid of ink or paint. When the disc was rotated by a turntable, a stylus cut into it a spiral groove that corresponded to the sound being picked up by a diaphragm. Berliner called his first machine the "gramophone" and imagined that it could be used to supply voices for dolls or to reproduce music.

1896, United States. Windup mechanical turntables were introduced to play disc recordings.

1897, United States. By this time, the disc gramophone was gaining acceptance, and people like Berliner had begun to use recording discs from which copies, or imprints, of master recordings could be printed. Gramophone records made available at this time were usually made of thick, brittle shellac, operated at 78 rpm, and had recording on only one side.

1898, Denmark. Valdemar Poulsen of Copenhagen built the first magnetic recorder. It was called the telegraphone and recorded crosswise (vertically) on a steel piano wire as it was rotated between the poles of an electromagnet. Unlike modern tape recorders, which use iron-oxide-coated tape as a medium, the uncoated metal wire itself was the medium. Calling his device an "apparatus for electromagnetically receiving, recording, reproducing, and distributing articulate speech," Poulsen took the 1900 Paris Exposition by storm and won the Grand Prix for scientific invention. He envisioned the device as an office dictation machine. Poulsen had two versions of the telegraphone. The most widely known was the one that used wire as the recording medium. Because the twisting of the wire caused distortion in the sound, he next tried to use steel tape as a medium. The American Telegraphone Company as formed around 1900 to produce and sell Poulsen's wire model, which had two spools to transport the wire, a 100-volt motor and manual rewind. It could record for thirty minutes on a wire moving at 7 feet per second. It was monitored by earphones, since amplifying tubes were still in the developmental stage at this time. The machine was a marketing failure, largely because of the inferior quality of its sound when compared with the gramophone. ATC ceased operation in 1909. A Dutch firm also licensed to sell the device folded in 1916. Other wire recorders, primarily those made by Air King in Brooklyn, New York, appeared during the 1940s, but were soon superseded by magnetic tape recorders.

1905, United States. By this time, various forms of sound boxes had been developed for use with the gramophone. These ranged from simple diaphragms connected to large horns, to delicately balanced "tone arms" with spring-mounted styli, mica diaphragms, and horns that could be either internally or externally mounted.

1906, United States. Lee De Forest invented what was, perhaps, the single most important device of an electrical nature of

The original magnetic recorder, the telegraphone of Valdemar Poulsen, circa 1907. This model was made by the American Telegraphone Company. (Smithsonian Institution photo no. 77187.)

this century, the vacuum tube. Sometimes called the thermionic valve, audion, or triode tube, this vacuum tube was capable of controlling electrical current with precision. A vacuum tube could be used for the generation, modulation, amplification, and detection of current and was thus useful for everything from amplifying the sound of gramophones to detecting radio waves and generating audio signals in tube oscillators.

1912, United States. In an experiment that largely went unnoticed, Lee De Forest succeeded in amplifying the magnetically recorded sound of a Poulsen telegraphone by using his triode vacuum tube.

1917, United States. G. A. Campbell built an early frequency filter.

1919, United States. A. G. Webster published his paper "Acoustical Impedance and Theory of Horns and Phonograph," which alluded to the possibilities of applying electrical theory to the design of microphone systems and reproducing systems.

Early 1920s, Germany. Kurt Stille, in yet another effort to salvage the telegraphone, organized the Telegraphie-Patent Syndikat Company to sell licenses to produce magnetic recorders in Europe. Several firms took part, a number of them using the improved version of the telegraphone that used steel tape instead of wire. The device was considered for use in the production of sound for movies, and some experimental films using synchronized sound were actually produced in England.

1925, United States. Electrical amplification was first used to improve the recording of sound.

1926, United States. J. P. Maxfield and H. C. Harrison successfully built electrically operated recording and reproducing devices.

Mid-1920s, United States. The AC bias technique for recording sounds was first tried by W. L. Carlson and G. W. Carpenter of the United States Navy. They used it to send recorded telegraph messages. Until that time, all attempts at recording had used DC methods. The AC technique eliminated the background noise found in earlier DC recordings and is still the principal method used today.

1929, United States. Special oversized disc recordings were introduced for broadcast use. Called "transcriptions," these ran at 33⅓ rpm and could carry a fifteen-minute program on one side of a 16-inch platter. These were the first long-playing records but required special playback equipment and were not available to the general public.

Early 1930s, Germany. Due to Kurt Stille's licensing activity, many varieties of wire and steel-band recorders were being sold in Germany. The Echophone Company produced a cartridge-loaded unit that simplified operation of the machine. ITT eventually acquired this company, but resold it to the

German firm of C. Lorenz Company, which redesigned the recorder and introduced it as the textophone in 1933. The Nazi party and secret police began to acquire large numbers of such magnetic recording devices.

The German scientist Pfleumer began experimenting with a number of new recording mediums in an attempt to improve on the basic design of magnetic recorders. He tried paper and plastic tapes coated with iron oxide particles as an alternative to wires and steel tapes. The Allgemeine Electrizitäts Gesellschaft (AEG) became interested in Pfleumer's work and bought all the rights to it. Such early recording tapes used large iron particles as coatings and had the feel of sandpaper. When run through a recorder, they immediately clouded the air with residue and dust.

AEG introduced the magnetophone in 1935 at the German Annual Radio Exposition in Berlin. This unit employed a coated paper tape instead of steel bands or wire. The supplies themselves cost a mere 15 cents per minute of recording time in comparison to the more than $1 cost of using steel tape. This fact, no doubt, contributed to the success of the device at the exposition.

1935, United States.   Bell Laboratories, one of the few American firms interested in magnetic recorders, designed the mirrorphone. This recorder employed steel tape and was used to broadcast weather reports over the phone lines.

1937, United States.   The Brush Development Company introduced the soundmirror, one of the first commercially available magnetic recorders in the United States. This steel tape unit could record only one minute of sound. Brush supplied the armed forces with many of these during World War II.

World War II.   While American firms like General Electric (GE) continued to improve the design of wire recorders for military use, the Germans shifted their attention to tape units. The AEG magnetophone was further developed, and when the victorious Allies moved into Germany in 1945, they were stunned to find the German tape units to be far superior to wire recorders. By 1945 the magnetophone had adapted AC-bias recordings and coated paper tape, and possessed a surprising frequency response of 10,000 cycles, which was much higher than earlier wire and steel tape units. These German recorders were capable of accurately recording midrange frequencies. The Americans quickly adapted the tape medium. Following the war, the United States alien-property custodian held all patents on the AEG magnetophone and licensed any American company that desired to build it. The only three small companies to earnestly take on the project were Magnecord, Rangertone, and the Ampex Electric Company. The first technical problem that needed to be solved was to replace the low-grade coated paper tape used by the Germans with something more durable and of higher quality. With the help of companies like Minnesota Mining and Manufacturing Company (3M), the tape problem was solved by 1948, and high-quality magnetic tape recorders became widely available.

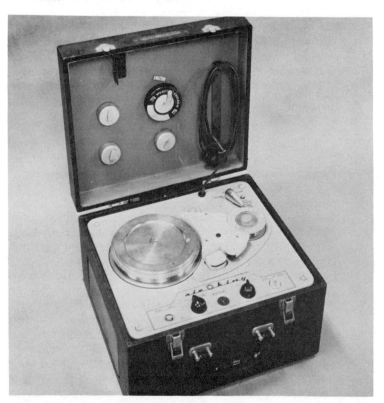

The Air King wire recorder, circa 1949. Sound recorders using only wire methods were displaced by magnetic tape recorders in 1950. (Smithsonian Institution photo no. 77360.)

1948, United States.   Bell Labs introduced the early transistor. This started another technological revolution, one that made it possible to use a miniature, solid-state component to perform the functions formerly associated with the vacuum tube.

Although the introduction of the tape recorder took nobody by surprise, it certainly made many modern composers who had been waiting for just such a development very happy. Until the late 1940s, the only practical means available for recording sound had been the phonograph. In spite of the fact that the phonographic medium was not suited to the editing and rearrangement of sounds, many composers had already used it to great effect. One of the earliest uses was certainly by Ottorino Respighi in 1924 when he called for a disc recording of nightingales during a performance of his *Pines of Rome*. By 1930, Paul Hindemith and Ernst Toch had toyed with experimental effects by using record turntables to change the speed of recordings and play them backward. During the mid-1930s, Varèse used multiple turntables with various speeds to play numerous discs simultaneously.

In 1939, John Cage composed *Imaginary Landscape No. 1*, the first piece to be written specifically for a recording medium. It consisted of sounds produced by playing audio test recordings on variable-speed turntables with speed clutches in combination with cymbal and piano-string sounds. This approach to manipulating recorded sounds preceded the availability of the tape recorder by nearly ten years.

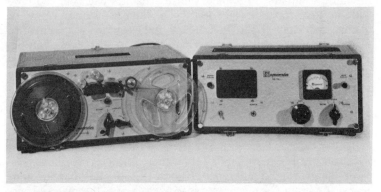

One of the earliest professional magnetic tape recorders, the Magnecorder, made in the United States in the early 1950s. (Smithsonian Institution photo no. 77135-C.)

INSIDE THE ELECTRONIC MUSIC STUDIO, CIRCA 1950 TO 1965

Prior to the development of solid-state, modular studio equipment in the middle and late 1960s, the electronic-music studio was simply a collection of miscellaneous audio contraptions thrown together by the creative will of composers and technicians. (The one notable exception was the Columbia-Princeton Electronic Music Center, with its RCA synthesizer, discussed below.) Of course, recording studios also existed for the entertainment industry and broadcast mediums. In some countries, like France and Germany, these facilities were often supportive of composers' sound experimentation. This was generally not the case in America. To make equipment available for electronic music purposes in the United States, academic institutions and composers pooled whatever equipment resources they could muster and tried to devise some way of interconnecting or patching various components for ease of use and sound mixing. This required some innovative design work and was quite successful at times.

France and Germany

The first two formal electronic-music studios were created in 1951. One was sponsored by French radio in Paris and the other by German radio in Cologne. To say that there was a rivalry in the early days of these studios would be an understatement. Each studio was formed to promulgate the particular theories of its founding members. In France, Pierre Schaeffer had been working with musique concrète since 1948. (The full details of his work are discussed in chapter 8.) His fundamental approach was to manipulate previously recorded sound material to create pieces of music. The sounds were not electronically generated but were disc recordings of such things as boat and locomotive engines, spinning saucepan lids, coughs, and other ordinary sounds, many of which came straight from the sound-effects library of the broadcast studio in which Schaeffer worked. By changing the speed of the recordings, repeating the sounds, and juxtaposing different sounds, Schaeffer created new music that was daring and unusual. Until 1951, all of his experiments were done with disc recordings. Because he worked for French National Radio (Radiodiffusion-Television Française), he was able to have some of this material performed live over the airwaves, an occurrence that inspired equal amounts of excitement and dismay on the part of the public. Schaeffer and his colleagues were forming a new approach to the idea of musicality, and as an outgrowth of this important work, French National Radio created the Paris electronic music studio in 1951 when tape recorders were first made available.

While the French were initially interested in manipulating only sounds that could be derived from the natural world, the Germans had been exploring the potential and problems of creating scientifically precise music in the tradition of Arnold Schoenberg and Anton von Webern, using existing electronic instruments. Dr. Werner Meyer-Eppler, a distinguished German physicist and theorist, published in 1949 an important paper that outlined the development of electronic-music technology ("Elektrische Klangerzeugung"). At the same time, the composer and musicologist Herbert Eimert became interested in electronic instruments as a natural means to extend the compositional work of Webern and other serialists. The link between these two men was another composer and music theorist named Robert Beyer, who collaborated with Meyer-Eppler in 1950 to present a series of lectures on the possibilities of what they termed " Elektronischen Musik," or electronic music. These demonstrations resulted in a program that Meyer-Eppler, Beyer, and Eimert organized for West German Radio (NWDR, now WDR) in Cologne on October 18, 1951, and from that point, the broadcasting system sponsored the formation of an official studio under the direction of Eimert to perfect electronic music. Unlike the French, then, the Germans were interested in purely electronic music produced through the use of new instruments.

While the early musical approaches of both of these studios differed in principle, the fact that each began to work with tape recorders meant that their styles eventually began to sound similar, and the terms *musique concrète* and *electronic music* became synonymous with the idea of tape composition. In the end, the preferred approach was actually a combination of the purely electronic with sounds collected from the real world, leaving it up to the composer to determine how to make an interesting piece of music from these elements.

Together, these two studios represented the state of the art, at least technically, in the early 1950s. The Paris studio, with its original orientation toward pure musique concrète, mainly included a number of interesting tape-recording devices. Every studio in those days had an engineering genius employed to develop useful gizmos and construct a control console. For the Paris studio, this person was Jacques Poullin. The equipment in this studio, most of it carrying the Poullin mark, included multiple tape recorders; a "space potentiometer," a kind of mixing device that could move sounds in space; a "morphophone," which was a complicated ten-channel tape-loop system with an audio filter attached that could be used to construct various degrees of the echo effect ranging from the playing of a distinct series of repeating echoes to the use of closely spaced repetitions that could prolong the duration of a single sound; and two variable-speed tape-loop machines called "phonogenes." One provided a clutch-driven speed control that was continuously variable over the entire speed range, and the other provided up to twenty-four preset playback speeds that were switch-selectable for any taped sound.

The German studio had a predisposition for electronic musical instruments. Tying all of the components together was especially tricky, but this task was handled admirably by Fritz Enkel, who built the control console. The German studio contained a Monochord, an updated version of the Trautonium, although still monophonic, designed by Friedrich Trautwein during the late 1940s; audio oscillators for sine waves and sawtooth waves; one variable-speed tape recorder; one four-track tape recorder; audio filters, including band-pass filters; a control console for mixing and recording this material; and a melochord, first built for the use of Meyer-Eppler for his lectures and demonstrations and later installed in the studio. This instrument was designed by Harald Bode in 1947 and included two monophonic tone-generating systems with separate keyboard controls. Two notes could be played at a time, and the device also featured a touch-sensitive keyboard and envelope control. In 1953 the studio commissioned a second melochord, this time with dual three-octave keyboards and added control for the selective filtering of the tones. The Germans were using four-channel tape recorders long before the rest of the world. Most studios were still adopting the two-channel tape machine around 1957, while the Cologne people were already releasing four-channel works.

The establishment of these two studios inspired a flurry of activity in electronic music. Many composers in other countries became interested in the phenomenon, and as the 1950s came to an end, similar studios began to appear in all parts of the world. Some of the best known of these are the Studio di Fonologia in Milan, Italy, established in 1953, where Luciano Berio, Bruno Maderna, André Boucourechliev, John Cage, and Henri Pousseur did some of their early work; the studios of NHK, the Japanese broadcasting system, which were established in 1955 and included as equipment one melochord, one monochord, audio oscillators, tape recorders, and thirty-two band-pass filters; the Philips Research Laboratories in Eindhoven, the Netherlands (established in 1956), where Edgard Varèse and Henk Badings did early work; and of course, the Columbia-Princeton Electronic Music Center in New York, which began as an equipment pool in 1951 and developed into the showcase for the RCA synthesizer from 1955 through the early 1960s.

Until the development of synthesizers, all of these studios shared the same basic components: tape recorders, band-pass filters, audio oscillators, melochords, monochords, ondes martenots, theremins, mixing panels, and splicing blocks. As the powers of the studio became more evident, there began a movement to design special instruments that could offer the composer more than the simple monophonic voices of the "ancient" instruments of the 1920s and 1930s. In Germany the noted Trautonium virtuoso Oskar Sala devised a studio version of that instrument known as the Mixtur-Trautonium, which incorporated additional tone generators and white-noise generators for studio manipulation. During the mid-1950s, America finally made its first major contribution to the studio environment with the founding and development of the Columbia-Princeton Electronic Music Center.

The Columbia-Princeton Electronic Music Center

There was an abundance of magnetic-tape composition activity in the United States during the 1950s, but most of it was being done by independent composers who relied on their own resources to establish studios and pool equipment. On the one hand, there was John Cage and a group of composer friends who formed the Project of Music for Magnetic Tape (1951–1953), which included notables like David Tudor, Earle Brown, Christian Wolff, and Morton Feldman. They generally composed tape music in whatever studio they could gain access to, but often frequented the commercial studio of New Yorkers Louis and Bebe Barron. Here, Cage completed *Imaginary Landscape No. 5* between late 1951 and January 1952. Cage employed chance operations to combine sounds from "any 42 phonograph records" into a tape piece. He continued his radical approach and next realized *Williams Mix* in 1952. In this piece, he catalogued a wide variety of taped sounds "in terms of pitch, timbre and loudness" and then collected them onto tape according to a sequence derived by chance operations from the *I Ching*, the ancient Chinese book of oracles. The sounds themselves were of diverse aural content and included "city sounds," "country sounds," "electronic sounds," traditional musical sounds, vocal sounds, and amplified small sounds. One of the most important aspects of this tape music was Cage's method for notating the composition using a series of graphic charts depicting the organization of eight tracks of tape. The Barron studio did not compare with the elaborate facilities found in Paris or Cologne and primarily consisted of tape recorders with variable speeds and audio oscillators. The Barrons themselves became known for their movie music; the electronic material they provided for the movie *Forbidden Planet* in 1955 remains some of the most memorable music of the science fiction genre.

Other independents working in relative isolation included Gordon Mumma and Robert Ashley in Ann Arbor, Michigan, between 1956 and 1964. Their Cooperative Studio for Electronic Music was hardly even a studio in the early days and consisted of tape recorders that the two men shared between their homes, plus some of Mumma's own sound-generating circuits.

At Columbia University things took a more formal turn, and thanks to some initiative and hard work, a little luck, and some good politicking, America's first legitimate electronic-music studio was formed. The story begins in 1951. American composers Otto Luening and Vladimir Ussachevsky were both music instructors at Columbia University, which had acquired some tape equipment so that music programs could be recorded, including a dual speed Ampex 400 tape recorder, a Magnachord tape recorder, and a Western Electric microphone. As the story goes, Ussachevsky could not resist playing with the equipment and not only became its keeper but recruited a young engineer from the university named Peter Mauzey to give him some technical pointers. According to Luening, Mauzey also built a black-box device to aid Ussachevsky in creating echo effects. Ussachevsky worked on his tape pieces through the end of 1951 and into 1952, and presented his first recital of the results on May 9, 1952.

Luening became interested at this point, and he and Ussachevsky arranged to use the equipment during the summer of 1952 to explore fully its possibilities. Because they did not have any audio oscillators to generate electronic sounds, they resorted to taping sequences of flute and piano sounds as raw material and manipulating them with the tape equipment. The resulting experiments, although only played for a small group of friends, landed them on a concert program of new music at the Museum of Modern Art in October of that year. (A full account of this concert and of the approach of the two men is related in chapter 8.)

The museum concert catapulted Luening and Ussachevsky into the public eye. Although their approach was decidedly conservative, especially compared with the very abstract work being done by Cage, Tudor, and others, it had very good exposure in

New York City (including a live television appearance on NBC's "Today Show") and in the press. Luening and Ussachevsky were certainly willing to play the roles of electronic-music statesmen if that is what fate had in store for them, but they also set about to employ this sudden exposure for the furtherance of their efforts at the university. In 1955—after three more years of composing, lectures, demonstrations, and performances—the pair received a grant from the Rockefeller Foundation to study the field of electronic music in both Europe and America and to respond with a plan for establishing an electronic-music center in the United States.

In their travels in Europe, Luening and Ussachevsky visited all the major studios and met with some of the foremost composers and engineers in the field. They were most impressed with the personalities they encountered but came away knowing that the technology of the medium was still in a primitive state. They were pleasantly surprised, upon returning to the United States, to hear of a special electronic-music "synthesizer" that had been developed at the David Sarnoff Laboratories of RCA in Princeton, New Jersey. They immediately arranged for a demonstration.

The device was called the Olson-Belar sound synthesizer and was named after its inventors, Harry Olson and Herbert Belar. First introduced publicly in July 1955, the device was the first sound synthesizer in the modern sense. This meant that it was a single, modular system that could generate, modify, process, record, and present complex sonorities. RCA's hopes for the device were rather pedestrian and predictable. They hoped to use the synthesizer to imitate traditional instruments for the creation of pop music and, with the aid of trained musicians, to turn the device into a pop-music machine. In spite of RCA's commercial intentions, Luening and Ussachevsky were very impressed with the device's revolutionary musical capabilities and saw in it their dream come true. Discovering that the serialist composer Milton Babbitt, then at Princeton University, was also interested in experimenting with the device, Luening and Ussachevsky joined forces with him to lobby for some time on the machine. This was granted to them, and for the next three years the trio made regular trips to the Sarnoff labs to develop new musical material.

In 1957, Luening and Ussachevsky completed a 155-page report for the Rockefeller Foundation on their findings in the electronic-music field. In it they recommended the establishment of the Columbia-Princeton Electronic Music Center, the first institutionally sponsored studio in the United States. The result was a further grant from the foundation for $175,000 to be paid to both Columbia and Princeton universities over a five-year period. In

The RCA Mark I electronic-music synthesizer, as it appeared in the David Sarnoff Research Center of RCA in Princeton, 1955. The disc recording system is shown on the left. (Courtesy RCA.)

cooperation, RCA first rented their synthesizer to them and in 1959 donated an improved version (now called the RCA Mark II synthesizer) to the center on permanent loan. The operation committee of the center included Luening and Ussachevsky from Columbia and Milton Babbitt and Roger Sessions from Princeton. Ussachevsky was the chairman. The center was established in New York City and consisted of three studios—one for the RCA Mark II and related recording equipment and the others for postproduction editing and sound modification.

The RCA synthesizer was a large device that occupied the better part of the studio in which it was situated. This was not surprising, since its electronics were controlled with vacuum-tube components. Like early computers from the same era, a device of any ambition whatsoever was bound to be large because of the kind of circuitry required to make it function. Even so, it was designed for easy use and, to a large extent, applied the idea of computer control to the concept of creating electronic music. It was not a computer, but the sound synthesizer could be instructed to control all the basic parameters of sound: pitch, volume, duration, and timbre. In the first model, this was done through the use of punched paper-roll codes. This grand combination of the computer and the player piano permitted the composer to construct

The disc recording system of the RCA music synthesizer, circa 1955. In spite of the fact that tape recorders had been available for seven years, the Mark I designers decided to employ a disc lathe to record music created by the system. This component was replaced by a tape-recording unit when the synthesizer was moved to the Columbia-Princeton studio in 1959. (Courtesy RCA.)

and edit a piece of music from a typewriter keyboard. The system was later modified to accept tab-card input as well. The ability to store instructions was perhaps the greatest innovation of the device. This allowed the composer to experiment with the structure of a piece prior to having to record it and mix it. It also permitted the synthesizer to be used for highly complex serial-style compositions, which previously had been too burdensome for a composer to handle manually. This capability was ideally suited to the work of Milton Babbitt, who was instrumental in applying the unit to the composition of traditional modern music in the twelve-tone vein.

The sound-generating sources of the RCA synthesizer were simple tuning-fork oscillators. The unit was designed for the production of twelve-tone music using the traditional chromatic scale, a feature that was deemed a deficiency by many of the more experimental composers. The oscillators produced rich sawtooth waveforms, which could then be modified through filtering to produce the kinds of timbres desired. In the hands of a creative composer, the use of extreme tempo changes, envelope techniques, and timbral combinations could overcome the strictly twelve-tone effects of the system. The device also included white-noise generators that could be selectively filtered for special effects as well.

Using the paper-roll input device, the system could only play two notes at a time. The paper roll contained up to thirty-six columns of instructions to apply binary codes to the formation of any two notes. These codes were used to designate such elements as timbre, pitch, and duration of the notes, as well as repetitions of the notes over time in conjunction with alterations in their nature. Another unique aspect of the system was a disc-cutting lathe and playback turntable for the recording and reproduction of the sound material. The original system did not adopt magnetic tape like the rest of the world but permitted the composer to record any paper-roll sequence on a disc and later combine it with other sequences onto a new disc. This laborious system seemed entirely

The RCA music synthesizer as it appeared in 1959 upon being installed in the Columbia-Princeton Electronic Music Center. This photo shows a composer working at one of the punched-paper-tape input stations. (Courtesy RCA.)

effective from the point of view of inventors Olson and Belar but was thought entirely too awkward by the composers who worked with it. Milton Babbitt worked closely with RCA to attach a tape-recording system to the synthesizer by 1959 when the device was installed at the Columbia-Princeton Center.

One final feature of the RCA Mark II set an important technical precedent: microphone input could be input and processed by the synthesizer. This was probably the first electronic musical instrument with this capability and foreshadowed a similar application that has since become a standard feature of the modern voltage-controlled synthesizer.

When the Columbia-Princeton Electronic Music Center was chartered, internationally known composers were invited to use the facilities. In the first two years, the center was able to sponsor work by such composers as Mishiko Toyama from Japan, Mario Davidovsky from Argentina, Halim El-Dabh from Egypt, Bulent Arel from Turkey, and Charles Wuorinen from the United States. The center drew on this body of work when it presented its first public concerts on May 9–10, 1961, in the McMillin Theatre of Columbia University. The program consisted of seven works, six of which were later released on a Columbia record album (the missing piece was Wuorinen's *Symphonia Sacra* for chamber ensemble, three voices, and synthesized sound on tape). These works were either pure tape pieces or involved the interaction of live musicians with tapes of synthesized sounds. Among the other people associated with the studio in later years were Edgard Varèse (who completed a second version of *Déserts* at the studio in 1961), Luciano Berio, Ilhan Mimaroglu, Walter (Wendy) Carlos, Jon Appleton, Pauline Oliveros, and Jacob Druckman.

Other Studios

Following 1960, electronic-music studios began to proliferate throughout the world. Many of them were simply the private studios of composers, particularly in the United States. Others were sponsored by government media centers and universities.

The San Francisco Tape Music Center (SFTMC) is important not only because of the composers who worked there but because its history is emblematic of the dilemmas faced by devotees of electronic music in the early 1960s. The artistic climate in San Francisco in 1961 was ringing with new ideas. A number of adventurous composers, including Ramon Sender, Terry Riley, and Pauline Oliveros, had created an improvised electronic-music "studio" in the attic of the San Francisco Conservatory of Music. It

A state-of-the-art electronic music studio, circa 1965, was often a collection of miscellaneous components creatively linked together by ingenious technicians. This view of the San Francisco Tape Music Center shows the racks of tape recorders and various tone generators. All of this could be patched into the central control console. (Photo by Bill Maginnis, studio technician.)

was here that the group began to produce a series of concerts called "Sonics." Morton Subotnick, who was also dabbling in the medium while teaching at Mills College, got together with this group. They pooled their equipment and moved to another location to officially inaugurate the SFTMC in 1962. The center continued to grow until 1963, when it moved to bigger quarters and struck up a relationship with radio station KPFA of the nonprofit Pacifica Foundation. Tony Martin joined the group as their visual artist in charge of light projections for the performances, and William Maginnis joined as both technician and composer.

Maginnis defined the center as a "nonprofit cultural and educational corporation, the aim of which was to present concerts and offer a place to learn about work within the tape music medium." The center itself had very little equipment aside from tape recorders and some audio oscillators. This forced the composers to develop some novel approaches to making electronic music, including Oliveros' unique tape-loop and -delay systems. The composers were also very interested in creating music that could be presented live, which led them to the use of light projections to accompany tape pieces and theatrics with live musicians and interactive tape systems. Riley split from the group to pursue his own brand of minimalist performance music utilizing electric organs and tape systems.

The collective was highly successful and influential, and undertook regional and national tours during the mid-1960s. During 1966 and 1967 two important developments took shape. First, the engineer Donald Buchla collaborated with Morton Subotnick and Ramon Sender to develop the first Buchla analog synthesizer (more on this in the next chapter). Next, the SFTMC decided to accept a $15,000 grant to move to Mills College and become part of the Mills Center for Contemporary Music. The studio facilities were improved, but the organizational problems of being part of a large institution soon took their toll on the original core members of the SFTMC. By 1967, all of the SFTMC people had departed, and by the time Robert Ashley joined Mills in 1969 as the new director of the center, the electronic-music studios were gone and there was no equipment left. Ashley's revival of the studios took the form of a public-access music and media facility that was highly innovative but always dependent on the financial generosity of both the university and the granting foundation.

The need for institutionalized studios was particularly important in the United States because there was no government support as in other nations. With reluctance, many composers became associated with universities that were willing to fund the establishment of experimental music programs. The need for university-funded operations became even more important as the new and expensive breed of voltage-controlled synthesizers became available during the mid-1960s. University sponsorship, however, was tentative at best, and even though some major studios were established and flourished during the heyday of activity in the late 1960s, the composers themselves were often strapped by financial obligations to the institutions and by censorship that restricted the kind of music they could produce. It was a frustrating experience for many composers but one that they realized they could escape once the price of modular, voltage-controlled synthesizers came down enough to put the equipment in the hands of anyone who wanted it. That is the next step in this history of the technology: the development of the modern synthesizer.

the
SYNTHESIZER
ERA

During the mid-1960s, a revolution in the design of electronic musical instruments began. The arrival of an affordable transistor had as much to do with this as anything, facilitating a rapid move from the electronic music "instrument" or component to that of the "system." As an early synthesizer of the system variety, the RCA Mark II set some important precedents in the areas of system control and flexibility. One more developmental stage beyond the Mark II was still needed, however, to really get things rolling—the design of the first voltage-controlled components. This work was being done independently in 1964 by Robert Moog (rhymes with *vogue*) and Donald Buchla in the United States and by Paul Ketoff in Italy. When these systems began to appear in 1965, the word *synthesizer* suddenly became forever synonymous with the term *electronic music*.

A synthesizer is a self-contained electronic system for the generation, modification, and organization of sound in real time. When a synthesizer is combined with some amplifying, mixing, and recording equipment, one has the makings of a complete studio. The general characteristics of modern synthesizers can be summarized as follows:

- Synthesizers are capable of generating a wide spectrum of sounds, from the typically musical to the nonmusical. Some models are fully programmable by the operator, so that the entire range of sounds that can be devised is only dependent on the imagination of the composer and the range of the individual instrument. Some models employ presets, which automatically select predetermined types of sounds at the flip of a switch. This approach is useful for live-performance situations. A hybrid approach permits the composer to program the presets, a capability that lends another degree of flexibility to a system.

- The oscillators, amplifiers and filters of a synthesizer are activated and controlled through the use of voltage. The composer usually triggers the sound through the use of a keyboard. The keyboard sends a voltage signal corresponding to the desired tone to the sound-generating components, which are then activated to produce the sound. Because the same voltage signal can be used to trigger more than one sound generator, voltage control introduces the element of automatic programmable triggering of sound events to expand greatly the immediate control that a composer exercises over the material.

- Synthesizers are modular in design and can be expanded through the addition of other voltage-control components, effect units, and control devices.

- Synthesizers can produce sounds in real time. This is naturally limited by the immediate capabilities of a system, but generally speaking, modern synthesizers offer much more immediate response than previous studio methods for structuring and manipulating complex sounds.

- The primary components of a synthesizer include oscillators for generating audio waveforms; sound altering devices such as band-pass filters, ring modulators, amplifiers, frequency shifters, and reverberation units; and control voltage-triggering components such as keyboards, ribbon controllers, and envelope generators.

THE MOOG SYNTHESIZER

In 1963, Robert Moog was a student at Cornell University in Ithaca, New York. While getting his doctorate in physics, he helped make ends meet by selling do-it-yourself kits for building transistorized theremins. Moog and his wife, Shirleigh, ran this business from their apartment and, in one year, reportedly sold a thousand kits at the price of $49.95 each. One of Moog's customers was Herbert Deutsch, a composer and music instructor who used Moog's theremin in some of his music. The two first met in the autumn of 1963 at a conference of music teachers in Rochester. Moog was exhibiting his theremin at one of the display booths, and Deutsch invited him to attend one of his concerts in January 1964 to see how he was using the instrument. This led to conversation regarding the need for new types of electronic instruments that used solid-state technology. In June 1964, Moog recruited Deutsch as a kind of consulting composer, and the pair spent two weeks tinkering with circuitry and mulling over possible system designs. The result was a piece of music for demonstration purposes (*Jazz Images* by Deutsch) but no real system to play it on. By the end of the summer, Moog had his first complete prototype ready. He wrote a paper entitled "Voltage-Controlled Electronic Music Modules" and was invited to present it at a convention of the Audio Engineering Society that fall.

From this early exposure of his system, things moved gradually ahead for Moog and his machine. It was during this time that he formed the company bearing his name and geared up to begin manufacture of his unusual instrument. The first production model was available in the spring of 1966 and was purchased by Alwin Nikolais, the director of the Nikolais Dance Theatre. The next two models were used by Raymond Scott and Eric Siday for television and radio commercials, and a number of composers began to acquire Moog's modular systems to experiment with. Moog finally christened his product the Moog Synthesizer in the same year.

During this period, composers and other people in the music business began to recognize the potential of the Moog Synthesizer, but the device really had not made a tremendous impact on the public yet. What was really needed was a virtuoso or two to dem-

Robert Moog. (Courtesy Moog.)

onstrate the true power of the modern synthesizer. In 1968, Moog got his wish in the form of *Switched-On Bach*, a recording of Bach's music performed by Walter (Wendy) Carlos and released on Columbia Records. This record had unusual appeal because it was palatable to traditionalists in spite of being electronic. The avant-garde was not too excited about it but found the formidable instrument of Carlos to be quite compelling. With the release of this album, the word *synthesizer* suddenly became a household word. The interest generated by this one record was responsible for the sudden use of synthesizers in all music genres, from rock and jazz to classical and the avant-garde.

The basic studio version of the Moog was modular and could contain a variety of components to meet the specifications of the user. Except for the availability of additional effects units, control devices, and improved electronics, the studio model of the Moog has remained essentially the same over the years. Its typical characteristics include the following:

- A five-octave keyboard for voltage control. This can be set either to operate like a chromatic keyboard using the twelve-tone scale or adjusted for alternate pitch scales and microtonal systems.

- Monophonic operation (produces one note at a time from the keyboard).

The Moog System 35 studio synthesizer. (Courtesy Moog.)

- High-range voltage-control oscillators, with a frequency range of .01–40,000 Hz. Since the range of human hearing is really only about 20–20,000 Hz, the Moog provides many subaudio and ultrasonic frequencies that can be used for control voltage and modulation functions. The original Moog contained two VCOs as sound sources. Larger studio models like the Moog 55 contain up to seven VCOs for sound-generating purposes. Each VCO is switch-selectable for sine, sawtooth, triangular, and rectangular waves.

- Patch cords, used to make corrections between the different modules.

- The use of VCAs and filters.

- An envelope generator that provides control over the initial rise time, sustain time, initial decay time, and final decay time of the output signal.

- A ribbon controller, available as an optional trigger device.

- Popular accessories, including reverberation, pink- and white-noise generators, vocoder (analog voice processor), and frequency shifters.

The studio model of the Moog has always required some learning on the part of the composer, but it offers a wide variety of high-quality sound sources and control devices for the writing of complex music. While the typical Moog Synthesizer just described is fine for studio use, it is too cumbersome and temperamental to take on the road or use in performance situations easily. In 1969 the company set another precedent by introducing the Minimoog, a simple, compact monophonic synthesizer designed for live-performance situations. This model became the most popular and widely used synthesizer in the industry and was still in production early into the 1980s. Most of the patching between modules is hand-wired and controlled by the flick of rocker switches and the turning of dials. The keyboard features two unique performance controls that have been widely imitated: the "pitch wheel" for bending notes and the "mod wheel" for adjusting the degree of modulation of the output signal.

Moog's next innovation was the introduction of a truly polyphonic synthesizer, the Polymoog, in 1975. Designed to resemble the combo organ that was a familiar tool of rock groups, this powerful instrument pioneered the use of integrated-circuit chips to control the sound-generating hardware of an analog synthesizer. These control chips replaced the wiring and patch cords, and represented one of Moog's first efforts to use preset sounds as well as user-programmable sounds that could be changed at the touch of a button.

Moog Music continues to create a diverse line of synthesizer products. Some of the more recent innovations include the Moog Source, a small performance instrument with touch-sensitive controls and sixteen presets; the 1130 percussion controller, which permits a drum to act as a control input to an oscillator; the Taurus pedal synthesizer, which can be played with the feet; and the Moog Liberation, a solo instrument that can be slung from the shoulder like a guitar.

Robert Moog himself left Moog Music in 1977 after having lived through a period during which the company was acquired by first one, then two, larger corporations. Moog and his family moved to rural North Carolina where he continues work on the design of new control devices to be used by experimental music composers.

THE BUCHLA SYNTHESIZER

During the formative years of the SFTMC in 1961 and 1962, composer Morton Subotnick joined forces with other Bay Area electronic luminaries, including Pauline Oliveros, Ramon Sender, and Terry Riley, to pool their tape-composition equipment and establish a cooperative studio. According to William Maginnis, who served as a composer and engineer in the studio from 1964 to 1967, the equipment they had was barely more than six audio oscillators and some tape recorders—certainly not enough to produce sophisticated electronic music. The need for more capable equipment led to an association with engineer Donald Buchla around 1965.

Buchla was working along lines similar to those of Moog in developing a voltage-controlled synthesizer. He worked closely with Subotnick and Sender to design a system that would truly meet the demands of a composer, and the result was the Buchla Modular Electronic Music System. Maginnis remembers that although the official date of introduction for the system was 1966, the first prototype components arrived at the studio as individual modules "one by one as they were developed." Maginnis was one of the first people to produce a piece on the system. Called *Flight*, it was realized on the first night that the initial components arrived in 1965.

In its use of VCOs, amplifiers, and filters, the solid-state

The PolyMoog polyphonic synthesizer. (Courtesy Moog.)

Buchla was very similar in capability to the Moog. It differed primarily in two respects. First, it was the first synthesizer to feature a sequencer for programming and repeating a series of control voltages. This innovative approach offered composers an easy way to preset auditory chain reactions and introduced an element of automatic control that has since become a common option in most synthesizers. Second, instead of a keyboard, the early Buchlas employed sixteen touch-sensitive plates. These plates could each trigger sounds that had been manually programmed, using patch cords and the control panel, or they could be set to emulate an actual keyboard using the chromatic scale.

Since the traditional Buchla does not employ a keyboard (although some later models do), it has always been attractive to composers who are trying to avoid keyboard-oriented approaches to electronic music. Subotnick has become the foremost virtuoso of the device and, through his pioneering work, has demonstrated the magnificent power of the Buchla. Many of these releases are available on Nonesuch Records and include such exploratory works as *Silver Apples of the Moon* and *The Wild Bull*. (All recordings mentioned in the text can be found in the Discography in chapter 11.)

AFTER MOOG AND BUCHLA

Following the success of the Moog and Buchla systems by the late 1960s, many new manufacturers entered the market with variations on the modular voltage-controlled synthesizer. The primary target market was, and continues to be, that of the rock musician, so most new instruments have been designed for performance situations.

One of the leading makers of synthesizers has been Arp Instruments of Lexington, Massachusetts, whose first product was a large studio model called the Arp 2500, introduced in 1970. By 1971, though, the company shifted its emphasis to the performance instrument and introduced the Arp 2600, a lightweight, portable synthesizer that captured the fancy of musicians with such divergent interests as Henry Mancini, Pete Townshend of the Who, and John Lennon. The secret behind the popularity of both of the early Arp machines was the careful consideration the company gave to design factors that would be attractive to musicians. The Arp 2600 includes presets for all of the most common connections that are normally made using patch cords. Each preset connection is activated through sliding controls that can also vary the amount of action that each circuit sees. This matrix-switching approach is very convenient for the average keyboard musician but may be overridden through the use of patch cords if other connections are desired. The system also includes a built-in stereo amplifier with speakers for monitoring, an important feature for a portable unit. One slight deficiency of the system was that the frequency range (.03–20,000 Hz) did not include as rich a spectrum of ultrasonic waves as the Moog and other systems.

In addition to Arp, a number of other manufacturers have become familiar names during the past ten years. These include Oberheim (which introduced one of the first polyphonic synthesizers in 1975), Roland, Korg, and EMS. Most of these firms offer a wide variety of synthesizers and accessories, including portable units, studio models, monophonic and polyphonic instruments, effects units, and adaptations for guitars. For those interested in a build-it-yourself budget system PAIA Electronics of Oklahoma City, Oklahoma, offers a diverse line of synthesizer kits available through the mail.

COMPUTER MUSIC

We are currently entering an important phase in the history of electronic-music technology. By 1990, the use of analog synthe-

The Oberheim polyphonic synthesizer. (Courtesy Oberheim.)

sizers in the tradition of the Moogs, Buchlas, and Arps will have been entirely superseded by the availability of inexpensive, computer-based, digital synthesizing systems. This phenomenon is closely related to the popularity and development of the home computer and has already begun to have a great effect on the synthesizer market. In the interim, we will see both the emergence of an interesting assortment of approaches to digital synthesis and the development of hybrid analog systems that combine computer control with analog synthesizing components.

Digital Versus Analog Synthesis

Any type of analog system operates through the measuring of quantities. In this sense, the bathroom scale is an analog device. It translates a person's weight into a reading that is caused by the moving of a needle along a scale of measurement. The degree of movement of the needle is dependent on the amount of weight on the scale, and this movement is said to be analogous to the weight.

The electronic music devices described up to this point have all been analog instruments. Each produces sound by generating electrical vibrations that are then used to physically drive the components of a loudspeaker system. Voltage-controlled synthesizers are the ultimate analog-synthesizing devices because they introduce a high degree of control over the production of analog sequences of voltages for the production of sound. They have also been designed with a sensitivity to the needs of the musician.

Digital systems operate on the basis of counting. All quantities that are to be measured are represented by a two-digit binary code that, in electrical terms, represents no more than a simple on-off state. In a music system, such digital codes can be used to represent components of sound itself (frequency, amplitude, timbre, duration, envelope) or control measures for the organization of sound. Computers are the source of digital control.

Types of Computer Music

The term *computer music* refers to a number of approaches to the production of music using computers as aids:

- Computer composition, in which the computer actually aids the composesr in producing a score that can then be played on traditional musical instruments. When this practice was first experimented with by Lejaren Hiller and Leonard Isaacson at the University of Illinois in 1955, the computer was allowed to create sequences of notes that were then selected and organized by the composers and transformed into normal sheet music for a string quartet. This endeavor was met with hostility by most people because it seemed to be removing the art from the act of composition. In the place of human creativity was the production of random note sequences by an indifferent machine. While total composition by computer has never become extremely palatable, computer-assisted composition has become very important. In this activity, the traditional composer uses the computer as an aid in organizing and mapping the music he or she is trying to write. The result may be a piece of music for any kind of musical ensemble. The computer can store the score as information on a magnetic diskette, and the system may even be able to generate a printout of the material in the form of sheet music. Pioneering work has been done on this at Massachusetts Institute of Technology (MIT), and many software packages for home computer systems are now capable of providing rudimentary music-composition aids.

- Computer synthesis of sounds, in which the computer itself produces codes that can be used to generate sounds directly. This is done through the use of a digital-to-analog converter (DAC), which translates digital binary codes into analogous electric waves that can drive a loudspeaker system.

- Computer control over analog synthesizing devices. Here, the sound is produced by the normal components of an analog synthesizer—its oscillators, filters, amplifiers, and so forth—but a computer is engaged to provide control voltages to trigger and change the sounds. The computer may act merely as an elaborate sequencer to aid a performing musician, or it may control multiple aspects of the production of a piece of music that are really beyond the control of any single individual in real time. This area of involvement for the computer has blossomed during the late 1970s with the availability of inexpensive microprocessors. Whether using a detached, general-purpose home computer for control purposes or the built-in digital control functions of some state-of-the-art synthesizers, the marriage of the computer with the well-designed analog music machine possesses great potential.

- Computer sampling of audio input. This is the opposite of digital-to-analog conversion. In an analog-to-digital conversion, input from a microphone, tape recorder, or other analog electrical music device is converted into binary codes, which can then be processed and reorganized at will. This may be done for the sole purpose of analyzing the audio waveform of an acoustic sound and then reproducing it or for the manipulation of a sound that originates outside the computer.

- Hybrid analog-digital musical instruments. These combine normal, voltage-controlled synthesizing components with microprocessor-based control devices. Such integrated, digital components include devices like sequencers that the musician can actually manipulate but may also include sophisticated chips and memory modules that assist the synthesizer in carrying out its functions. For example, the original Polymoog employed microprocessors to divide and distribute the control voltages from each key in order to activate multiple oscillators to produce chords. In 1981, Arp introduced the Chroma, a polyphonic synthesizer that employs a microprocessor to gauge touch response on the keyboard. The Roland Corporation uses programmable memory to preset sounds on polyphonic synthesizers like the Jupiter 8.

Why Use Computers?

Mankind has been creating and composing music for centuries without the aid of computers, so why are they suddenly becoming so necessary? The answer lies in the nature of music that has developed during the twentieth century. Not only have certain schools of composition stressed a greater emphasis on the mathematics of music, but the sound palette available to the modern composer has been enriched by the introduction of electronic synthesizing instruments. Because computers are mathematical devices that communicate in the language of electricity, they serve as a natural adjunct to the efforts and desires of modern composers.

As sophisticated as analog voltage-controlled synthesizers are, they remain deficient in a number of ways. First, the creation and shaping of sound elements is purely a manual operation, involving the turning of dials, the adjustment of slide controls, and the prescribed placement of elaborate patch-cord arrangements. Even the most methodical synthesizer composer spends a lot of time in the trial-and-error stage, rearranging patch cords, fine-tuning the adjustments, and trying to devise an ingenious way to create the sounds that he has in mind. Second, this laborious process is often very difficult to repeat, which leads to the recording of many samples of sound that must later be edited and manipulated on tape and remixed to create a final version. In addition to these tedious technical tasks, the performing composer must also concentrate on keyboard technique and the actual playing of a piece of music. The combining of all of these responsibilities cannot always be successfully achieved by the composer. The unhappy result may be a piece that is performed well on the keyboard but lacks interesting tone color or is mixed poorly.

The interface of computer technology with electronic-music production can expedite many of the tasks associated with this kind of music. Some of the greatest advantages come in the area of musical organization, wherein a sequence of binary codes can be used to trigger voltage-controlled activity in an analog synthesizer. This not only provides the composer with additional control over the structural components of the music but provides a stored function that can be easily repeated anytime. The editing and mixing of a piece is also greatly simplified through the storage of information on magnetic diskettes. This information may be the musical notes themselves or control-voltage sequences for structuring the material. Since diskette storage provides random access to any of the captured information, retrieval and manipulation of this material are much easier than with sounds stored on reels of audio tape.

The actual computer generation of sounds, bypassing altogether the analog synthesizer, is a much more sticky problem. The pioneer experiments with this in the late 1950s by Max Mathews at Bell Labs indicated that in order to specify all of the relevant parameters of the desired sounds, even the most efficient of programs operating on the fastest computers required several seconds to calculate each second of sound. Over the years the solution has been aided by the development of faster computers and better programs, and now we are beginning to see the emergence of the first all-digital systems that can be used by the average composer or musician who does not have previous computer experience.

A Brief History of Computer Music

Following is a brief history of computer music, tracing the general developments in the various branches of the field:

1953–54 Romanian-born Greek composer Iannis Xenakis employed a computer to aid in the calculation of variable-speed glissandi for his orchestral work *Metastasis*.

1955–1956 Lejaren Hiller and Leonard Isaacson, research associates in physical chemistry at the University of Illinois, became involved in an assignment using an Illiac digital computer to solve a problem in statistical mechanics. Hiller had been trained as both a chemist and a composer, and had studied theory and composition with Roger Sessions and Milton Babbitt during the 1940s. He immediately understood the potential of the computer as a composition aid and, with Isaacson, developed a program to let the computer generate sequences of data that could be related to the notes and parameters of a musical score. The two men selected portions of this output and assembled it into the first significant piece of music composed by a computer, the *Illiac Suite* for string quartet (published in 1957). The piece was meant to be performed by a string quartet and does not involve any computer synthesis of sound.

1956   Two computer engineers at the Burroughs Corporation of California, Martin L. Klein and Douglas Bolitho, programmed a Datatron computer to compose popular songs automatically. Affectionately nicknamed "Push-Button Bertha," the unit reportedly composed some four thousand pop tunes after having been fed the characteristics of one hundred that were then popular.

1956–1962   In Paris, Iannis Xenakis gained access to an IBM 7090 computer at the European Institute for Scientific Calculation and wrote some probabilist programs to aid in the composition of music. Rather than having the computer itself compose a piece, Xenakis fed the device previously calculated information and employed the computer to work out complex parameters of scores for various sizes of instrumental groups. Works produced during this period include *ST/10—1,080262* for ten instruments, *Atrées (Law of Necessity), Morsima-Amorsima*, and *ST/48—1,240162* for forty-eight instruments.

1957   At the Bell Labs in New Jersey, researcher Max Mathews successfully demonstrated the computer generation of sound for the first time using a DAC. For Mathews this was the beginning of a long association with computer music that continues today. Bell's interest was in the computer synthesis of speech for use over the telephone network, entailing research that largely focused on devices like the vocoder. Mathews and others working with him at Bell extended such research into the synthesis of music.

1959–1966   Mathews and his associates James Tenney, John Pierce, David Lewin, and Newman Guttman experimented widely with computer-synthesized music. Their compositions ranged from mundane demonstrations (for example, *Pitch Variations* by Guttman, *Sea Sounds* by Pierce, and *Noise Study* by Tenney) to simple renditions of familiar tunes (such as Mathews' "Daisy" and "Happy Birthday") and more complex pieces (*Five Stochastic Studies* and *Ergodos* by Tenney). Mathews and the others had developed a series of programs for automating the digital processing and organization of such works. These programs began with Music I in 1957 and were updated regularly with improved versions. Music IV (1962) was used widely during the 1960s. Many of these pieces were available in the 1960s on a record, *Music from Mathematics*.

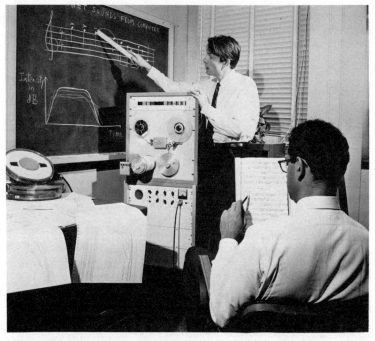

Jean Claude Risset, French physicist and composer, demonstrates a trumpet tune synthesized by a computer at Bell Labs in 1965. (Courtesy Bell Labs.)

1965   At Bell Labs in New Jersey, the French physicist and composer Jean Claude Risset employed a program by Max Mathews and Joan Miller to digitize the sound of a trumpet. This experiment in analog-to-digital conversion was particularly important because previous programs had been unsuccessful in faithfully reproducing the sound of a brass instrument. In this experiment, the sound of a trumpet was recorded on magnetic tape and then converted into digital form. It was analyzed on an IBM 7094 computer. A press release from Bell in November 1965 proclaimed the results of the experiment: "In listening to the computer-generated tones, 20 persons, several of whom were professional musicians, were unable to tell the difference between the computer trumpet sound and the real one."

1966   At Bell Labs in New Jersey, the availability of computers began to permit researchers to analyze analog input more

Computer analysis of audio waveforms at Bell Labs in 1966. This technique
of working with real-time computers led to speech synthesis and musical-
sound synthesis. (Courtesy Bell Labs.)

quickly. Progress in the synthesis of natural sounds acceler-
ated rapidly.

1967   At the University of Illinois, John Cage and Lejaren Hiller
collaborated on a massive multimedia piece called *HPSCHD*.
The work is scored for seven harpsichords and fifty-one computer-generated sound tapes. It was prepared by Cage and
Hiller with a computer to assemble sound patterns based on
calculations derived from *I Ching* chance operations.

1969–1974   At Bell Labs in New Jersey, Max Mathews, F. R.
Moore, and Jean Claude Risset released their Music V program, an improved version of the earlier Bell programs for
efficiently developing computer-generated sounds. In response to a call for a computer-music program that could be
used in performance situations, the group developed the

Groove program, which permitted a computer to be used as a voltage-control device for an analog synthesizer.

1975–1982   Mini- and microcomputers began to be used as control devices for analog synthesizers. Developments in microprocessor technology introduced the use of sound synthesizing "chips" in consumer musical instruments and professional synthesizers. The first all-digital synthesizers for the commercial market were introduced. Computer-music programs became commonly available for use with home computers made by such companies as Apple, Commodore, and Atari.

DIGITAL SYNTHESIZERS

The first commercially available portable digital synthesizer was introduced in 1975, developed by the composer Jon Appleton and the engineers Sydney Alonso and Cameron Jones. Called the Synclavier, the instrument was performance-oriented and included the capacity to store tracks of sound that could be used interactively with real-time keyboarding. This instrument was a vital contribution to the realm of electronic performance instruments and set the early standards for computer-based synthesizers.

Since the mid-1970s the digital synthesizer has begun to appear in many forms. These range from inexpensive consumer products with built-in keyboards, preset sound settings, and loudspeakers, to full-scale minicomputers with full control over the designing and synthesis of all sound parameters. Many types of systems will begin to appear on the market during the next few years. Market activity has settled for the moment into three basic areas: consumer-oriented products (especially compact hand-held systems), devices that attach to personal computers, and fully integrated systems with self-contained microcomputers.

Consumer Music Products

Up until 1979, the Casio corporation of Fairfield, New Jersey, was primarily known for its wide line of pocket calculators. In its experiments in the mass marketing of such devices, it discovered a new application for the microprocessor chip: sound synthesis. Around 1980 it introduced its first portable electronic musical instrument, the Casio VL-Tone. Selling for about $70, this small instrument with its 2.5-octave keyboard contained presets for rhythms and instrument voices and permitted the player to store a sequence

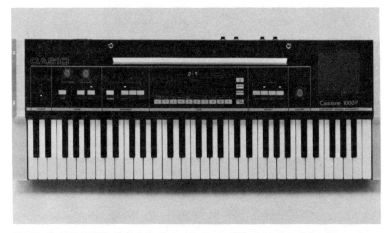

The Casio CT-1000P digital keyboard is a portable instrument for the serious musician. It features 1,000 user-programmable voices in addition to 10 preset sounds. (Courtesy Casio.)

of up to a hundred notes in memory. The secret behind this device was compact computer technology. All of the sounds produced by the instrument were generated by tiny electronic chips and converted into analog waveforms for broadcast over its built-in loudspeaker. This revolution in the design of portable consumer musical instruments led to the development of many other products using the same general principles. The more expensive systems, those costing between $500 and $1,000, are of sufficient quality to be used by professional musicians and compete effectively with analog synthesizers, which are often more expensive.

The more impressive Casio devices include the following:

- The Casio PT-20: A thirty-one-key monophonic instrument with 2.5 octaves, it includes seven preset voices such as piano, organ, violin, and flute and offers seventeen background rhythms. To play chords, chord buttons are provided with designations for chords such as major, minor, and seventh. Using a feature called an "automatic judging chord generator," the keyboard can be played with one finger and the PT-20 will automatically play the accompanying chord. The keyboard can also store up to 508 notes for playback. This device was introduced in January 1983 at a retail price under $100.

- The Casiotone CT-1000P: This is a five-octave polyphonic keyboard instrument for the novice or professional musician. Through the combination of various tone controls, up to a thousand different timbres can be selected. Ten presets are also included, as well as a sequencer and effects such as sustain, vibrato, delayed vibrato, and heavy vibrato. When first introduced, this device cost $699.

- Bar Code Input: A number of recent Casio instruments have incorporated bar-coded input options to permit the units to play automatically music being read by a light pen. The user merely passes the scanning wand over the bar-coded sheet music and the system memorizes it for play-back. This rather novel feature for the nonmusician is representative of the unusual turns that digital electronics can offer—a player piano that can be held in one hand.

Many other companies have entered the consumer market for small digital music systems. Among these are Yamaha and Roland.

Music Using Personal Computers

The proliferation of home computers is destined to have a tremendous effect on the availability of digital synthesizing equipment. The current desktop microcomputer totally outclasses its distant relatives from the prehistoric 1950s in every way, including sound-synthesis capability. With the availability of chips and circuits that can convert digital codes into signals that can be translated into audible sounds, the world of the synthesizer is suddenly open to anyone who can afford a small computer. While many inexpensive software packages are available to create simple music using a personal computer, one of the earliest companies to offer a total digital music system for a home computer was Syntauri Corporation of Palo Alto, California.

The alphaSyntauri system by Syntauri uses a 48K Apple II computer as its brain, one or two disk drives for storage, and a video monitor. The digital audio oscillators are contained in a circuit board developed by Mountain Computer. Syntauri then provides the software, a four- or five-octave piano-type keyboard, interface hardware, and plenty of ideas to help one get started with digital music.

When dealing with a digital system such as this, one selects

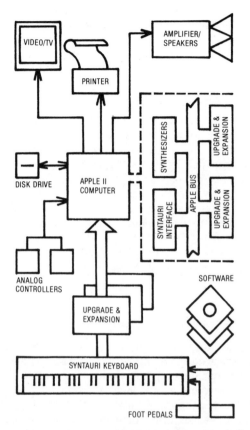

Configuration diagram for the alphaSyntauri digital synthesizer used in connection with an Apple II microcomputer. (Courtesy Syntauri Corporation.)

sounds by either designing the waveforms graphically on the video monitor or by selecting one of the many preset sounds that are available. Although the system is oriented toward a keyboard, unusual timbres and sound effects can also be generated by devising and mixing sound waves at will. The desired sounds can be played via the keyboard and recorded on a "floppy disk" for storage. The floppy disk replaces magnetic tape and may be used to accompany other sounds being played. The entire approach may seem abstract to the person who is accustomed to turning dials and moving patch cords on an analog synthesizer, but the potential is there once one adapts to the available means of control.

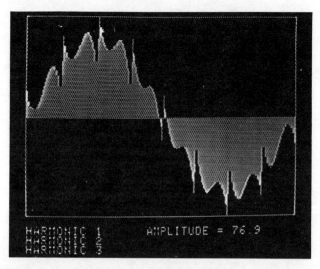

The CRT display of the alphaSyntauri digital synthesizer allows the analysis and design of waveforms for synthesis. (Courtesy Syntauri Corporation.)

The typewriter keyboard of the Apple computer becomes a significant tool when using the Syntauri system. Through the keyboard, it is possible to provide instructions to the computer to design waveforms, store information, manipulate recorded sounds, and play back any sounds. Up to sixteen oscillator voices (eight per channel) can be used. The video display can depict the shape of a wave graphically, and once a composer becomes familiar with the various waveforms, he or she will be able to begin to design new waveshapes to match an anticipated result. A light pen is also provided for hand-drawing waveforms on the screen, which can then be permanently stored by the system on disk for later recall.

In a live performance, the alphaSyntauri system can be used to fetch prerecorded sounds and play them back. This can be done by hitting a key or two on the typewriter keyboard. Other capabilities that can be predetermined and called up at will include special presets for the keyboard, different musical scales, and special effects such as vibrato, timbre scanning for creating sequencer rhythms, and pitch sweep, which creates rising glissandi.

One very attractive feature of the alphaSyntauri and other similar units is the ability to create new pitch scales easily by giving

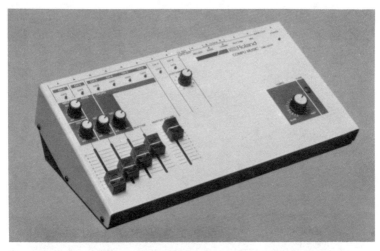

The Roland Compu Music CMU-800R, a device for adding fundamental percussive and harmonic synthesis capability to an Apple computer. (Photo from Roland Corporation U.S.)

simple instructions to the computer. On the alphaSyntauri it is possible to do this with up to thirty-two intervals per octave. It is even possible to play back a previously recorded keyboard track using a newly devised pitch system. As the final touch for any composing job, the alphaSyntauri will also let the user print out the musical score using a standard matrix computer printer.

Perhaps the most startling aspect of the alphaSyntauri is its price. The most elaborate package of equipment, including a five-octave keyboard, a hundred preset sounds, and special software, costs around $2,000. That does not include the cost of the Apple computer, which would be an additional $1,500 to $2,000. For a total of about $4,000, then, one can acquire a complete digital synthesizing package and a computer. This is really very good news for the composer who has been saving up to buy a studio synthesizer of some type. One is compelled to examine digital equipment such as the Syntauri prior to making the leap into any kind of system, especially an analog one.

A less expensive way to use the Apple computer for music is with the Compu Music system by Roland. This device is an external add-on to the computer and provides six digital tone generators and seven rhythm sounds. The unit is plugged into the computer through an interface circuit board and is "played" or programmed through the typewriter keyboard of the computer.

External controls are also provided for the envelope and volume of the melody, chord, and rhythm components of the sound. While its capabilities are limited, at the price of $500 it serves as an excellent introduction to computer synthesis of sound.

Fully Integrated Computer Music Systems

Even more impressive than the alphaSyntauri is the Fairlight Computer Musical Instrument (CMI). It is also six times more expensive. Developed and first built in Australia in 1979, the Fairlight CMI has become one of the most popular new instruments to be taken on tour by rock groups. Like the alphaSyntauri and other digital synthesizers made for use with personal computers, the Fairlight provides a full complement of control and wave-design capabilities. It comes with its own dedicated computer, as well as dual 8-inch disk drives, a six-octave touch-sensitive keyboard, and some very powerful software for the creation and manipulation of sounds.

One of the most striking features of the Fairlight is its ability to accept incoming signals from other sources such as a microphone. Using a process called sampling, the system can then analyze the sound and store it on disk in digital form for later reproduction. This permits the incorporation of any sound into a composition and allows the composer to change and alter sounds that are collected. Perhaps the greatest implication of sampling is the ability to use the timbre or nature of a natural sound as the form for musical sounds being played by the instrument. For example, one could sample the sound of a violin and then accurately reproduce it, or one could take the sound of a jet airplane and transform it into a musical sound. The possibilities are endless and have applications not only in pure musical composition but in the making of sound effects for motion pictures.

Another of the Fairlight's features is the ability to use an external sound signal as a controlling device, which would allow an electric guitar, for example, to trigger sounds in the CMI. Further, like the alphaSyntauri, the Fairlight comes with a light pen for drawing new waveforms on the display. It also features sequencing capability, four hundred preset sounds, and the ability to create new tonal scales tuned in increments as small as one one-hundredth of a semitone. As a recording device, live tracks can be merged with recorded passages to create overdubbing effects. In the studio, the system can act as a controller for synchronizing up to fifty-six parts on an eight-track tape recorder.

The Fairlight is a professional system and, unlike some of its

The Fairlight Computer Music Instrument, one of the first full-featured computer-based digital music systems. Its features include a six-octave keyboard, floppy-disc drives for the storage of audio material in digitized form, and the ability to convert analog sounds picked up by a microphone into digital representations. (Courtesy Fairlight.)

home-computer counterparts, is rugged enough to withstand road trips with a rock band. Artists including Stevie Wonder and Keith Emerson were some of the early proponents of the system. The potential is limitless for a device that can literally store and reproduce any sound that can be recorded as well as create a few that have never been heard before. That is the true fascination of these sophisticated devices, and even though an average Fairlight now sells for $25,000–$30,000, the cost of such digital systems will naturally come down as more units are developed in the market and hardware becomes less expensive.

The Synclavier II, made by the New England Digital Corporation, is the current digital synthesizer model offered by the company that pioneered the field in the mid-1970s. It features the same general capabilities as the Fairlight CMI but is designed more as a musical instrument than as a computer. The control panel features dozens of buttons that are logically arranged by functions such as volume envelope, recorder control, vibrato, and timbre

Synclavier II digital music synthesizer, one of the most popular digital synthesizers in use today.

bank. The unit features sixteen digital oscillator voices and sixteen-track recording. The sampling feature is extremely powerful and digitizes analog sounds using a greater bandwidth (frequency range) than the Fairlight instrument. Its digital memory recorder can store a sequence of two thousand notes, and can be expanded to record fifteen thousand notes. The Synclavier II is the premiere product in the digital synthesizer market but costs anywhere from $28,000 for a basic configuration up to about $55,000 for a fully equipped system.

OTHER COMPUTER DEVELOPMENTS

In 1984, a significant step toward a standardized industry approach to digital synthesizer interface was reached with the development of MIDI—Musical Instrument Digital Interface. The MIDI interface permits instruments made by different companies to be linked electronically for control purposes during performance. Through using MIDI-compatible components, it is possible, for example, to control the output of two or more synthesizers using a single keyboard. In this case, the control signals from the single keyboard are transmitted through MIDI interface communications to the other synthesizers that are linked to it. Other applications of MIDI include linkage to personal computers to provide program control of multiple synthesizers and the manipulation of electronic percussion boxes in the accompaniment of keyboard music. MIDI promises to broaden the control of the performer and the industry has quickly rallied around this standard in an attempt to widen the application of computers in the field.

The introduction of sound recording using digital coding will certainly supplant the reel-to-reel tape recorder that we know today. Digital "mastering" of recordings became common during the early 1980s, as did the first commercially available digital "compact discs" and players for the consumer. The next stage to watch for will be the availability of digital sound recording and mixing devices for general distribution to the consumer and professional markets.

COMPUTER-ASSISTED MUSIC—A NEW TRADITION

Many electronic tinkerers who have made reputations for themselves as electronic-music composers have turned to the use of microcomputers for the making of music. Whether it is Pierre Boulez in Paris, Morton Subotnick in California using the first Buchla digital unit, or any one of dozens of other composers who are exploring the field, one goal seems to have come to the fore: to put the human being back into computer music. Laurie Spiegel, a composer who creates rich soundscapes that are uncharacteristic of traditional computer music, probably summed it up best in the liner notes to her album *The Expanding Universe*: "Computers had a negative and dehumanizing image as long as they were only seen as inaccessible threatening tools of large bureaucratic organizations. They were popularly imbued with the characteristics of those organizations. Now that computers are increasingly becoming the personal tools of ordinary individuals, this image is changing." So is the music.

One of the most interesting goals of the new composers of computer music is to create an interactive performance situation between the musician and the computer. Joel Chadabe has done this by developing a program that will compose rhythmic sounds in response to incoming sound signals, like the clapping of a hand or the playing of a percussion instrument. Some examples of this can be found on his 1981 album *Rhythms*. In this case, a percussionist improvises with a computer that is capable of hearing what he is playing and responding accordingly with spontaneous rhythmic sounds of its own. The Synclavier computer-based digital synthesizer made by New England Digital Corporation is used in this project. The results are a wide variety of short pieces containing a multitude of harmonic and percussive rhythmic sounds.

The Macrofusion Computer Music Laboratory in Oakhurst, California, is one of the best-equipped private computer-music studios in the world. Operated by Peter Spoecker, the studio includes a fully equipped Synclavier II, five analog synthesizers, Teac and Revox mastering tape machines, an Osborne computer for data base management, and a full array of effects and treatment devices. (Courtesy of Peter Spoecker, Macrofusion Computer Music, Oakhurst, California.)

Another composer who has devoted much of his work in music to creating installations for use by musicians and nonmusicians alike is David Behrman. Prior to his current involvement in the development of a kind of interactive computer music game, he was working with Kim-1 microcomputers and homemade sound-generating circuits. In his piece *On the Other Ocean*, the computer can sense specific pitches that are played by a flutist and a bassoonist. The computer responds to this input by producing sets of harmonies emanating from the sound-synthesizing equipment. This interactive situation adds life to computer music and puts the human being back in the forefront.

Computers have become so accessible that they have finally become just another tool for creating music, like a piano, a penny whistle, or a pipe organ. With interactive systems that permit the performer to exercise control over the spontaneous output of digital equipment, it would be more accurate to say that we have entered the age of computer-assisted music.

3

EXPERIMENTAL MUSIC

Because it often deals with unusual new sounds and new methods of organizing music using technology, electronic music has been linked with experimental music from the early days. Many of the first composers to embrace electronic music, like Edgard Varèse, John Cage, and Henry Cowell, were experimental thinkers in search of new tools to work with. They were interested in extending the sound barrier of the traditional orchestra through new textures, instruments, and tonalities. Electronic music offered them an opportunity to do that.

Electronic music blossomed under the guidance and exploration of avant-garde composers. Most of the breakthroughs in the design and use of the equipment began with modern composers who dared to be venturesome. It is within the context of experimental music that the most startling capabilities of electronic music can be discovered. Because the development of the instruments is so intimately connected to the ideas of the avant-garde, it is important to examine the experimental music movement of the twentieth century in order to fully understand the origins and applications of electronic music.

Seven

ORIGINS
of the
AVANT-GARDE

This history of the avant-garde predates somewhat the

introduction of electronic music and traces the work of

many classical composers. It closely parallels similar rev-

olutions in the art world such as impressionism, dadaism,

cubism, and futurism. These movements, whether in music

or in the visual arts, questioned seriously the traditions of the past. The influence of the industrial revolution on society and a growing militarism that pushed more and more nations to the brink of war cast grave doubts on the state of humanity. Artists and composers responded through a revolution of their own in their art and music.

ALTERNATE PITCH SYSTEM, NEW SCALES, AND ATONALITY

In 1887, a young Parisian named Erik Satie wrote his *Trois gymnopédies* and *Sarabandes* for piano. After having dreamed away several years at the Paris Conservatoire and become bored with the contrivance of major-minor tonality as found in Germanic symphonies and operas, Satie set forth to create a new music of lucid clarity, stripped of ornamentation and "sauce," as he called it. He was also disconcerted by the embellishments of impressionist music—then still a quite young movement—and sought to avoid its overwrought, self-conscious approach. The result was a blow for simplicity straight from the heart of this strange fellow. He was later to comment on his experience at the Paris Conservatoire, "My harmony professor thought I had a gift for the piano, while my piano professor considered that I might be talented as a composer."

In the *Gymnopédies* and *Sarabandes*, Satie first applied medieval scales and the modes of Gregorian chant to his music. These haunting and unforgettable pieces employed delicate melodies in conjunction with floating harmonic blocks and unresolved chords to suspend the sound in a kind of mystical aura. Some of the scores for Satie's early piano works omitted bar lines as well as time and key signatures. More than any other composer of his time, Satie represented the mood of the movement toward a new musical aesthetic. Although his work received only a fraction of the attention bestowed on contemporaries like Claude Debussy, Darius Milhaud, and Maurice Ravel, it was Satie who most strongly opposed tradition and who inspired the great body of French composition through the 1920s. His acerbic wit and penchant for unusual titles (such as *Veritable Flabby Preludes, Chapters Turned Every Which Way,* and *Old Sequins and Old Cuirasses*) made his presence almost ridiculous. Yet the experiments he undertook to free French music provided the force underlying much of the impressionist movement. Debussy, for instance, went on to employ the pentatonic and other medieval scales and to a large extent receives credit for developing these techniques, which were in fact first attempted by Satie.

Debussy became a pivotal figure in the modern music movement of France. In 1889 he attended the Paris Exposition, which marked the one-hundredth anniversary of the French Revolution. There he heard Balinese gamelan music for the first time. His exposure to this led him to a favored view of the whole-tone scale, which is suggestive of Far Eastern modes. Debussy was brimming over with creative enthusiasm and seized every experience, every influence, as a means for mobilizing his own ideas. He was a marvelous assimilator of concepts and matured into one of the most familiar modern composers.

Debussy first met Satie in 1890. Satie was acting as pianist at a well-known cabaret in Montmartre, Le Chat Noir. Satie, twenty-four, and Debussy, twenty-eight, took a liking to each other and developed a relationship that proved to be mutually beneficial. Both men were disillusioned with the current state of music, and as they watched their peers wallowing in the mire of Wagnerian influence, each laid down plans to change the state of music. By this time, both men had experimented with unusual tonal scales, had suffered through an academic environment in which their ideas were met with indignation, and had turned to the attractive avant-garde life of Paris for camaraderie and support. It was probably during one of their discussions at a French club that Satie uttered his famous line "We ought to have our own music—if possible, without sauerkraut!" Satie also shared some thoughts with Debussy on a lyric opera he was considering. As the story goes, Debussy was so influenced by these ideas that he went on to compose his only completed opera, *Pelléas et Mélisande* as a result. It took him ten years to complete, and in the meantime, Satie continued to sculpt his whimsical and concise piano works with such titles as *Pièces froides* (*Cold Pieces*, 1897) and *Trois morceaux en forme de poire* (*Three Pieces in the Form of a Pear*, 1903).

Together, Satie and Debussy became known for several distinct experimental approaches to music. These included the use of organum, in which two or more melodies are written in parallel so that they rise and fall in equal steps simultaneously; the application of the whole-tone scale and other scales consisting only of primary intervals and lacking major and minor steps like the half notes of the chromatic scale, as found on the piano; and the use of repetitive chords in a steady rhythmic pattern to achieve a suspension of motion and tension. Perhaps the foremost preoccupation of both composers was their effort to free melody from its traditional key and chord underpinning, allowing it to move and develop independently of any presupposed melodramatic superstructures. This last characteristic of their music gave it a mystical, serene quality.

During the same period that Satie and Debussy began using whole-tone scales, a number of other composers and theoreticians began to suggest even more elaborate approaches. The microtonal scale employs intervals that are smaller than the traditional half tones of the chromatic scale. Early supporters like Shohe Tanaka and Carl Fitz proposed microtonal scales having from 20 to 104 notes per octave. The only problem was that there were not any instruments that could play such music, which forced some of these men to try to build new instruments to suit the purpose. This problem was never satisfactorily solved until the introduction of modern electronic musical instruments that can be tuned in variable scales.

In 1888 a fourteen-year-old American named Charles Edward Ives wrote his first song, called "Majority." In the piano accompaniment, he used a "tone cluster," which is the simultaneous playing of multiple adjacent keys on the piano—a rather disharmonious act. This is probably the first documented use of a tone cluster in a score. Ives went on to use tone clusters throughout his career. From this curious beginning, Ives developed into one of America's most original and prolific modern composers. Among his credits are the developments of polytonality (the use of different keys simultaneously), polyrhythms, and polymeters (layers of differing rhythms and rapidly changing meters), and microtones. In order to use quarter tones for a piano work, the resourceful Ives once tuned two pianos a quarter tone apart so that he could perform his *Three Quartertone Piano Pieces* (1923–1924).

Following the early work of Satie, Debussy, and Ives, the exploration of alternatives to the standard chromatic tonal scale was championed by many composers. They included Ferruccio Busoni, Bela Bartok, Arnold Schoenberg, and Anton von Webern. In 1907, Busoni, a well-known Italian-German pianist, composer, theoretician, and teacher, read about the telharmonium of Thaddeus Cahill in the July 1906 issue of *McClure's* magazine. He was inspired by the possibilities of using such an instrument to develop new tonal scales and was prompted to write about it in his famous manifesto *Entwurf einer neuen Ästhetik der Tonkunst* (*Sketch of a New Esthetic of Music*):

> I refer to an invention by Dr. Thaddeus Cahill. He has constructed a comprehensive apparatus which makes it possible to transform an electric current into a fixed and mathematically exact number of vibrations. As pitch de-

pends on the number of vibrations, and the apparatus may be "set" on any number desired, the infinite gradation of the octave may be accomplished by merely moving a lever corresponding to the pointer of a quadrant.

It really was not that easy, but Busoni never had the benefit of using the instrument himself. Even so, he came the closest to recognizing the value of the telharmonium as a precursor of an experimental age of music. It took nearly sixty years for this vision of electronically generated microtonal scales to become truly practical.

In 1906 the Hungarian composer Bela Bartok began to incorporate elements of his native folk music into his modern composition. This folk music impressed him with its use of old musical modes, lack of major and minor keys, and use of pentatonic scales. His *Twenty Hungarian Folksongs* (1906) began to exhibit some of this influence. Bartok went on to experiment and became noted for using polymodality (combining different modes), polytonality (combining major and minor keys), percussive dissonance (anticipating Stravinsky), droning bass lines, repeated notes, repetitive rhythmic structures, and dissonance.

In 1907 the Austrian composer Arnold Schoenberg composed his last piece to use a major or minor key signature, the String Quartet No. 2 in F-sharp Minor, and moved into twelve-tone music. With its emphasis on using series of the twelve notes of the scale in tone rows, this music avoids the use of familiar chord and melody structures, and employs a highly organized, mathematical approach to building a piece of music from blocks of sound. To do this, Schoenberg avoided using musical keys, which released all of the notes from a tonal center so that they could each be treated independently without regard for normal rules of harmony. Because this music does not follow conventional rules of Western harmony, it is called "dissonant" or "atonal." Schoenberg refined the technique of twelve-tone music during the 1920s. Berg and Webern were some of the immediate disciples of this form of composition. Serial music—employing random but fixed series of notes and developed in the 1950s through the work of composers Milton Babbitt, Pierre Boulez, and Karlheinz Stockhausen—is the ultimate refinement of this approach.

Anton von Webern became known for his unique, sparsely orchestrated compositions. He suppressed all repetition in his music. Like Ives, he used unusual combinations of instruments and concentrated on putting traditional instruments in odd groupings in order to develop new sound textures. He was concerned with the qualities of sound for sound's sake, a devotion later echoed by Cage and others. He extended the twelve-tone system beyond the limits of pitch to seek total control of timbre and rhythm as well. In so doing, he developed serial music as a natural extension of Schoenberg's twelve-tone theories.

THE USE OF NOISE IN MUSIC

By 1910 the public was politely humoring the eccentric approaches to tonality that had begun to pop up in the works of Ives, Schoenberg, Debussy, Satie, Webern, and others. They were not prepared, however, for the next onslaught: the use of noise as an element in music. This movement began, appropriately, with the piano. In his *Allegro barbaro* (1911), Bartok suddenly began to pound loud, dissonant "chords" on the keyboard. Even more alarming, though, were the antics of a young composition student at the University of California named Henry Cowell. In 1912, Cowell took Ives's tone cluster and made it the center of a musical controversy. His clusters were not quaint little diatribes using two or three notes simultaneously. Cowell banged on the keyboard with his forearm, the flat of his hand, or any convenient length of wood in order to depress an entire range of adjacent keys at the same time. Then he went a step further and began to pluck and strike the strings on the inside of the piano. His techniques were so well developed that he published a book called *New Musical Resources* in 1930 (first written in 1919) to document his efforts. Cowell became one of the more durable members of the avant-garde in America and gained notoriety for his performances during the 1920s and 1930s.

Even more startling, however, was the futurist movement, which sprang up in Italy in 1909. It was conceived and organized by poet Emilio Filippo Tommaso Marinetti, and while its primary focus was in the visual arts, some of its members became interested in new musical ideas. In 1911, the composer Francesco Balilla Pratella published a manifesto on *Futurist Music*. In this work, he expressed sentiments not unlike those being put forth in Germany, France, and the United States. He was interested in expanding the range of harmonic music through the use of semitones and agreed with the use of a "chromatic atonal mode" as previously introduced by Schoenberg. He called this the "enharmonic mode," and although he felt he could embrace this development as "a magnificent conquest by Futurism," his formula does not seem to be vastly different from theories being considered elsewhere at that time. In addition, Pratella hoped to "crush the domination of dance rhythm" in order to create a freer approach to tempo, and take charge of polyphony as a way of "fusing harmony and counterpoint."

In 1913, Pratella introduced his music at a concert at the Teatro Costanzi in Rome. He conducted his piece called *Musica Futurista* for orchestra, much to the delight of his futurist compatriots. One painter, Luigi Russolo, was so inspired that he quickly wrote his own manifesto called *The Art of Noise* (1913). Although it was clear that Pratella remained interested in working with traditional orchestral instruments and that his goal was to develop new pitch and rhythm systems to expand the potential of existing tools, Russolo addressed his own, more extreme views to Pratella. Russolo was compelled to take Pratella's ideas a step further to include various kinds of noises in music. He not only put his ideas on paper but immediately abandoned painting and devoted his full time to the design and invention of new mechanical noisemakers to produce his music.

Russolo's manifesto is an impressive document and certainly an influential precursor of modern experimental music. In it can be found the following statements boldly emblazoned:

- THIS EVOLUTION OF MUSIC IS PARALLELED BY THE MULTIPLICATION OF THE MACHINE.

- IT IS NECESSARY TO BREAK THIS RESTRICTED CIRCLE OF PURE SOUNDS AND CONQUER THE INFINITE VARIETY OF NOISE-SOUNDS.

- WE TAKE GREATER PLEASURE IN IDEALLY COMBINING THE NOISES OF TRAMS, EXPLOSIONS OF MOTORS, TRAINS AND SHOUTING CROWDS THAN IN LISTENING AGAIN, FOR EXAMPLE, TO THE "EROICA" OR THE "PASTORALE."

- WE WANT TO SCORE AND REGULATE HARMONICALLY AND RHYTHMICALLY THESE EXTREMELY VARIED NOISES.

His simple purpose was to extend the accepted musical spectrum a little further by introducing nonmusical sounds in a controlled fashion. With the help of the painter Ugo Piatti, Russolo began to design and build various mechanical noise-producing instruments. He called them *intonarumori* ("noise-intoners") and built them to produce the following "families" of sounds:

1. Roars
   Thunders
   Explosions
   Bursts
   Crashes
   Booms

2. Whistles
   Hisses
   Puffs

3. Whispers
   Murmurs
   Grumbles
   Buzzers
   Babblings

4. Screeches
   Creaks
   Rustles
   Hums
   Crackles
   Rubs

5. Percussion noises using: metal, wood, skin, rock, terra cotta, etc.

6. Voices of animals and humans: shouts, shrieks, moans, yells, howls, laughs, groans, etc.

Outwardly, each noise-intoner consisted of a wooden box with a megaphone. Internally, there were various electromechanical devices used to generate the desired sounds. There were different noise-intoners for the different families of sounds.

By August 1913, an entire orchestra of these strange boxes had been completed, and concerts began in Rome. A year later, in June 1914, Russolo presented a concert in London. A critique of the event in the *Times* of London aptly summed up the public's reaction to this music. The writer likened the sounds to those "in the rigging of a channel-steamer during a bad crossing" and suggested that it had been "unwise" of the musicians to proceed after their first piece was greeted by "the pathetic cries of 'no more' from all parts of the auditorium."

It probably took the compulsiveness of a nonmusician like Russolo to venture so recklessly into the use of noise in music. He did so without much restraint, and although in years to come others like Varèse and Cage gained notoriety for similar efforts, Russolo's unhappy fate was to be considered a kind of avant-garde clown like Spike Jones. He continued to develop his instruments, however, and they eventually were accepted by the theatrical world as a means for producing sound effects.

Back in France, Erik Satie had joined forces with the playwright Jean Cocteau to present a "ballet" called *Parade* in 1917. With sets by Pablo Picasso and choreography by Leonid Massine, this unusual work was a pivotal piece of avant-garde craftsmanship. Cocteau characterized the ballet as a manifesto of cubism. The stage was filled with a variety of nonsense activities, including the antics of a Chinese magician, a dancer who mimed the riding of a horse and swimming in a river, and a troup of acrobats flying across the stage. It was Satie's music that caused the biggest uproar.

The Futurist Art of Noise: Luigi Russolo (left) and his assistant, Ugo Piatti with noise intoners (*intonarumori*). (Courtesy of the Philadelphia Museum of Art, the Harry Lewis Winston Collection.)

Not only did it nonchalantly move from ragtime to classical motifs, but it included such nonmusical sounds as the pounding of a type-writer, a steamship whistle, a siren, and an airplane motor. The audience, naturally, rioted. In a reply to a critic, Satie simply wrote:

> *Sir and Dear Friend,*
>
> > *You are not only an arse, but an arse without music.*
> > *Signed, Erik Satie*

THE ARRIVAL OF VARÈSE

Edgard Varèse (1883–1965) went to live in New York City in 1915. He was the first composer to recognize that the natural extension of avant-garde music was into the use of electronics. Although his most respected and experimental work still lay before him, he showed that he possessed an uncanny sense of the future when in 1916 he made the following statement in the *New York Morning Telegraph*: "Our musical alphabet must be enriched. We also need new instruments very badly. . . . In my own works I have always felt the need for new mediums of expression . . . which can lend themselves to every expression of thought and can keep up with thought." In 1917 he wrote in the periodical *391*: "I dream of instruments obedient to my thought and which with their contri-bution of a whole new world of unsuspected sounds, will lend themselves to the exigencies of my inner rhythm." Thus did Varèse set the stage for the entrance of electronic music.

By 1930 all of the fundamental principles of classical Western music had been openly questioned by the unusual international collective of composers known as the avant-garde. Their origins were different, as were their languages, but their goals relating to music were precisely the same: to create a new music that was not a remnant of vastly different days gone by but a music that was of their own time, entirely of their own invention. By 1950 new tech-nology in electronic music made it easier for them to explore these ideas.

Eight

ENTER
ELECTRONIC
MUSIC

Electronic musical instruments invented prior to 1950 were

performance instruments designed to be played live. De-

vices like the theremin, ondes martenot, and Trautonium

were indeed unique, but in trying to write for them, most

composers reduced the devices to the role of a solo in-

strument in an otherwise familiar instrumental ensemble.

The titles of early works for these instruments—such as Joseph Schillinger's *First Airphonic Suite* for RCA theremin with orchestra (1929) or Bohuslav Martinu's *Fantasy* for theremin, string quartet, oboe, and piano (1945)—generally attest to the parochial nature of the music. Men of vision, like Varèse and Cage, certainly anticipated the use of electronic instruments in those pre–World War II days, but the hardware to carry out their dreams simply did not exist yet. With the availability of the tape recorder in 1948, electronic music suddenly became a medium. It was during this time that a true aesthetic of the music began to take shape.

AESTHETIC CHARACTERISTICS OF ELECTRONIC MUSIC

The aesthetic attributes of electronic music simply extend in some ways the basic trends that were set in motion by the avant-garde in the early part of the twentieth century. Whereas the idea of twelve-tone or serial composition encouraged the exercise of great control over each element of a piece of music, electronics offered the composer the technical means to achieve this to a far more exacting degree. In addition, it opened the doors to alternate pitch systems through the use of pitch ranges that could be variably adjusted. Finally, because of its ability to capture and treat non-musical sounds, electronic music fostered the use of noise and ambient sounds in either a controlled format or a freer style.

Electronic music is also unique in some special ways. First of all, it does not have to breathe. As Robert Ashley learned early on, "It can go on as long as the electricity comes out of the wall." Electronic music also offers more control over the total production and performance of music than was ever before possible when working with traditional instruments. Whether working in a studio with tape equipment or with an interactive synthesizer that can be programmed with preset sequences, one person can have total control of the music.

Because electronic music is, by its nature, capable of being recorded and manipulated, it also provides unique command over the space-time fabric of music. Music is a seeming nonentity, existing only as sound waves that can be detected and interpreted through the ears and the mind. With electronic-music devices, however, sound patterns can be stored on magnetic mediums and revived at will. This is the most revolutionary aesthetic feature, and challenge, of electronic music and provides the composer with considerable power over the fundamental nature of music. Our understanding of this power is still immature. We have barely begun to realize the potential of using these space-time aspects of music.

Lastly, the inherent ability to invent and synthesize new sounds offers the composer the most versatile aural palette ever created. Using sophisticated digital synthesizers, one can even capture, analyze, and manipulate any sound that can be heard, whether the sound of a traditional instrument like a violin or an ambient sound like that of a speeding car. This unique control over the physical nature of sound unleashes untold power and wonder for the fulfilling of man's most ambitious musical dreams. The adaptable nature of electronic music permits every composer to produce work that is distinctly different from that of any other composer.

The arrival of the tape recorder following World War II sparked a surge of activity in experimental music. Composers such as Varèse and Cage had been anxiously awaiting something like magnetic tape recording for many years. Cage defined the significance of the tape recorder in the following way: "It made one aware that there was an equivalence between space and time, because the tape you could see existed in space, whereas the sounds existed in time. That immediately changed the notation of music. We didn't have to bother with counting one-two-three-four anymore. We could if we wanted to, but we didn't have to. We could put a sound at any point in time."

In the early years of the tape recorder, there was a distinct difference in approach between the major schools of electronic music. In France, the studio of Pierre Schaeffer became known for musique concrète, which manipulated recordings of nonelectronic sounds. This music developed out of experiments with phonograph recordings and tape recorders, and did not use any electronic musical devices whatsoever. In Germany, on the other hand, the studio of Dr. Herbert Eimert focused on the use of only electronically generated sounds. The only commonality between the two studios for a number of years was that they both used tape recorders to organize the material. By the middle of the 1950s, however, electronic music had come to embrace a combination of electronic and nonelectronic sounds, and all differences between the two schools of thought vanished. Over the years, then, the various approaches to producing electronic music have settled on a few very broad categories: musique concrète, electroacoustic music, studio composition, and live electronic music.

MUSIQUE CONCRÈTE

Pierre Schaeffer was responsible for a new-music movement that strove to treat everyday noises and sounds as musical material. This was not unlike the radical concepts of futurism some thirty-five years earlier, except that Schaeffer had the technical means to work with recordings of actual environmental sounds, whereas the futurists depended on the use of mechanical devices that were designed to make various noises. Schaeffer, like his futurist predecessor Russolo, was not a trained musician. He succeeded, though, in revealing the full musical spectrum to the world at large, an amazing feat that perhaps could only have been accomplished with so much bravado by a nonmusician possessing no special predispositions.

Schaeffer coined the term *musique concrète* to describe his work. He actually began in 1948 by using phonograph recordings of sound effects as source material. This was not easy. Using multiple turntables, Schaeffer would cue desired sounds from existing recordings and rerecord them using a disc lathe to produce a complete work. His only means for altering the sounds of the discs were through changing the speed of the turntables, creating repeating loops or grooves in the discs, superimposing two sounds by playing them simultaneously, and adjusting the volume and playing sounds backward. His first composition, *Étude aux chemins de fer* (*Étude for Railroad Trains*), was completed in 1948 using these techniques applied to recordings of steam locomotives.

He soon followed with other works for such things as saucepan lids or even the unsuspecting piano. His cohorts were intrigued by his experiments, and on October 5, 1948, a "concert of noises" was broadcast over French radio. Five pieces were presented: *Étude aux chemins de fer, Étude aux tourniquets* (for xylophone, bells, and whistling toy tops called tourniquets), *Étude au piano I, Étude au piano II* (both using piano material recorded for Schaeffer by Pierre Boulez), and *Étude aux casseroles* (using the sounds of spinning saucepan lids, boats, human voices, and other instruments). These pieces represent a vast development from the mere presentation of interesting sequences of sounds and rhythms to an attempt to deal musically with his newly discovered techniques.

In 1949, Schaeffer invited composer Pierre Henry to join him in his work. This marked the beginning of a healthy collaboration that brought more artistic consciousness to the musique concrète phenomenon. The works generated by the studio began to exhibit more musical overtones, if by title alone, and the pair began a crusade to transform modern concepts of music. *Symphonie pour un homme seul* (1949–1950) was the first major work completed by the duo. Although the twelve-movement work underwent many revisions over the years, the original recording, composed using phonograph machines, is a striking and ambitious piece, even by today's standards. It freely employed a wide variety of sounds, including spoken voice, broadcast music, prepared piano, and various mechanical or natural noises. Disc loop (repeating grooves) were employed effectively to create rhythmic passages of spoken words. The piece was originally structured as a series of twenty-two movements or expositions on certain combinations of sounds. It grows in complexity from movement to movement, creating greater and greater abstractions of recorded sounds until a finale of booming instrumental sounds brings the work to a close. It is emotional and fraught with tension, a trademark of early musique concrète that often inspired severe reactions on the part of the listening public.

In 1951 the French National Radio responded to the work of Schaeffer and Henry by establishing a "modern" studio for them, complete with tape recorders, filters, and other equipment. With the help of technical assistant Jacques Poullin, they devised a number of additional studio devices to give them greater control over the manipulation of sound.

The studio attracted many through its ambitious productions of electronic music and collaborations with live performances. *Symphonie pour un homme seul*, for example, in 1955 became the basis for a ballet by the choreographer Maurice Béjart. Even more awe-inspiring was the Schaeffer-Henry composition for the "concrete-opera" *Orphée 53*, produced in 1953. In this controversial production presented at the annual Donaueschingen Festival in Germany, the fairly routine presentation of two arias and musical themes was juxtaposed with tapes containing thunderous, sweeping sonorities and distorted human voices.

The studio of French radio was the center of electronic music activity in 1951. Schaeffer began to present lecture-demonstrations of the studio's work, and during the next few years many composers went to try their hand there. Among these were Pierre Boulez (who had already assisted Schaeffer by providing piano fragments for two works), the German Karlheinz Stockhausen, Marius Constant, Darius Milhaud, and Olivier Messiaen. A research assistant named Abraham A. Moles also joined the group in 1951. He was somewhat of an intellectual and set about analyzing the kind of work being done in the studio. Schaeffer and Moles developed one of the first formal aesthetic handbooks for electronic music. In it, they catalogued sounds, described the various tape-editing techniques that formed the basis of musique concrète, and expounded on some philosophical matters regarding the nature of the new medium. Among these were the interesting, although now rather obvious, observations that recorded music was permanently captured, that it could be reproduced mechanically without the need to engage musicians, and that the ability to manipulate the material provided some sort of illusory control over space and time.

Pierre Henry became the most prolific composer associated with the studio. By 1954 he had composed no less than forty-four pieces, most as solo works. He worked for French radio until 1958, when he left to start his own establishment, the Studio Apsome, with the choreographer Maurice Béjart. He continued in the tradition of musique concrète but gradually began to bring more lyricism and dynamic variety to the medium, which had always been characterized by extremities, contrasts, and choppy effects. Two of his best known works, *Le voyage* (1961–1962) and *Variations pour une porte et un soupir* (*Variations for a Door and a Sigh*, 1963), are among the most mature pieces of musique concrète ever realized.

Pierre Schaeffer, on the other hand, began to compose less and less as other trained composers spent time in his studio. He seemed to be satisfied to observe the development of the medium at arm's length but continued to serve as the guiding influence of the group by bringing in other talents to produce works. In October 1954, at Schaeffer's invitation, Edgard Varèse worked in the studio to complete the electronic portion of his piece *Déserts*.

The era of classic musique concrète lasted from the first Paris experiments in 1948 to the late 1950s. The French had a penchant for romanticism that was revealed in the dark mood of many of the works. Because the medium was so new, much of the music in the early years was inhibited by the problems of splicing pieces of recording tape together. The resulting music was characterized by angular changes in dynamics and the juxtaposition of contrasting sounds to effect sharp changes in mood and tension. By 1959 the nature of musique concrète had changed dramatically. In contrast to its original credo, it had already become acceptable to include electronically generated sounds in combination with the recorded noises that had originally been its sole source of material. In the hands of new composers and new thinkers like Luc Ferrari and Iannis Xenakis, it gradually lost its heavy-handed air of contrivance and manipulation. Equally important were the experiments in studio composition that had sprung up around the world, including the United States, Netherlands, Japan, and Italy. The novelty had worn off. A freer approach was needed. What remained was a studio in which people could dream up new forms of music and put the pieces together. Schaeffer himself shifted his focus to what he called "musical experiences," an approach to composition that remained open to interpretation.

The culmination of classic musique concrète came with the presentation of experimental music that was part of the Brussels World's Fair in 1958. For this exposition, the noted architect Le Corbusier was contracted to build a pavilion for the Philips Radio Corporation. Edgard Varèse was asked to provide some music on tape, and together the two men collaborated on one of the most ambitious presentations of new music ever conceived. Le Corbusier actually designed the pavilion for the express purpose of presenting Varèse's eight-minute tape piece. It was built in the shape of a circus tent with three peaks. Inside were four hundred loudspeakers to broadcast the sound in sweeping arcs throughout the pavilion. The music was accompanied by visual projections selected by Le Corbusier. Varèse called *Poème électronique* a work of "organized sound." This was, in effect, his version of musique concrète, but he went well beyond the structural barriers usually employed by his friends at the French radio studio. The piece combines passages of familiar sounds with starkly electronic effects and treatments. Church bells toll and metallic scrapes cut the space in shreds, and organlike tones drone quietly as ominous electronic sounds build to a threatening crescendo. A voice moans, thunderous crashes interrupt, and dark timbres lurk in the background. All of this is accented by a brilliant use of pauses and silence, ever increasing the tension and awe that this work inspires. *Poème électronique* is probably the most powerful piece of musique concrète ever produced. It represented the French approach in its most mature state. With this piece, Varèse succeeded in introducing the French to the next stage in the evolution of electronic music, which had already been embraced by most other practitioners—a full discourse in sound using all of the tools of the studio.

STUDIO COMPOSITION AND "ORGANIZED SOUND"

While the French developed musique concrète, electronic music was being explored from a number of different angles in other countries. In Germany the electronic-music studios of Nordwestdeutscher Rundfunk (Northwest German Radio, or NWDR) in Cologne were also established in 1951. Because these studios already had the use of a number of familiar electronic musical instruments, including a monochord by Trautwein, composers there were predisposed to experiment with using only purely electronic sound sources. This was a satisfactory approach at first because all of the modern German composers were already preoccupied with updating Webern's serialism, and electronic music provided them with an experimental medium with which to test their grandiose theories of control and manipulation.

Herbert Eimert, a musician and musicologist who was intensely interested in twelve-tone music, became the director of the Studio for Electronic Music of NWDR. His partners in this venture were the composer Robert Beyer and the physicist and mathematician Dr. Werner Meyer-Eppler. One of their disciples was a young composer named Karlheinz Stockhausen. Eimert, Beyer, and the others were naturally aware of the work being done in Paris. Stockhausen himself composed his very first piece of electronic music—*Étude* for sine-wave generators—in 1952, while visiting the French radio facilities. Because the Germans initially avoided the use of nonelectronic sounds, they concentrated on controlling the rhythms, pitches, and timbres of pure sine waves. The work was important but rather uninteresting when compared with the highly emotional and often contrived sounds of musique concrète. Of this body of initial experiments spanning the years 1951–1953, only Stockhausen's *Studie I* (1953) emerged as an example of new music worth remembering. It was composed using serial composition techniques and three sine-wave oscillators through a process of additive synthesis. It was also one of the first pieces of electronic music to be notated for a score. In 1954, Stockhausen's *Studie II* went slightly beyond pure sine tones and incorporated some white noise as additional source material. From that moment on, the German approach broadened its scope to include nonelectronic sounds in combination with its pure sine waves.

Stockhausen's first piece to follow his pair of electronic studies was the remarkable *Gesang der Jünglinge* (*Song of the Youths*, 1955–1956). Compared with the work of his peers in France and Germany at the time, *Gesang der Jünglinge* was dramatically more advanced and developed. It was neither musique concrète nor purely electronic, but a hybrid exposition of sounds using any facility and technique that was necessary to elicit the desired emotional impact. The piece calls for the use of sung sounds and electronic sounds and was presented publicly using a five-track recording with speakers surrounding the audience. It was one of the first electronic works to employ the concept of sound movement in space as a central part of the form. With this magnificent work, Stockhausen moved from the restrictions of twelve-tone compositions into a more organic form that has become characteristic of much electronic music. Rhythmic structures are only occasionally present, no formal repetition of motifs exists, and sounds are placed in time and space according to intuition rather than science. Some call it collage work, but collages employ an element of indeterminacy. Varèse's phrase "organized sound" is probably more applicable here, for it rightfully implies that the composer has exercised great control over the movement and placement of sounds in space. In so doing, he has created a work that plugs directly into the listener's senses of anticipation, surprise, and beauty. The freshness and strangeness of much electronic music makes it difficult for the work to appeal to a mass audience. The experience becomes a subjective one, a private one, with each individual responding emotionally as required by his or her sensibilities. Varèse probably said it best when he stated, "My experimenting is done before I make the music. Afterwards, it is the listener who must experiment."

Following Stockhausen's successful foray into organized sound, a number of noted European composers went to experiment in Cologne. Each of these composers was compelled to deal more freely with a discourse in sounds, and the results were varied and interesting. György Ligeti produced a violent tape piece based solely on vocal sounds (*Artikulation*, 1958) as well as one of his initial experiments in the use of sound masses ("Glissandi," 1957). Mauricio Kagel composed *Transición I* in 1958 as an experiment in maintaining a continuity of timbre from one sound to another. Finally, the Briton Cornelius Cardew began his work in electronic music in 1958 by completing two exercises at the Cologne studio.

Stockhausen succeeded Eimert as director of the NWDR studios in 1963 and continued to bring a sophisticated approach to the work being done there. He further developed his approach to organized sound but also began to explore the possibilities of using electronics in live settings.

During the 1960s, Stockhausen became the focus of electronic-music activity. He is an extremely prolific composer, and his work from the 1960s spans many projects and many objectives. On the one hand, he continued to work with mildly serial techniques in conjunction with orchestras, producing such works as *Momente*, with four choral groups and instrumentalists spatially deployed around the auditorium; *Stop* for orchestra; and *Adieu* for wind quintet. In the area of electronics, he worked with pure studio composition (*Hymnen* and *Telemusik* primarily), electronics combined with other instrumentalists (*Solo* for one melody instrument with feedback; *Spiral* for one soloist and shortwave receiver; *Kontakte* for electronic sounds, piano, and percussion), and live electronic music for improvisational settings (*Kurzwellen* for piano, tam-tam, viola, and shortwave radios; *Prozession* for tam-tam, microphones, instruments, and filters; *Aus den sieben Tagen* [*From the Seven Days*] and *Für kommende Zeiten* [*For Times to Come*]), each for any kind and number of instruments.

Stockhausen's *Hymnen* from 1966–1967 is the seminal work of studio composition of the 1960s. It is both free-flowing in its exposition and tightly controlled and edited for maximum effect by the composer, an unusual blend of styles that combines the tension of a chance piece with the dramatic impact of a serialist composition. The word *Hymnen* means "anthems." The piece is 113 minutes long, occupying four album sides. Each side, or "region," focuses on a number of national anthems as source material and inspiration. These are sometimes reproduced by playing recordings of the anthems, which are then modified and processed. On other occasions, the composer generates the entire sound of an anthem through electronic means. Stockhausen used a combination of pure electronics and musique concrète to construct this marvelous work. It has the atmosphere of a collage at times but moves in precise, well-planned stages, developing itself musically through the changing of sounds and textures. The piece is replete with broadcast sounds, miscellaneous noises, shortwave radio interference, crowd sounds, and brilliant moments of purely electronic origin.

Stockhausen underscored his personal indebtedness to a number of composers by dedicating each of the four regions to one of them: Pierre Boulez, Henri Pousseur, John Cage, and Luciano Berio. *Hymnen* was presented many times using a quadrophonic sound setup, and Stockhausen also composed a concert version that included parts for six soloists. Following his work on *Hymnen*, Stockhausen himself became highly interested in meditative and intuitive music (most of us would call it improvisation), and his works in pure studio composition tapered off in favor of music that combined electronics with live performers. In *Hymnen*, he gave us with one of the few authentic electronic masterworks, a piece that continues to inspire new composers.

THE UNITED STATES: ORGANIZED AND UNORGANIZED SOUND

Even though electronic music was first being explored in America during the same period as in Europe, composers in the United States did not experience the same spiritual dilemma that had befallen the French and the Germans. Musique concrète, as such, never really existed in the United States. From the beginning, there

John Cage. (Photo by Roberto Masotti.)

was an open attitude about electronic music that encouraged anyone at all with any interest to join the fray. This led to some
divergent but equally interesting activities.

John Cage and Friends

In 1951, John Cage organized the Project of Music for Magnetic Tape. With the technical assistance and studio facilities of
Louis and Bebe Barron in New York, Cage, Earle Brown, Morton
Feldman, Christian Wolff, and David Tudor all began to explore
the tape medium. Using hundreds of sounds from the audio library
and studio of the Barrons, Cage completed his first two tape pieces
in 1952. The first was *Imaginary Landscape No. 5*, followed by the
better-known *Williams Mix*.

Unlike his contemporaries, Cage was not interested so much
in the finite control and manipulation of sound as in serial music,
but in the effects that result from combining material in an indeterminate fashion. In 1950 he first began to use chance operations
derived from the *I Ching* to "organize" his compositions in a manner that excluded subjective decision-making. His approach to tape

composition was similar. *Williams Mix* began with a library of five hundred or six hundred sounds, each classified by given categories like "city sounds," "country sounds," "electronic sounds," and so forth. Over a nine-month period, Cage, Tudor, and Brown assembled the material using chance operations to denote how the tape pieces should be edited and combined. The result was a work that opened the world of music to any and all types of sounds and that avoided a sense of control or manipulation in the presentation of such sounds. While many composers found Cage's compositional methods a bit too radical for their taste, the influence of this and other Cage works nonetheless began to broaden their opinions about what was or was not musical.

By 1954 the Project of Music for Magnetic Tape had run its course. The participants became disenchanted with the restrictions of formal tape composition. Brown, Feldman, and Wolff returned to experimental music using acoustic instruments, while Cage and Tudor extended their interest into the use of electronics in live settings.

Cage himself composed only a few purely tape pieces. One of these was *Fontana Mix*, completed in 1958 at the Studio di Fonologia in Milan. This was not intended to be only a tape piece but rather a composition for any instruments. Because the results of each performance of *Fontana Mix* are unknown ahead of time, indeed unknown even during the performance, committing the piece to tape seemed to defeat the purpose of creating indeterminate or chance music. Thereafter, Cage rarely dealt with the tape medium in isolation, although he frequently used it as a source for sounds in live-performance situations.

Cage and Chance Music

John Cage is without question one of the most important and influential composers of the twentieth century. His work has had a ripple effect that permeates not only the fields of classical and modern music but jazz and rock music as well. The fact that he often uses electronics in his work is almost incidental because the true impact of his music has been in the changing of people's opinions about what is musical and what is not. In 1937, he said, "Wherever we are, what we hear is mostly noise. When we ignore it, it disturbs us. When we listen to it, we find it fascinating." His dissatisfaction with strict tape composition in 1958 is amplified by his thoughts about indeterminacy in music delivered in a lecture entitled "Composition As Process" and published in his book *SILENCE*, which is essential reading:

John Cage and David Tudor during a performance of *Indeterminacy*, 1971.
(Photo by permission of F. C. A. Lagrange.)

An experimental action is one the outcome of which is not foreseen. Being unforeseen, this action is not concerned with its excuse. Like the land, like the air, it needs none. A performance of a composition which is indeterminate of its performance is necessarily unique. It cannot be repeated. When performed for a second time, the outcome is other than it was. Nothing therefore is accomplished by such a performance, since that performance cannot be grasped as an object in time. A recording of such a work has no more value than a postcard; it provides a knowledge of something that happened, whereas the action was a non-knowledge of something that had not yet happened.

John Cage at the Memorial Concert of the Marcel Duchamp exhibition, Museum of Modern Art, Seibu Takanawa, Japan, August 1981. (Photo by Norihiko Matsumoto.)

In conversation with the author, Cage summarized his experience with chance music as follows:

> I think the thing that underlies my works since the use of chance operations—whether it's determinate or indeterminate—is the absence of intention. I've used the chance operations as a discipline to free the music precisely from my taste, memory, and any intentions that I might have. It's a discipline equivalent, I think, to that of sitting cross-legged, but the cross-leggedness would carry one, so to speak, in toward the world of dreams, the subconscious and so forth, whereas this discipline of chance operations carries one out to the world of relativity.

The use of chance operations in music can be highly disciplined in the hands of composers like Cage, Wolff, Feldman, Tudor, Mumma, and others. They may also operate purely as inspiration, leading more to free-form improvisation, the use of noise in music, and a more open state of mind regarding the nature and structure of music. In his willingness to experiment on the outer edge of the avant-garde, John Cage's music has been used as the most powerful and dramatic demonstration of changing artistic ideals and methods in our time.

Luening, Ussachevsky, and the Columbia Studio

The development of the Columbia-Princeton Electronic Music Studio is traced in chapter 5. The music being produced by this squad was decidedly different from that of the Cage group. During 1951 and 1952, music teachers Otto Luening and Vladimir Ussachevsky of Columbia University began to experiment with the use of tape recorders to transform sound. Like the earliest French experiments, these first exercises did not make use of any electronically produced sounds from oscillators. Instead, Luening and Ussachevsky turned to the manipulation of recorded instrumental sounds. This was an important choice for them to make. Luening states in his autobiography, "We had a choice of working with natural and 'nonmusical' sounds like subway noise and sneezes and coughs, or widening the sound spectrum of existing instruments and bringing out new resonances from the existing world of instruments and voices. We chose the latter."

Their very first exercises were all composed on tape, using flute sounds. When invited to present some electronic music at the Museum of Modern Art in New York, the pair hastily gathered their resources and set to work on their first electronic masterworks. These included *Fantasy in Space, Low Speed,* and *Invention in Twelve Tones* for Luening's flute and *Sonic Contours* by Ussachevsky using the piano. Both composers experimented with altering the nature of the sounds through tape-speed changes. Luening also employed some twelve-tone composition techniques in his work and used multiple tracking to superimpose separate tracks of flute sounds that were played with slight differences in pitch. *Low Speed* used these techniques to synthesize overtones in much the same manner as that used with sine-wave oscillators.

Luening and Ussachevsky became well known for their experiments with tape composition. Together with Milton Babbitt and Roger Sessions of Princeton, they founded the Columbia-Princeton Electronic Music Center and continued their research using such elaborate equipment as the RCA Mark I and II synthesizers. Sticking close to the classical tradition, the work of these men often explored the modern elements of music using electronics in combination with traditional instruments. Some of their most important achievements centered on the synchronization of live performers with electronic music played on tape. In 1954, Luening and Ussachevsky composed *A Poem in Cycles and Bells* for tape recorder and orchestra, which was, along with Varèse's *Déserts* of the same year, the first work to attempt to coincide the live performance of a symphony orchestra with tape music. This approach constituted the standard procedure in the field for adding electronic music to a live instrumental performance until the development of portable synthesizers in the late 1960s.

Compared with the truly unusual work of the Cage group, the Columbia-Princeton composers at first seemed rather tame. Their early contributions were important, however, in bridging the aesthetic gap between the extremists of the avant-garde and those who were still unsure about electronic music. When the Columbia-Princeton studio opened its doors to the world in 1959, the kind of music being produced there took on the variety and fluency of the organized-sound movement exemplified by Varèse and Stockhausen. Composers who made fine use of the facilities included Luciano Berio, Mario Davidovsky, Walter (Wendy) Carlos, Mel Powell, and Ramon Sender. Varèse himself revised his earlier tape for *Déserts* at the studio during 1960 and 1961.

Process and Meditation

In addition to movements to bring to musical indeterminacy (Cage), organized-sound exposition using electronics (Stockhausen), and the classical tendency toward serialism, there arose a movement in American music whose goal was to strip away the embellishments of instrumental music and concentrate on extremely simple rhythmic, melodic, and harmonic structures. Generally known as the minimalist movement, this tendency has taken many forms on both the East and West coasts of the United States. While the movement itself is not necessarily dependent on electronics, many of its proponents have used electronic instruments as their means of expression.

In California a number of individuals became interested in some form of minimalism. Pauline Oliveros, the noted composer and guiding light of the SFTMC, in the early 1960s, became interested in meditative aspects of music. Some of her tape pieces show an interest in additive synthesis of simple sound waves and the resulting dronelike effects, often associated with chants and meditation. Another early regular of the center, Terry Riley, went on to become known for his melodic works set to pulse rhythms. After having learned how to explore the use of tape-delay systems and loops, Riley began to perform solo instrumental concerts ac-

Composer and electronic-music innovator Pauline Oliveros in Lencadia, California in 1979. (Photo by Becky Cohen, Lencadia, California.)

companying himself with a tape recorder. One of his most noted works, *In C*, was originally developed in the SFTMC in 1961 as an electronic piece. An instrumental version was introduced in the mid-1960s. In 1980, after a long absence from the recording studio, Riley released a record album called *Shri Camel*, on which he updated his performance techniques through the use of a Yamaha electronic organ tuned to a nontempered scale, modified and accompanied by a digital delay system. His music has always exhibited an Indian influence, and through the use of electronics he has succeeded in broadening the control he can manage as a solo performer.

Another Californian, La Monte Young, was perhaps the strongest proponent of chantlike meditative music with his Theatre of Eternal Music in 1964. This group used instruments in combination with droning sine-wave oscillators to weave a music of repetitive stasis.

In New York both Steve Reich and Philip Glass have employed electronic organs and synthesizers to develop their brands of process music. In the mid-1960s, Reich was an ardent composer of tape pieces that he used to demonstrate what he called "phase" processes to create music. His approach was to begin with a simple sound fragment and then to extend and develop it gradually, using tape repetition, reverberation, and multitracking. One of these works, *Come Out* (1966), uses a spoken phrase as its primary source of material. The phrase is first played simultaneously on two channels, but as the second channel begins to speed up slightly, the phrases go out of phase and create an interesting interplay of rhythms and colliding sounds. Reich used this same approach with his *Piano Phase* and *Violin Phase* pieces before moving away from tape composition and into instrumental works that employ the same phase processes.

Philip Glass has been primarily interested in melody, harmony, and rhythm as a unit structure that cannot be subdivided. His works have always used electronic organs to generate the long, sonorous tone rows and textures he employs. Works such as *Music with Changing Parts* (1971) use long, repetitive structures to create a feeling of suspension. The music is keyboard-based and takes advantage of the electronic organ to sustain tones and change tone color.

The minimalist composers have had an unexpectedly strong influence on a number of rock-music performers. These include some of rock's more experimental performers like Brian Eno, Talking Heads, and David Bowie as well as mainstream acts such as the Who, Police, and Genesis. This influence is largely due to the availability of electronic keyboard instruments that can store and recall patterns of sounds in accompaniment to other performers in a rock band.

Organized Sound In America

The development of organized sound, or electronic exposition in the manner of Stockhausen and Varèse, has always been present in American electronic music. During the heyday of the studios in the late 1950s and 1960s, there was always a stable of composers devoted to this style of composition. In Ann Arbor, Michigan, Gordon Mumma and Robert Ashley founded the Cooperative Studio for Electronic Music in 1958. There both com-

Morton Subotnick of the San Francisco Tape Music Center, July 1965. (Photo by Bill Maginnis, studio technician.)

posers created a body of impressive tape pieces. Although each soon moved on from pure tape composition to concentrate on live presentations of new music, each made important contributions to the medium. At the SFTMC many composers began their careers by experimenting in the tape medium. One of these was Morton Subotnick, who has since worked closely with analog and digital Buchla systems and who has distinguished himself as one of the medium's most prolific sonic virtuosos. Subotnick and others worked at the center prior to the availability of synthesizing equipment and used classic studio techniques and equipment to produce important experiments. Other members of this group included Pauline Oliveros, Ramon Sender, and Terry Riley.

LIVE ELECTRONICS AND
ELECTRO-ACOUSTIC MUSIC

Prior to the postwar age of the tape recorder and studio music, electronic music had been a performing medium. Every electronic instrument invented prior to 1950 was devised for live performance. The coming of the tape recorder amplified the need for more sophisticated studio devices, leading directly to the development of synthesizers. These machines were neither easy to use nor portable, however, and during the 1950s and most of the 1960s, electronic music could easily have been confined to the studio. Many resourceful composers, however, felt they could not work in the medium unless they could take it with them, so many interesting approaches to using electronics in a live setting developed.

The first "performances" of modern electronic music—such as the presentation of works by Eimert and Beyer at the Cologne New Music Festival in 1953 or the Museum of Modern Art concert in New York featuring works by Luening and Ussachevsky—involved no more than playing tapes through loudspeakers. Stockhausen and others tried to make the most of this situation by using multitrack recordings and elaborate loudspeaker arrangements, but the situation was clearly unacceptable to both the audience and the composers. It was not that it did not accurately represent the music: after all, what better way was there to present a piece that had been assembled from little pieces of recording tape strewn across a table? It was simply boring and lacked sufficient visual stimulation to keep people awake. Even so, the loudspeaker tradition has survived all these years and remains as a final alternative when no other is available to the composer.

Live electronic music as we wish to discuss it involves performance in the presence of an audience. A broad distinction to make here is between music produced using purely electronic performance-oriented instruments, such as the synthesizer, and music produced using specially designed circuitry or electroacoustic arrangements. There are obviously many electronic performance instruments available to the musician today, especially those designed for keyboard players. These are available in both digital and analog form, and may be used as needed for the making of live music. Many of the most innovative composers, however, have relied on their own ingenuity to devise equipment and systems for the presentation of their music. The latter approach, using whatever instruments or circuits have been devised, may be purely electronic or may be electroacoustic and interact with ordinary sounds in the ambient space of the concert hall in order to produce the desired effects.

Theatrics and Mixed Media

Theatrical and multimedia presentations have been associated with new-music ideas since the early years of this century.

We have already looked at the Italian futurist movement, which made an attempt to concertize a music of noise. The avant-garde ballet *Parade*, with music by Satie, sets by Picasso, and story by Cocteau, was mind-shattering to the average Parisian of 1917. Between 1916 and 1920 the German writer Hugo Ball established the Cabaret Voltaire in Zurich as a "center for artistic entertainments" and the hub of the dada movement. This club was the site of regular performances of poetry and music, including presentations of "phonetic" and "simultaneous" poetry, text-sound pieces and random poetics generated by scrambling scraps of paper with words printed on them.

It was only natural that electronic music coming from the experimental community would have a leaning toward similar theatrics and mixed-media orientations. As association with modern dance has been particularly strong, beginning in the early days of musique concrète with productions such as *Symphonie pour un homme seul*, by Schaeffer and Henry and choreographed by Maurice Béjart in the early 1950s. Other examples range from the mildly adventuresome, such as Remi Gassmann's music for George Balanchine's ballet *Electronics* (1961), to the more abstract combinations of sound and movement involving composers such as John Cage, who has had a thirty-year association with Merce Cunningham's dance company.

John Cage began an association with dancers as long ago as 1938, when he wrote his first piece for "prepared piano," *Bacchanale*, to accompany a dance by Syvilla Fort in Seattle. Soon thereafter, he met Merce Cunningham and became musical director for his dance company in 1943. When electronic music became more feasible to produce, Cage and Cunningham often presented wildly extravagant multimedia events. Joined by David Tudor, Gordon Mumma, and others, a typical Cage-Cunningham performance during the 1960s would place the dancers in a setting populated by objects such as helium-filled pillows and projected visuals while the musicians in the pit busily adjusted all forms of audio devices. *Variations V* (1965) was one of the most clever of these. The "score" was written after the first performance, and as Cage has said, it merely consists of "remarks that would enable one to perform *Variations V*." The sound system consisted of continuously operating tape machines (at least six) playing sounds composed by Cage and Tudor, shortwave receivers (at least six), audio oscillators, and optional electronic devices that could be activated at will. The sounds of these devices were all fed into a central mixer and controlled by a triggering device prior to being sent to the loudspeakers. The sounds were triggered (made audible) through the physical movement of the dancers as they came close to prox-imity-sensing rods or interrupted light beams angled across the space.

One of the most complex multimedia events ever staged oc-curred in 1969 at the University of Illinois. John Cage and Lejaren Hiller teamed up to present a joint composition called *HPSCHD*. Using a computer-derived extrapolation of the *I Ching* developed for Cage, the two assembled fifty-one sound tapes generated by computer and combined them in a live setting with the activities of seven harpsichordists. The work was presented in a sports arena, with the electronic sounds amplified by fifty-one individual speak-ers mounted along the ceiling. Seven additional speakers were also used to amplify the harpsichords. For visual stimulation, fifty-two slide projectors provided streams of unrelated imagery, which was projected onto a large hanging screen measuring 100 feet by 160 feet as well as a semicircular screen which ran 340 feet around the inside rim of the ceiling. For five hours, hundreds of people sat in the bleachers and milled around on the main floor of the arena experiencing this sensory chaos. It was big and absorbing and live.

Not all of Cage's presentations have been this complicated, but all have been interesting. For *Reunion* in 1968, all of the sounds that were heard (as created by David Tudor, Lowell Cross, David Behrman, and Gordon Mumma) were triggered for release to loud-speakers through photoelectric switches located in a chessboard. The piece was "performed" by Cage and the painter Marcel Du-champ, who were engaged in a game of chess on stage. An equally amusing avoidance of musical control took place in 1967 when a Cage presentation consisted of the amplified sounds of a five-course dinner being served on stage.

John Cage, of course, is not the only person to have employed theatrical settings to fortify a performance of electronic music. It became a common practice during the early to mid-1960s and was put to good use by many composers, including Pauline Oliveros (*Double Basses at Twenty Paces* for Bertram Turetzky in 1968, *Canfield* for the Cunningham Dance Company in 1969) and Robert Ashley (*The Wolfman*, 1964). The music-theater tradition contin-ues as evidenced by the stage version of one of Ashley's more recent works, *Atalanta* (1982), which combines a reading with mu-sicians and a live video presentation.

The ONCE Festivals

The most important ongoing experiments in the production of new music-theater were the ONCE Festivals. Beginning in 1961 in Ann Arbor, Michigan, composers Robert Ashley, Gordon Mumma, Roger Reynolds, George Cacioppo, and Donald Scavarda joined forces with the local Dramatic Arts Center of Wilfred Kaplan to produce the first ONCE Festival of contemporary music. Ann Arbor had already gained a reputation as an experimental music center because of the work of Mumma and Ashley in the Space Theatre of Milton Cohen. The Space Theatre was a performing space where electronic music had been presented since 1958 in combination with elaborate light systems and eventually dance or group-motion activities. The interest of this core of musicians and artists in new music inspired the creation of the ONCE Festivals as a showcase for contemporary music. Prior to ONCE, the only periodic showcase for new music had been in Darmstadt, and that was a fairly formal program backed by substantial funding. The creation of ONCE grew out of the devotion of its artist-performers and was sustained both by the efforts of Kaplan as the initial organizer and by the tremendous public support that the series gained.

The first ONCE Festival took place in a two-hundred-seat Unitarian church in Ann Arbor. Contrary to its name, the festival did occur more than once, and it continued to grow year by year into successively larger auditorum settings. The festivals were presented on an annual basis from 1961 to 1968. Each consisted of about seven days' worth of performances spread out over two weeks in early February. According to Robert Ashley, only one performance during the entire eight years had less than standing-room-only attendance. Apart from the festivals themselves, there were also year-round concerts and performances given by individual members of the collective.

The first five years of the ONCE Festivals were centered on performances of new instrumental music. These used the familiar concert setting and were focused more on the music itself than on special settings or multimedia collaborations. Over the course of the first five years, there developed in Ann Arbor a kind of repertory of artists and musicians who were interested in new music as well as a theatrical performance group under Mary Ashley. Many of the regulars on the Ann Arbor scene were not necessarily trained musicians but rather artists, filmmakers, and theater people whom Robert Ashley describes as being "extremely musical people." It was under the influence of this creative force that the ONCE Festivals acquired a more music-theater orientation beginning in 1966.

The ONCE Festivals were some of the most important showcases for new music, music-theater, and electronic music during the 1960s. Sustained for eight years, they were the most durable festivals as well. The programs became progressively more ambitious as the years went on, and many important new composers were eager to participate. Each festival had numerous guest artists. The first included a new-music group headed by Luciano Berio as well as a performance by the pianist Paul Jacobs. By 1964 the program included a variety of performers, such as the Judson Dance Theatre, a new-music ensemble from the University of Illinois, the Brandeis Chamber Choir, and the Creative Associates ensemble from Buffalo, New York. It was also through the ONCE Festival that Ashley and Mumma first met Alvin Lucier and David Tudor, which led to the formation of the Sonic Arts Union performing group following the end of the ONCE experience.

In spite of the perennial ribbing of media music critics (many of whom enjoyed beginning reviews, as Robert Ashley recalls, with a line such as "Once is enough."), the ONCE Festivals served as a major influence on the contemporary-music scene. By the end of the festivals in 1968, many other, related activities had blossomed in other parts of the United States, especially the work in San Francisco by Pauline Oliveros and her associates at the SFTMC. This group had activities that largely paralleled those of the Ann Arbor movement, including instrumental and electronic performances using tape or live electronic modification, theater and dance pieces, and unusual visual projections. William Maginnis, who served as a composer and engineer at the SFTMC, makes special note of the work done by the composer and artist Tony Martin, who worked as a kind of "visual composer" to help plan and expand the performances through multimedia approaches (better known as "light shows"). The ONCE and SFTMC groups developed an ongoing correspondence and shared many ideas related to their common experiences. This led to some interesting collaborations in the late 1960s between veterans of both groups, including Oliveros' production of *Valentine* (1968), which was commissioned by the Sonic Arts Group of Ashley and Mumma.

Valentine was presented in the same year as *Reunion* by John Cage, the piece mentioned earlier that featured the amplified sounds of a game of chess. In her piece, Oliveros staged a game of hearts during which the heartbeats of the four card players were amplified as well as the sounds of card playing. In addition, the stage setting included a person reading aloud the history of playing cards, a croquet player who occasionally hit a ball (but without wickets), a large projection of the queen of hearts that gradually changed into the queen of spades, and two men building a picket fence. During the piece, there was no interaction among these various performers, but the simultaneity of the actions presented a complex of experiences that encompassed visual, aural, and environmental factors. For Pauline herself, *Valentine* is an associative piece that recollects the kinds of activity and energy by which she was surrounded as a child—in particular, those evenings when the family would gather in the living room to play games and listen to radio melodramas.

Open and Closed Systems

Many performance pieces involving electronic music have been centered around the completion of a given process. This process may be directly dependent on the design of the equipment being used, the acoustics of the room, or something as arbitrary as a time limit imposed on a performance. An "open" approach to such a system permits relative freedom to create within the bounds of the defined activity. A "closed" system is one in which little freedom of choice exists once the system has been set in motion.

A simple example of an open system is *Cartridge Music* (1960) by John Cage. This was another early attempt to bring live electronics to a performance as a desirable alternative to taped music. Cage took this approach after having had several disheartening experiences. The first was his attendance at an early presentation of German electronic music in Cologne. He noticed that "even though it was the most recent electronic music, the audience was all falling asleep. No matter how interesting the music was, the audience couldn't stay awake. That was because the music was coming out of loudspeakers." He then experienced his own frustration with tape recorders by trying to transfer his chance operations to tape compositions like *Fontana Mix*. The problem with this was that once the material was committed to tape, it no longer existed as a piece of indeterminate music; it lost its spontaneity once it became a fixed entity. This realization became quite clear to him during a 1958 rehearsal that included a presentation of his tape *Williams Mix*. While the tape was being played, "the piano tuner came in to tune the piano, and everyone's attention went away from the *Williams Mix* to the piano tuner because he was live."

Cage composed *Cartridge Music* at Stony Point, New York, where he and David Tudor had set up an ad hoc electronic-music studio. The score itself consists of numerous transparent sheets with markings on them such as "a complex of points, circles, biomorphic shapes, a circle representing clock time and a dotted curving line." These sheets can be superimposed in any way possible by the performers. The resulting patterns of the sheets are then interpreted as instructions to enable "one to go about his business of making sounds." These sounds are produced through the amplification of small sounds through the use of phono cartridges and contact microphones in conjunction with objects such as slinkies, tacks, chairs, tables, waste baskets, and so forth. The resultant performance is about as close to improvisation as a "system" can come. I categorize it as an open system for three reasons. First, there is a score. Second, the means for producing sounds (through contact microphones and phono cartridges) is restricted. Third, the reading of the score will often compel one of the performers to adjust the volume of the sound, creating a contingency that affects the other performers and is beyond their control. As fanciful as the entire process is, each performance is going to have similar characteristics and will be bound by the same rules (as anarchic as they may be). Because of its freewheeling approach to live performance, *Cartridge Music* served as an inspiration to many of the avant-garde improvisational groups that came later.

A closed system is a little easier to recognize than an open one. Once set in motion by the performer, a system like this will run through a predestined set of operations and bring itself to a natural conclusion, with or without further participation by the performer.

Steve Reich's *Pendulum Music* is a simple example of a closed system. Composed in the summer of 1968, the only requirements for this piece are microphones on long cables, loudspeakers, and amplifiers. The score is actually a short set of instructions to the people who will set the action in motion. The mikes are hung from the ceiling by their cables and are suspended "the same distance from the floor and are all free to swing with a pendular motion." Each mike is connected to an amplifier, and a speaker for each microphone is placed on the floor directly beneath its mike. The amplifiers are set to the point of feedback for each microphone and its associated speaker. Each mike is then pulled back "like a swing," and then all are released in unison to swing like pendulums. As the mikes swoop over their respective loudspeakers, the feedback is heard. This begins as quick pulses but gradually becomes longer and more intense as the mikes lose momentum. The "performers," after having released the mikes, sit back and observe the activity with the audience. The piece ends after the mikes slow to a stop and the feedback is continuous. The final act of the performers is to pull the power cords on the amps.

Tape recorders have often been used in live settings to provide systems for structuring a piece of music. A closed system can be created that employs tape delay and echo circuits in combination with real-time action. The use of echo itself is as old as the invention of the tape recorder, and many creative composers have extended its use into an effective technique for building interactive layers of sound. Beginning with her days in the early 1960s as part of the SFTMC, Pauline Oliveros became adept at designing unusual pieces around the use of the tape recorder. Her piece *I of IV* is a real-time performance piece using two tape recorders and a battery of twelve audio oscillators triggered by a keyboard. She developed the technique for this piece during 1965 and demonstrated that the deployment of some extremely simple principles of tape composition could be used to create a very complex soundscape. In this piece, a single reel of recording tape is threaded through two tape recorders. Tape recorder 1 is set to record and tape recorder 2 is set to play back. The sounds of the oscillators are fed directly into channel A of tape recorder 1. This channel is then fed directly into channel B of the same tape recorder and then back to channel A to create a "double feedback loop." The sounds that are recorded on the first tape recorder are then played back on the next tape machine after an eight-second delay. Once played, this sound is fed directly back to the record channels of the first tape recorder. With the addition of reverberation, the result is a barrage of slowly unfolding undulations that change dynamically as sounds continue to be repeated. Every sound that enters the loop is slowly transformed as other sounds are continuously layered over the top. This system imposes some strenuous controls and restrictions, but it also relies on the performer to trigger the activity through the use of the keyboard and the oscillators.

Another composer who has become widely known since the mid-1970s for his tape-delay approaches is Brian Eno. Eno earned his reputation first as a synthesizer player for the rock group Roxy Music and then as a solo artist and producer of esoteric rock acts. His 1975 piece called *Discreet Music* and the album which bears that title make his intentions perfectly clear: "Since I have always preferred making plans to executing them, I have gravitated towards situations and systems that, once set into operation, could create music with little or no intervention on my part. That is to say, I tend towards the roles of planner and programmer, and then become an audience to the results." Eno's passive approach to his own music is rather curious and lends a rather Cagian acceptance of fate to his work. His composition exists as a diagram of the devices used to generate the music. His approach is identical with that of Oliveros except for the fact that the sound material is melodic in nature and is filtered somewhat prior to its entering the tape loop. The result in this case is a slowly unfolding exercise in steady-state energy. The music is nearly as passive as the composer's attitude toward it. Eno has continued to employ a closed-systems approach to many of his later works, particularly his efforts to create "ambient" music that is subsumed and resonated by the given performance space.

Many other approaches to open and closed systems are certainly possible and have indeed been tried over the years. Tape-delay networks can be devised in various levels of complexity, depending on the number of tape recorders one wishes to employ. One can also add acoustic input via microphones to the looping

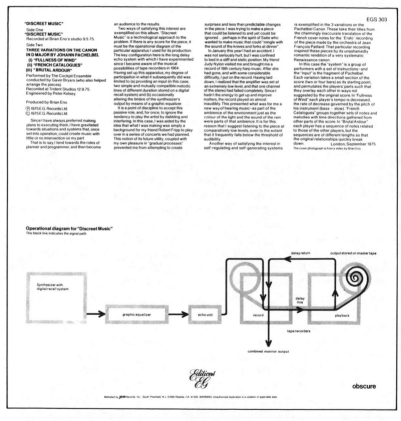

The back cover of Brian Eno's *Discreet Music* depicts the tape-delay configuration used to create the music. Through this technique the system itself will create music once it is set into motion. (Courtesy E. G. Records, Ltd.)

circuit and allow the resonance of the acoustic space to modify further the given sounds. Charles Amirkhanian has used this technique effectively in many of his text-sound compositions, changing the sound of the spoken word into a ghostly incantation colored by layers of room noise and ambient events.

Performance Groups and Improvisation

The live performance of electronic music has always been with us. It may have gone into hiding for a brief period just after the appearance of the tape recorder, but even then, composers working in the Paris and Cologne studios made attempts to present their tape music on the radio or in front of audiences through the use of loudspeakers. Current synthesizer technology, with its vast assortment of keyboard devices and control units, has made life easier for the practicing electronic musician. Until the late 1970s, however, most of the well-known electronic performance groups relied on their own ingenuity to create special homemade instruments to suit their special needs. Many of the graduates of this school of thinking continue to tinker today, never settling for the limitations imposed by state-of-the-art commercial instruments.

Some of the earliest live performances of electronic music in the post-tape-recorder era were those presented in Ann Arbor, Michigan, at the Space Theatre of Milton Cohen. The theater was actually a loft in which Cohen, a sculptor, and Harold Borkin, an architect, had devised an elaborate projection space for visual presentations. Robert Ashley joined the group and installed a sound system, mixed the concerts, provided some taped music, and designed acoustic resonators with Borkin. Gordon Mumma then joined the group to compose tape music and create home-brew sound-generating circuits that could be used in live performance along with prerecorded material. Beginning in 1957, and for the next five years, they held concerts there twice a week. Similar experiments soon began in California, where Pauline Oliveros, Ramon Sender, Terry Riley, Phil Windsor, Ellis Gans, and Dave Talbot collaborated to produce a series of concerts called "Sonics," beginning in 1961. These were held in a small electronic music studio in the attic above the San Francisco Conservatory of Music and attracted people like Morton Subotnick and Luciano Berio, who later helped the group create the SFTMC.

A number of instrumental performance groups evolved during the early 1960s, including Larry Austin's New Music Ensemble in Davis, California, and La Monte Young's Theatre of Eternal Music in New York. Electronic music began to take to the road

Robert Ashley, whose pioneering work in music-theater has led to his recent work in the video field. (Photo by Mimi Johnson.)

during this time in the capable hands of John Cage and David Tudor and then later in the form of the Sonic Arts Group (later, Sonic Arts Union), which grew out of the ONCE Festivals in 1968. The Sonic Arts Group consisted of Gordon Mumma, Robert Ashley, David Behrman, and Alvin Lucier. This band of electronic wizards often lent a hand to the Cunningham Dance Company and the Cage-Tudor extravaganzas that accompanied it, but it also traveled the world on its own, displaying its unusual brand electroacoustic music. Each composer contributed a different element to the mix: Ashley with his mixed-media pieces involving text and music; Mumma and his electroacoustic improvisations; Lucier with his scientific oddities, like the amplification of brain waves or ionospheric disturbances; and Behrman with his audience-accessible installations for the making of electronic music.

The art of new-music improvisation was embodied in the work of two groups that sprang up during 1966. The first, Musica Elet-

Gordon Mumma performing *Hornpipe 1967* at the Metropolitan Museum of Art in New York in 1972. Mumma is one of the true originals in experimental music and performs works using special devices and of his own design. (Photo by Jumay Chu.)

tronica Viva (MEV), was founded in Rome by four American composers: Alan Bryant, Alvin Curran, Frederic Rzewski, and Richard Teitelbaum. Also joined by Italian Ivan Vandor, MEV specialized in electronic-music improvisation. Among its instruments were the Moog synthesizer, devices homemade by Bryant, and the use of "organic" triggering sources such as the voice, heartbeats, brain waves, or skin-resistance sensors. Its music was a free-association exercise using both electronic and acoustic source material.

Another group to arise in 1966 was the British faction, AMM. Headed by the composer Cornelius Cardew, the group consisted of musicians who were primarily schooled in jazz: Lou Gare, sax-

David Behrman, who not only produced some of the most influential recordings of experimental music on the Columbia label during the 1960s but has become widely known as a designer of interactive, computer-based music systems. (Photo by Terri Hanlon.)

ophone; Christopher Hobbs and Edwin Prevost, percussion; and Keith Rowe, electric guitar. Under the guidance of Cardew, with his disposition toward "informal" rather than "formal" sound, the group developed into a respected avant-garde ensemble and gradually acquired a more electronic flavor.

The activities of such groups as the Sonic Arts Union, MEV, and AMM laid the groundwork for many other groups to follow. They not only made electronic music more mobile and accessible,

Alvin Lucier, who has a knack for making experimental music using everything from amplified brain waves to subways to room resonances. (Photo by Mary Lucier.)

they provided an aesthetic example for others to emulate. Whereas improvisation in the jazz sense has always implied the maintenance of certain rules of rhythm and harmony, experimental-music improvisation returns to the fundamental characteristics—and mysteries—of sound itself as its basis. An evaluation of such music has little to do with comparisons to traditional music and everything to do with the way in which we perceive sounds, associate thoughts with them, and use them to form an impression of our environment. The adventurous tours of these pioneering groups, and the strange, kinetic music they each produced, truly set the stage for the wave of electronic performance groups that emerged in the 1970s. Whether we think of the work of Philip Glass, Steve Reich, and other minimalists, of rock music, or of jazz, it is apparent that each field owes some debt to the first steps taken by Mumma, Tudor, Cardew, Teitelbaum, and others associated with the early electronic performing groups.

Intuitive Music

During the late 1960s, as interest grew in transcendental meditation and other Far Eastern spiritual disciplines, composers in the West began to incorporate ideas borrowed from the East in their approaches to music. Much of the minimalist sound of folks like La Monte Young and Terry Riley originated in a desire to create music of even temper and tension, music that could elicit a steady state of meditation in the mind of the listener. Other composers, like David Rosenboom, actually tapped into the energy of the brain to produce music by amplifying alpha waves. This was perhaps one of the most acutely organic means for generating meditative music but seemed to be of more value to the participants than to the listeners.

During 1968, following the completion of a number of works that placed instrumentalists in a controlled-improvisational circumstance, Stockhausen took a gigantic leap into what he called "intuitive music" with the fifteen compositions that constitute *Aus den sieben Tagen*. The compositions themselves are not scores at all but simple text instructions that elicit certain reactions on the part of the performers. The instructions for the piece "Aufwärts," for example, contain the following guidelines: "Play a vibration in the rhythm of your smallest particle. Play a vibration in the rhythm of the universe. Play all the rhythms that you can distinguish today between the rhythms of your smallest particles and the rhythm of the universe one after another and each one for so long, until the air carries it on." It should be noted that the people who originally performed these works for Stockhausen had been working very closely with him, in some cases for many years. The pieces do not specify any type of instrumentation, although recordings of them have included ensembles using piano, viola, tam-tam, trombone, filters, shortwave receiver, metal Japanese temple cups, electronium, and other instruments, both acoustic and electronic.

Stockhausen for the most part has tried to remove control and leave the production of the music purely up to the impulses

of the participants. His intention in creating such "musique intuitive" is very clearly stated in Stockhausen's instructions for the
piece "Es":

> Within the cycle, the text "Es" reaches an extreme
> of intuitive playing in the instruction to play only when
> one has achieved the state of nonthinking, and to stop
> whenever one begins to think. By this means a state of
> playing should be achieved in which one acts and reacts
> purely intuitively. As soon as a player thinks of something
> (e.g., that he is playing; what he is playing; what someone
> else is playing or has played; how he should react; that a
> car is driving past outside, etc.) he should stop, and only
> start again when he is just listening, and at one with what
> is heard.

This almost religious approach to producing music through
pure spiritual concordance with the universe did indeed pose some
problems for Stockhausen and his group. They continued to work
at it for a number of years, though, wrapping up the exploration
with the set of pieces that make up *Für kommende Zeiten* in 1970.
For Stockhausen, who for most of his career exercised total and
complete control over every aspect of sound in his music, the idea
of intuitive music was at once bold and fraught with sacrifice on
his part. It was perhaps characteristic of him to have taken the
original idea to such extremes. The result was a greater awareness
on his part of the power of impulse and intuition in music, an idea
that has continued to play an important role in his composition.

Interactive Computer Systems

With the recent proliferation of microcomputers, we can only
expect to see more and more sophisticated computer-music aids
being made available to the amateur and professional alike. Unlike
early computer music, which often required hours of laborious
programming and instruction to yield minimal musical results, the
latest systems are geared toward real-time performance. To borrow
the language of the computer world, we are now talking about
interactive computer music systems.

Interactiveness in a live setting can be achieved in various
ways. Using a digital synthesizer like the Synclavier or Buchla,
one can store previously created musical passages or control signals
and activate them at will to accompany other live actions. Morton
Subotnick (on the Buchla) and Jon Appleton (on the Synclavier)

are two composer-performers who have worked this way. Another form of interactiveness allows the computer to respond automatically to audio activity that it recognizes. It may be instructed to respond to given chords, harmonics, tones, or rhythms, and its response can be in a random or predetermined sequence. Joel Chadabe and David Behrman have pioneered this approach.

Another important approach to live electronic music is to combine traditional with electronic instruments. This can be done very simply by playing a tape as accompaniment to the players. Many composers who enjoy traditional composition methods turn to this approach when they wish to add electronic sounds. They do not yield any control over the sound while working in the tape medium, and they can go about creating a piece using the same rules and regulations that apply to their instrumental composition. Composers who have distinguished themselves in this field include Otto Luening, Vladimir Ussachevsky, Mario Davidovsky, Edgard Varèse, Edwin Dugger, Roger Reynolds, and Luigi Nono.

Other composers have gone a step further by using electronics to modify the sounds of acoustic instruments. This is a fairly common approach today and is expedited by the use of modular synthesizers that are supplied with input ports for microphones or line inputs from instrument pickups.

The piano was an early victim of the urge to electrify, and it seems that every major composer who has dealt with electronics has dabbled with the piano somewhere in his career. Schaeffer and Henry first used the piano as a sound source back in 1950 when they did some of their early musique concrète. John Cage's *Variations II* (1961), although not specifically scored for any particular instrument, was often realized by David Tudor at the piano. Using only contact microphones and amplification, Tudor was able to dramatically transform the sound of the piano. Composer Richard Maxfield composed his own piece to display the talents of Tudor in 1961. Called *Piano Concert for David Tudor*, it consists of three tracks of electronically modified piano sounds improvised by Tudor beforehand, in addition to a live performance part played in combination with the tapes.

Karlheinz Stockhausen became noted in the mid-1960s for modifying and processing instrumental sounds in a real-time situation. He came back to the piano in 1970 after many years of working on large-scale electronic compositions and composed *Mantra*. This hauntingly gentle piece for two pianos uses ring modulation and amplification to color a series of variations on a thirteen-note tone series. Work with the piano continues, of course, and a fine example of recent advances is *And Out Come the Night*

David Tudor, composer, performer, and virtuoso of avant-garde piano works and electronics presentations. His recent works include electroacoustic pieces that amplify the sounds of specially constructed moving sculptures in a performance space. (Photo by Lowell Cross.)

Ears (1978) by the Californian David Rosenboom. The piece combines an "improvisationally developed solo for piano" with an electronic system provided by Donald Buchla. The electronics are set to recognize and respond to various frequency ranges of the piano. The incoming piano tones trigger sound-modifying electronics while still maintaining a real-time relationship with the performer's activities.

The number of examples of works for other types of instruments modified with live electronics is virtually endless. *Hornpipe* (1967) by Gordon Mumma combines unusual sonorities performed on the French horn with electronics that continually modify the amplified output in keeping with responses of the sound to the ambience of the performing space. Joel Chadabe has recently been working with interactive computer music systems, but prior to that he produced works like *Echoes* (1975), which amplified, altered, and distributed instrumental sounds (percussion, violin, guitar, or trombone) through an electronic delay system. This piece, too, added dimensions of room resonance to the final output of the music. Another interesting approach has been that of David Behrman and his pieces for performers and interactive computers. *Figure in a Clearing* (1977) uses a microcomputer to trigger patches of electronic harmonies to which a cellist can play. The computer initiates chord changes using sixteen preset triangle wave generators. The rhythm or tempo of the changes is somewhat randomized through a triggering program that is "modelled after the velocity of a satellite in falling elliptical orbit about a planet." The cellist improvises in relation to these computer-controlled changes.

EXPERIMENTAL MUSIC AND ELECTRONICS TODAY

The availability of more affordable electronic music devices has inspired a great interest in avant-garde music since the late 1970s. We can see activity today in virtually all of the classic genres of the medium; tape composition, serial music, collage and chance music, and live electronic improvisation. Many of the familiar performers—Stockhausen, Cage, Ussachevsky, Subotnick, Ashley, Behrman, Mumma, Tudor, and many others—are still working with electronics, while an entirely new cast of characters has also emerged since the mid-1970s. Tape composition is more prevalent than ever, with work being done in the United States by independent producers like Mnemonists in Colorado, Negativland in California, Michael William Gilbert in New England, and the collective of composers recording for the Palace of Lights label in Seattle, Washington. From other countries come the work of Roger Doyle, the Nocturnal Emissions, both of England; Der Plan of Germany; SPK of New Zealand; and Merzbow of Japan, to name only a few.

In addition to the forms of experimental music discussed in this chapter, there continues to be much activity in the translating of classical music to the electronic medium. This was begun in 1968 by Walter (Wendy) Carlos, who continues to contribute to the field, and has been broadened by numerous artists playing everything from the music of Satie and Debussy to Stravinsky and Prokofiev. One of the most fluent composers in this field has been Isao Tomita, who since the 1970s has created many impressive albums of highly charged and skillfully adapted classical music. There will undoubtedly be more activity in this area in the future as more and more classically trained musicians gain access to affordable and easily used synthesizing equipment.

4

ROCK MUSIC
AND
ELECTRONICS

Rock music has always been electronic. Since its inception it has relied on the power of amplified instruments to drive home its energy and emotion and on the recording studio and engineering methods to enhance and alter the sound of the music. The development of the rock idiom into a recording art closely parallels the appearance of the classic electronic-music studio. This culminated in an explosion of activity during the late 1960s when psychedelic rock began to make full creative use of some very abstract electronic-music techniques. Since those days, the technology of rock has continued to grow in sophistication, and the development of new electronic-music devices has been intimately linked with the rock world.

Unlike experimental music, rock music is geared for mass consumption. It is a popular song medium for telling stories, for relating emotions, for inciting action, for inspiring pleasure. In order to accomplish these goals, it uses familiar motifs in songwriting, attractive melodies and harmonies, clearly defined rhythms and instrumentation, and a penchant for what is called the "hook" to capture one's attention. Rock songs are designed to entice repeated listenings and sell records through the infectious excitement that the music inspires. The hook is no more than a special effect, an aural anomaly that is memorable and catchy. It may be purely instrumental (like a guitar line), vocal, or a special combination of both. Every form of popular music has relied on hooks. What is interesting is that rock music is more dependent on the novelty of sound for its popularity than it is on compositional innovation.

The very heart and soul of rock music is a devotion to an experimentation with sound. This preoccupation with the sound of rock is so clearly at the core of the music that it helps distinguish one rock group's sound from another, and it recognizes certain individual performers for their own personal contributions to this sound. The sound of Jimi Hendrix, for example, is distinctly different than that of Buddy Holly, although both musicians used similar Stratocaster guitars. The difference was made by each individual's methods for modifying the sound of the guitar, performing on it, and recording it. Even record producers become known for the styles they impart on record. The famous Phil Spector "wall of sound" was perhaps one of the first true acknowledgments of the talents and power of the producer. The tradition is carried on by producers like Brian Eno (for David Bowie, Ultravox, Devo, Talking Heads, and himself), Todd Rundgren (for Meatloaf, Patti Smith, Psychedelic Furs, Utopia, and himself), and countless others who have developed their own personal styles in the shaping of rock sounds for recordings.

Rock music is as seriously concerned with the nature and quality of sound as avant-garde and classical music. Its audience might be broader and musically less sophisticated, but it is also in demand of uniqueness and novelty. This popular quest for special innovation is really in the same spirit as that of the avant-garde. It is not surprising, then, that electronic-music techniques have long served as one of rock's most formidable weapons in its search for identity.

Nine

ROCK-MUSIC INSTRUMENTS and OTHER HARDWARE

The classic electric instruments of rock include the electric

guitar, electric bass, and electric piano and organ. With

the addition of drums, these instruments still remain the

keystones of rock instrumentation, although since the early

1970s the synthesizer has come into great prominence as

an alternative keyboard or effects device.

ELECTRIC GUITARS AND BASS GUITARS

Electric guitars and bass guitars use an electromagnetic pickup to sense the vibrations of wound steel strings and translate them into an electric current, which can then be amplified. The principle is very simple and has been in use with various types of stringed instruments, including pianos, since the 1930s. The modern electric rock guitar, perhaps epitomized by the Fender Stratocaster, first introduced in 1954, has changed little during the past thirty years. The "Strat" is a six-stringed instrument featuring three magnetic pickups, a volume control, two tone controls, and sometimes a tremolo arm for bending notes by physically leveraging the strings. A standard bass guitar features four strings, a couple of pickups, and three or four tone and volume controls.

The sound of any standard guitar must be amplified, and here is the first opportunity for the musician to color the voice of the instrument in some unique way. This way be through the use of an effects device, such as a fuzz box or chorus unit, or through the creative use of the guitar amplifier. A seasoned performer can use the simple tone controls of guitar and amp and the power of feedback distortion to create wildly distinct variations in guitar sounds.

TRADITIONAL KEYBOARDS

The acoustic piano was one of the original tools of the rock musician and continues to maintain its position of prestige in many hands. A number of electric keyboards have become popular over the years as well, including electric pianos and organs of various designs.

Electric pianos are electromechanical devices like guitars. Magnetic pickups of various designs are used to translate the vibrations of strings that are hammered by the keys into an electric current, which can be amplified. The Fender Rhodes is one of the original, and most popular, electric pianos. Featuring fairly natural piano action, the Rhodes is commonly used by both rock and jazz keyboardists. Other popular variations on the electric piano include the Clavinet (made famous by Stevie Wonder on such hits as "Superstition") and models made by Wurlitzer, Yamaha, Crumar, and Hohner.

The first organs to gain popularity with rock bands were those being made by Hammond. The "traditional" Hammond being used in the 1950s, 1960s, and 1970s still used the same tone-wheel principle first introduced back in 1930 and demonstrated by Thaddeus

Cahill as long ago as 1900. The sound is full and rich, and when combined with a rotating Leslie speaker system, the instrument provides a body and a depth rarely reproduced by any other electronic techniques. One of the beauties of this instrument is that sliding tone bars are used to vary the timbre of the sound to any degree within the range of the given preset "voices," thus making the organ quite versatile in the production of unique sounds. The most popular Hammond organ with rock performers was the model B-3. It was an instrument like this that appeared on some of the early Beatle songs ("Mr. Moonlight," "Dizzy Miss Lizzy") and later very effectively on the unusual "Blue Jay Way." The group that probably did the most to popularize the Hammond sound was Procol Harum. Behind the inspired organ playing of Matthew Fisher, this unknown group emerged in May 1967 with a surrealistic adaptation of a Bach cantata that they called "A Whiter Shade of Pale." Their first three albums continued to spotlight the Hammond organ and to set their sound clearly apart from that of all other rock acts.

Other popular organs of the 1960s included the Vox Continental (featured by Alan Price of the Animals on "House of the Rising Sun") and the Farfisa. Both organs were less expensive than the Hammond models but only featured a limited repertoire of timbres, and both went out of production during the 1970s. The Farfisa remains a highly collectible organ and has experienced a revival of sorts through the music of the minimalist experimenters (Steve Reich, Philip Glass) and various rock groups.

The mellotron is another keyboard instrument, but it is neither an organ nor a piano. The sounds produced by the mellotron are actually played from tape loops stored within the cabinet of the machine. The instrument features two 35-note keyboards. The right-hand keyboard can play approximately three octaves of sounds in the voices of eighteen different instruments previously recorded on tape. The left-hand keyboard controls prerecorded rhythms and chords to accompany the melodic line. The sounds themselves were recordings of individual acoustic instruments, such as flutes and violins, as well as combos, brass bands, string quartets, and choirs. Through its ability to bend notes (which on the mellotron is like suddenly bending the sound of an entire string section), its sustain features, and the unearthly quality of its orchestral renderings, the mellotron continues to be one of the most unique contraptions of rock. As for proponents, Mike Pinder of the Moody Blues became the embodiment of the mellotron player back in the 1960s. The instrument was also featured by such varied artists as the Beatles ("Flying," "Strawberry Fields Forever," and "I Am the Walrus,"

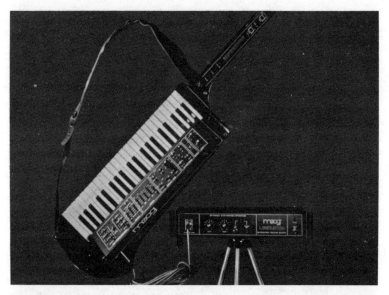

The Moog Liberation, a guitar-style performance synthesizer. (Courtesy Moog.)

to name a few), the Rolling Stones ("2000 Light Years From Home"), the Bee Gees (their first LP in particular), and the debut effort by King Crimson.

SYNTHESIZERS

Even before Robert Moog could produce his first portable synthesizer, the Minimoog, in 1970, adventurous rock performers had begun to employ his large, studio models. Most of their work with the large models was done in the recording studio, but the very courageous Keith Emerson (then of Emerson, Lake, and Palmer) insisted on taking his modular system on tour. By the early 1970s the synthesizer had begun to revolutionize the position of the keyboard in the rock combo. Instruments like the Arp 2600 became widely used not only for the rendering of melodic riffs and solos but for special effects and processing of other group instruments. The aural horizons of the performing musician were suddenly extended.

Synthesizers are designed for various purposes. Some are still oriented toward sound coloring and atmospheric effects, offering a wide variety of patching capabilities and oscillators. Some are strictly preset devices designed to play a number of specific instrumental voices, like strings or horns. Still others are meant to replace the electromechanical electric piano or organ. Following is a rundown of the various types of synthesizers employed by rock groups:

Monophonic synthesizers   Capable of playing only one note at a time, they are generally used for lead keyboard work but may also feature a wide range of oscillators, filters, and amplifiers for the creation of special effects. Usually operated using patch cords to set sounds.

Polyphonic synthesizers   They are capable of playing two or more notes at the same time. Some systems may only play two notes, but others play four, six, or eight. They are generally used in place of organs or pianos because they can play chords as well as melodies and usually incorporate extensive preset sounds.

String synthesizers   These are monophonic or polyphonic and incorporate extensive preset sounds to replicate the sounds of acoustic instruments like violins and cellos and can create orchestral effects. They closely approximate electric organ sounds.

Organ and Piano Synthesizers   Designed to replace electromechanical organs and pianos, they offer sounds that are an electronic approximation of their more traditional keyboard brethren. For electric pianos, computer monitoring is often used to rate the

The Roland Jupiter-8 is an eight-voice polyphonic analog synthesizer designed for performance situations. It uses sixteen oscillators and has sixty-four user-programmable memories that can store preset sounds. This full-featured analog synthesizer is representative of the state of the art in analog machines. (Photo from Roland Corporation U.S.)

The Moog 16-Channel Vocoder. (Courtesy Moog.)

sensitivity of touch on the keys in order to duplicate the dynamic feel of a true piano keyboard.

Guitar Synthesizers The guitar synthesizer employs a modified electric guitar to trigger sounds in a monophonic or polyphonic synthesizer. The guitar itself can be equipped with as many as six individual magnetic pickups (one for each string), which can be controlled separately while patched into a foot-controlled synthesizer module. Through the synthesizer, the guitarist can modify the sounds that are played by applying additional electronic sounds, filtering, enveloping, and pitch alteration. Another familiar effect is the "duet," in which the guitar sound is split into two harmonious signals. The guitar synthesizer is used frequently to add body and depth to the guitar sound and can be heard in recordings by such artists as Andy Summers of The Police, Robert Fripp, and Jimmy Page.

Vocoder This device accepts voice input through a microphone and processes it through synthesizing components. The result is a distortion and modification of the voice that can be modulated musically by using instrumental triggers. The vocoder was used very early by Wendy Carlos and Rachel Elkind in the soundtrack to the film *A Clockwork Orange* but has also been used by such diverse artists as Electric Light Orchestra, Neil Young, Kraftwerk, and Laurie Anderson.

Rhythm boxes Synthesized percussion devices produce electronic rhythms equivalent to ɹe sounds of drums and crashing cymbals. They permit the selection of various types of sounds from a preset repertoire and the variance of the tempo as needed to accompany the music. They may be linked to other instruments for the automatic triggering of rhythm or tempo changes. They typically produce a cold, mechanical rhythm, as used in the music of groups like Kraftwerk, Devo, and other technorock bands.

Digital synthesizers   The digital synthesizer is now emerging as a common tool of the rock performer. Some are simply the digital equivalents of commonly used analog synthesizers, featuring preset sounds and standard organlike voices (like those of Casio and Yamaha). Others are programmable by the user and may be employed to generate entirely unique sounds or even to analyze and "digitize" nonelectronic sound sources. Because of their computer nature, some digital devices are also designed to act as controllers for the triggering of sounds from multiple inputs, most will have built-in sequencing features, and many can be used to alter the sounds of outside sources, such as a guitar. The most elaborate varieties of digital synthesizers, like the Fairlight CMI and Synclavier, became available in the early 1980s but cost more than $25,000. Other, less expensive variations on the digital synthesizer have appeared in conjunction with home computers like the Apple and Commodore.

Effects Units   An effects unit is a black-box contraption that is designed to alter, modify, and enhance the sound being produced by an instrument. An industry began to develop during the late 1960s when innovative performers began to tinker with their guitars and in some cases commissioned engineers to produce special devices for them. Normally associated with guitars, many effects units can also be adapted for use with keyboards, horns, or other instruments.

Echo devices   We have already seen how the use of tape echo effects became a standard part of the menu for classic electronic music during the 1950s. This technique for using the standard tape recorder was adapted very early for studio use in the pop-music idiom and has been featured prominently on pop and novelty records since the early 1950s. During the 1960s, a number of companies began to manufacture "echo boxes" that were designed for easy use in the studio or on stage. Still in wide use and preferred by many to its electronic counterpart, the echo box consists of a tape recording and playback machine that is threaded with a short loop of magnetic tape. Sounds are patched in from sources such as a guitar or microphone, recorded on the tape, and then played back as the tape passes the playback head. The original sound is rerecorded on a second track and then played back again. The cycle is repeated over and over as needed, with the rate or pace of the echo dependent on the space between the record and playback heads of the echo box. Each time the original sound is re-recorded, it is somewhat diminished until finally all that remains is a pulsing hiss known as echo frizz. The performer can control the volume of the output, which will either extend or reduce the number of echoes that occur, and may adjust the distance between the machine heads to alter the rate of the echo somewhat. Tape echo is noted for its clean and distinct reproduction of sound. The Echoplex by Maestro has been one of the most durable tape echo boxes on the market. Echo continues to be a very popular recording technique with rock bands.

Electronic echo systems are currently being made available. These provide circuitry for digitizing analog sounds and then repeating them as needed through a playback of the digital sound in an echo pattern. This method does not introduce a diminishment of the sound unless it is desired. Digital echo will become so affordable that it will one day supplant tape echo, but the accuracy or feel of the digital reproduction may never be satisfactory to some aficionados of traditional echo techniques.

Reverberation   Reverb that is intended to replicate a highly resonant listening room rather than distinct echoes or sounds has traditionally been produced with spring reverberation devices, which actually drive the audio signal through a taut metal spring to add depth and hollowness to the signal. This simple technique is very effective and can be incorporated in a portable unit to accompany a rock act. Another interesting feature of spring reverb is its sensitivity to being bumped or knocked. A casual kick or shove is all that is needed to reproduce thundering bellows of unearthly quality.

Fuzz and distortion   As rock performers of the 1960s began to perform in larger and larger venues, they turned up their feeble little tube amplifiers and caused quite a racket. The racket was not caused so much by high volumes as by overloading the power of the amps and distorting the sound. Guitarists wanted a device that would provide them with the proper amount of distortion without blowing their amps to obtain a rich, fuzzy tone from their speakers. The new device, affectionately known as the fuzz box, was reportedly used for the first time in 1965 by Jeff Beck on the Yardbirds' hit "Heart Full of Soul." Various fuzz boxes became available, and by 1966, everyone was using one. Some of the more prominent singles of that era to feature fuzz tone on lead guitars and bass guitars included "I Had Too Much to Dream Last Night" by the Electric Prunes, "Hey, Joe" by the Leaves, "Psychotic Reaction" by the Count Five, and "Sunshine of Your Love" by Eric Clapton and Cream. An interesting example of actual speaker distortion—the thing that fuzz boxes were meant to duplicate—can be heard during the primal guitar break in the middle of the single "Pushin' Too Hard," played by Jan Savage of the Seeds in the summer of 1966. Modern fuzz boxes, more properly called distortion units, feature controls to adjust the degree of fuzz used, the treble of the sound, and the loudness of the distorted sound balanced against the unscathed sound of the guitar.

Wah-wah and filters   The wah-wah pedal was another unusual device for altering the sound of the guitar. It first appeared around 1967 and was used early on by Frank Zappa, who was producing some bold music with the Mothers of Invention at the time. The wah-wah pedal is really a primitive band-pass filter, with the lower frequencies of the guitar sound being filtered out as the pedal is depressed with the toe. Using a rocking motion of the foot on the pedal, the player can make the characteristic "wah" sound of the device. Modern wah-wahs are usually called envelope filters, in keeping with the language of synthesizers. They may be controlled by a rocking foot pedal, as in the early models, or triggered by variances in the strength of the incoming guitar signal. The envelope filter by MXR features a "threshold" control for adjusting the sensitivity of the filtering action and an "attack" control for varying the actual attack time of the signal. A wah-ing effect can be created by setting a longer, or sliding, attack.

Phasing   Phasing is actually a tape-recorder technique in which two identical tapes are played simultaneously but one is sped up slightly to overtake the other and make the two sets of sounds go out of phase by minute degrees. The result is a luscious, whooshing effect that can be controlled by continuously varying the speed of one tape to make it go in and out of phase with the other. The effect was used for the first time in the 1967 Small Faces hit "Itchycoo Park." Others began to experiment with this novel technique, and by 1968, Jimi Hendrix was using it in his albums, top-forty singles such as "Open My Eyes" by the Nazz featured it prominently, and even the Beatles gave it a go through George Harrison's "Blue Jay Way" on *Magical Mystery Tour*. Today, solid-state versions of phasing—or "flanging," as it is often called now—can be produced by phase shifters, which sweep an incoming signal to electronically cause the whispy washes of interfering sounds. Using one of these devices, the performer has much greater control over the dgree of phasing, which may range from a subtle vibrato, to the sound of a rotating Leslie speaker, to dramatic whooshing effects.

Signal Delay   Sometimes called chorus, a signal delay system is used to add body to the sound of an instrument by adding a mirror image of it that is ever so slightly delayed. The result can be adjusted from the kind of slight delay that would give a six-string guitar the resonance of a twelve-string, to a more pronounced double-tracking effect to produce the illusion of two instruments playing the same note line.

Frequency Shifter   Developed by Harald Bode and marketed early on by Moog, the frequency shifter takes an incoming audio signal and modifies it through the shifting of its entire frequency spectrum. This may be done within a range of plus or minus 5,000 Hz. The device can be used for a number of purposes, including the detuning of drum sounds, the creation of clangorous tones from perfectly harmonic ones, the creation of chorus effects, the suppression of feedback so that microphone gain can be increased, and the creation of special spiraling echo effects when used with tape echo units. One of the first uses of a frequency shifter by a rock group can be found on the Frank Zappa album *Waka/Jawaka*, released in 1972.

A variation on the frequency shifter is the harmonizer. The harmonizer produces new frequencies that maintain a harmonic relationship with the original signal, a feat that allows guitar players seemingly to carry on duets with themselves, a sort of lazy man's version of the two-part guitar solos made popular by the Allman Brothers in the early 1970s.

STUDIO EQUIPMENT

In addition to the instruments themselves, the recording studio is vital to the perfection of the rock sound. The use of electronic-music techniques in pop music goes back to the 1950s when special effects like sped-up tapes were used in novelty records like "The Purple People Eater" by Sheb Wooley (1958) and "The Chipmunk Song" by David Seville (1959). Multitracking of voices and/or instruments was explored as early as 1948 by guitar player Les Paul and became the stock in trade of much of the pioneering work of Buddy Holly with producer Norman Petty. The use of echo and reverb in the studio was also common in the 1950s and accounts for the remarkably ambient and bouncy sound of many an early rock-and-roller. Guitar distortion was also being explored in the early days by groups like the Ventures, the Tornadoes, and the Chantays, and many of their records were enhanced by studio effects to create the outer-space sound of the Sputnik age. These quiet revolutions were merely seeking novelty in most cases and were not matched by a predisposition for new music. Much of the rock music of the 1950s and early 1960s was far from adventurous in anything but melody and harmony.

By the mid-1960s, however, there arose a number of influential groups and individuals who would prove to have a lasting effect on the aesthetics of rock. Their techniques and innovations embraced the technology of rock—many were skilled songwriters and gifted thinkers—and the novel approaches made possible by technology provided them with the means to express themselves fully in music. The accomplishments of the Beatles, Jimi Hendrix, Frank Zappa, Pink Floyd, and countless others are well known. Their contributions to electronic music need not be detailed in this chapter, for the record guide in chapter 11 offers a concise review of the major influences in this area.

The creative use of the recording studio by rock musicians can be summed up by activity in the following areas:

Sound effects   The use of natural sounds and noise as a part of the music or as atmospheric material. The Beatles were responsible for making this popular (note the use of crowd sounds and barnyard animals on *Sgt. Pepper's Lonely Hearts Club Band* in 1967), although countless groups used sound effects during the 1960s and 1970s and continue to do so today.

Tape effects   The traditional studio effects of musique concrète were directed at an entirely different audience beginning in the mid-1960s. The intricate assembly of songs using tape editing, the use of tape reversal, and the use of variable-speed tape recorders became standard fare in the work of many rock artists.

Multitracking   Most records today are made using sixteen- and twenty-four-track tape-recording facilities. This permits the simultaneous recording of two or more tracks, which can then be remixed and modified to perfect the finished product. Two-track tape recorders were frequently used in the 1950s when multitracking was still a novelty. The Beatles used only a four-track tape machine to create the *Sgt. Pepper* album. Once a complicated operation, the management of multitrack recording has now be-

come simplified by the use of computer-assisted controls to iden-
tify, retrieve, and mix separately recorded tracks.

Electronic effects   The studio offers an environment in which
all sounds can be carefully controlled and modified. The use of
audio filters, distortion devices, reverb, echo, and synthesizer modulation are common in today's studio. The rock musician uses the
very same technology and techniques that were once only associated with avant-garde composers.

With the design and availability of easy-to-use portable synthesizers in the 1970s, electronic sounds became an increasingly
common component of rock music. This has resulted in the development of a new strain of rock that was described by various
names, including progressive, art rock, and new wave. As an abstract offshoot of this activity, a number of artists took their music
a few steps further and began to create an experimental form that
vacillated between avant-garde and rock. European artists such as
Tangerine Dream and Klaus Schulze evolved from rock musicians
to weavers of minimalist synthesizer orchestrations. Brian Eno
moved from the eccentric pop sounds of Roxy Music to create an
entire body of ambient electronic works and minimalist guitar-
synthesizer unions. Others, like Père Ubu and Talking Heads, used
language as a means of abstract expression while surging electronic
rock pounds out odd harmonics. The record guide in chapter 11
serves as a summary of this widespread activity and of rock music
of the 1980s, which continues to explore the experimental use of
electronics.

5

AN
ELECTRONIC
MUSIC
RECORD
GUIDE

The record medium has been an essential component of the electronic-music field. Without recordings, the popularity of electronic music would never have spread. It is a field in which a record album may be the only copyrighted representation of a piece of music, music that is sometimes too complex even to commit to a score. Most electronic music is produced with the record medium in mind.

The following record guide to electronic music is a compendium of all types of work, including musique concrète, studio composition, live electronic music, and rock. I have attempted to select some of the most important contributions to the field, plus a few odds and ends that may never have received their due amount of critical acclaim.

The organization of the discography is simple. The first part lists important collections of electronic music featuring the works of many artists. The second part lists albums by individual artists or groups and is arranged in alphabetical order by the artist's name. In most cases, the titles, dates, and identification numbers for all albums are shown. Finally, after the main body of the record guide, there are two additional sections devoted to recordings of "ancient" electronic-music instruments, such as the theremin and the ondes martenot, and a listing of rare, out-of-print recordings of electronic music.

Ten

ELECTRONIC MUSIC COLLECTIONS

COLLECTIONS OF CLASSIC TAPE COMPOSITION AND MUSIQUE CONCRÈTE

JOHN CAGE, (*Fontana Mix*), LUCIANO BERIO (*Visage*), ILHAN MIMAROGLU (*Agony*).

Electronic Music (1966), Vox Turnabout TV 34046S

Cage's indeterminate composition dates from 1958. The striking influence of Cage can be recognized in the works by Berio and Mimaroglu. The latter pieces are carefully controlled compositions but contain the flash of chance events that Cage instilled into experimental musical thought. *Visage* features the voice of Cathy Berberian, and explores vocal events that are articulated as words or consist of inarticulate utterances. Mimaroglu's *Agony* is purely electronic, although the textures and sonorities are reminiscent of musique concrète. A stark, vivid piece.

This collection represents an important era in tape composition. These composers had eluded the semantic battleground of the French (musique concrète) and Germans (purely electronic) to produce their strikingly original works. Cage worked in the Studio di Fonologia in Milan, as did Berio. Mimaroglu realized *Agony* at the Columbia studio.

LUCIANO BERIO (*Momenti, Omaggio a Joyce*), BRUNO MADERNA (*Continuo*), LUC FERRARI (*Visage V*), IANNIS XENAKIS (*Orient-Occident*), JEAN BARONNET and FRANÇOIS DUFRENE (*U 47*).

Images Fantastiques (1968), Mercury Limelight LS 86047

Classic works of musique concrète dating from 1955 to 1960. Works from France and Italy. Originally released by Philips of Europe as *Panorama des Musiques Experimentales* in 1960.

OTTO LUENING and VLADIMIR USSACHEVSKY (*Concerted Piece for Tape Recorder and Orchestra*), USSACHEVSKY (*Of Wood and Brass, Wireless Fantasy*), MEL POWELL (*Events for Tape Recorder, Improvisation, Second Electronic Setting, Two Prayer Settings*).

Music For Electric and Older Instruments (1968), CRI 227 USD

Classic works of American tape composition from the early 1960s. These folks represented the more conservative strain of contemporary music, as opposed to Cage, Tudor, Mumma, Ashley, and other stratospheric peers. *Concerted Piece* is notable for Luening's attempt to produce a blend of electronics and orchestral instruments that would be acceptable to the average listener. Valiant efforts like this seldom worked, mainly because the idea of having to listen to a tape recorder was even more offensive to most people than the sounds that were coming from it. A fine collection, nonetheless, of important contributions to the growing movement toward electronic instrumentation.

PIERRE SCHAEFFER (*Objets lies*), FRANÇOIS-BERNARD MACHE (*Terre de feu*), MICHEL PHILIPPOT (*Étude III*), FRANÇOIS BAYLE (*L'oiseau-chanteur*), LUC FERRARI (*Tête et queue du dragon*), IVO MALEC (*Dahovi*), BERNARD PARMEGIANI (*Danse*).

Musique concrète (1968), Candide CE 31025

Classic musique concrète from the French studios of the Groupe de Recherches Musicales, O.R.T.F. in Paris. Works date from 1959 to 1963.

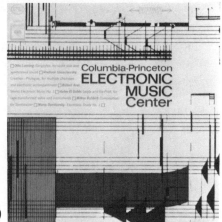

(Courtesy CBS Records.)

PIERRE HENRY (*Entite*), GYÖRGY LIGETI (*Artikulation*), HERBERT EIMERT (*Selection I*), MAURICIO KAGEL (*Transition I*), ANDRÉ BOUCOURECHLIEV (*Texte I*), HENRI POUSSEUR (*Scambi*).

Panorama Électronique (1968), Mercury Limelight LS 86048

Classic studio composition from the Paris and Cologne studios. Includes the musique concrète of the French, the pure electronic sounds of Eimert from Germany, and combined approaches by others like Kagel and Pousseur. Works dated from 1958–1960 and were originally released in Europe by Philips in 1960.

BULENT AREL (*Stereo Electronic Music No. 1*), HALIM EL-DABH (*Leiyla and the Poet*), VLADIMIR USSACHEVSKY (*Creation*), MILTON BABBITT (*Composition for Synthesizer*), MARIO DAVIDOVSKY (*Electronic Study No. 1*), OTTO LUENING (*Gargoyles*).

Columbia-Princeton Electronic Music Center (1964), Columbia MS-6566

Compositions from 1961 made in the Columbia-Princeton Electronic Music Center using the RCA Mark II synthesizer. A wide variety of forms and styles represented, all quite different from European work from same era.

ANDRES LEWIN-RICHTER (*Study No. 1*), ILHAN MIMAROGLU (*Le tombeau d'Edgar Poe, Intermezzo, Bowery Bum*), TZVI AVNI (*Vo-*

calise), WALTER CARLOS (*Variations for Flute and Electronic Sound, Dialogues for Piano and Two Loudspeakers*).

Electronic Music (1965), Vox Turnabout TV 34004S

> Studio composition from 1964 using the RCA Mark II synthesizer at the Columbia-Princeton studios.

LUCIANO BERIO (*Thema; Omaggio a Joyce*), JACOB DRUCKMAN (*Animus I*), ILHAN MIMAROGLU (*Piano Music for Performer and Composer, Six Preludes for Magnetic Tape*).

Electronic Music III (1968), Vox Turnabout TV 34177

> Studio composition from 1966–1967 by Druckman and Mimaroglu, plus a classic tape piece composed in Milan by Berio in 1958 using the voice of Cathy Berberian as the main sound source.

HERBERT BRUN (*Futility 1964*), LEJAREN HILLER (*Machine Music*), KENNETH GABURO (*Lemon Drops, For Henry*), CHARLES HAMM (*Canto*), SALVATORE MARTIRANO (*Underworld*).

Electronic Music from the University of Illinois (1966), Heliodor HS-25047

> Studio composition from the Studio for Experimental Music at the University of Illinois, circa 1964–1966. Mostly formal and stiff, although a couple of innocent tape pieces by Gaburo stand out in contrast to what was happening in most of academia at the time.

VICTOR GRAUER (*Inferno*), JEAN IVEY (*Pinball*), JOHN ROBB (*Collage*), HUGH LE CAINE (*Dripsody*), WALTER OLNICK-SCHAEFFER (*Summer Idyl Noesis*), MYRON SCHAEFFER (*Dance R 43*), VAL STEPHEN (*Fireworks, Orgasmic Opus*).

Electronic Music (1966), Folkways 33436

> A variety of studio works from independent composers in Canada, the USA, and Australia. Le Caine's is one of the earliest Canadian tape pieces.

ROBERT ASHLEY (*She Was a Visitor*), JOHN CAGE (*Solos for Voice 2*), ALVIN LUCIER (*North American Time Capsule*), PAULINE OLIVEROS (*Sound Patterns*), TOSHI ICHYANAGI (*Extended Voices*).

Extended Voices (1968), Columbia Odyssey 32 160156

> Electronically modified voice pieces by the kingpins of the American avant-garde. The work by Lucier from 1967 features a vocoder, perhaps the earliest on record.

HENK BADINGS (*Capriccio for Violin and Two Sound Tracks, Genèse, Evolutions*), DICK RAAIJMAKERS (*Contrasts*).

Evolutions and Contrasts (1968), Mercury Limelight LS 86055

Early electronic works from the Netherlands dating from 1952–1959. Composed in the Philips studios in Eindhoven. Originally released in 1960 by Philips in Europe.

JOHN CAGE (*Variations IV*), HENRI POUSSEUR (*Trois visages de Liège*), MILTON BABBITT (*Ensembles for Synthesizer*).

New Music From Leaders of the Avant-Garde (1968), Columbia MS-7051

A remarkable album assembled by David Behrman for Columbia. Includes one indeterminate piece by Cage, some serialist music by Babbitt, and a classic example of studio composition by Pousseur.

JOHANNA BEYER (*Music of the Spheres*), ANNEA LOCKWOOD (*World Rhythms*), PAULINE OLIVEROS (*Bye Bye Butterfly*), LAURIE SPIEGEL (*Appalachian Grove I*), MEGAN ROBERTS (*I Could Sit Here All Day*), RUTH ANDERSON (*Points*), LAURIE ANDERSON (*New York Social Life, Time to Go; For Diego*).

New Music for Electronic and Recorded Media (1977), 1750 Arch S-1765

Electronic works by women, mostly from the mid-1970s. There is a realization of a rare work by Johanna Beyer that dates from 1938, as well as one of Oliveros' tape flings from 1965.

STEVE REICH (*Come Out*), RICHARD MAXFIELD (*Night Music*), PAULINE OLIVEROS (*I of IV*).

New Sounds in Electronic Music (1968), Columbia Odyssey 32 16 0160

Varied electronic works by three independent composers, produced by David Behrman. One of Reich's early recordings, *Come Out* was an early exploration into process pieces that later evolved into the minimalist movement. A splendid album.

ARNE NORDHEIM (*Epitaffio for Orchestra and Tape, Response I*), ALFRED JANSON (*Canon for Chamber Orchestra and Tape*), BJORN FONGAARD (*Galaxy for Three Electric Guitars in Quarter-Tones*).

Response: Electronic Music from Norway (1967), Mercury Limelight LS-86061

> Collection of electronic music from Norway produced during the mid-1960s. Interesting experiments in combining tape with orchestra. Not as stiff and academic as the Americans. Standout piece is *Galaxy* for electric guitars.

REMI GASSMAN (*Electronics*), OSKAR SALA (*Five Improvisations on Magnetic Tape*).

Electronics (1962), Westminster WST-14143

> This disc documents two works created on the Studio Trautonium, Oskar Sala's advanced version of the Trautonium, which was widely used during the 1940s and 1950s. *Electronics* was used by the New York City Ballet for a ballet by George Balanchine. The music was composed on tape using purely electronic sound sources from the Studio Trautonium.

PIERRE HENRY (*Concerto des ambiguïtés*), PIERRE HENRY and PIERRE SCHAEFFER (*Symphonie pour un homme seul*).

Symphonie pour un homme seul (1972), Philips 6510 012

> These marvelous recordings date from the earliest days of musique concrète experiments in Paris (1949–1950). These pieces were composed using only disc recordings as sound

(Courtesy of Philips Records, a division of PolyGram Classics, Inc.)

sources and disc lathes as recording devices; no magnetic tape recorders were available. As works of musique concrète, they are unsurpassed and illustrate the excitement once captured by this style.

ROBERT ASHLEY (*Sonata*), PHIL HARMONIC (*Timing*), PAUL DEMARINIS (*Great Masters of Melody*), JOHN BISCHOFF (*Rendezvous*).

Just for the Record (1979), Lovely Music VR 1062

A diverse collection of keyboard music performed by "Blue" Gene Tyranny. Aside from the Ashley piece, which is acoustic, the works are all electronic and use Polymoog, Hohner clavinet, and electronic modification. An interesting blend of structure and improvisation pervades these works.

ALVIN LUCIER (*Vespers*), ROBERT ASHLEY (*Purposeful Lady Slow Afternoon*), DAVID BEHRMAN (*Runthrough*), GORDON MUMMA (*Hornpipe*).

Electric Sound (1971), Mainstream MS-5010

The only recording documenting some of the work of the Sonic Arts Union, the famed quartet of electronic music performers formed in 1966 after the disbanding of the ONCE group. Each of these artists has been extremely influential on the American avant-garde scene. Their music represents the most extreme tendencies of the experimental music movement.

This was one of the final albums released by Earle Brown on his important Mainstream label. Now out of print, it is valuable disc for the collector of new music. As a collection, it contains a text-sound work by Ashley, an electroacoustic improvisation using French horn by Mumma, a spatial piece using roving performers by Lucier, and a sound installation to be played by nonmusicians by Behrman.

GORDON MUMMA (*Music from the Venezia Space Theatre*), ROBERT ASHLEY (*Crazy Horse Symphony*), GEORGE CACIOPPO (*Time on Time in Miracles*), DONALD SCARVADA (*Landscape Journey*).

Music from the ONCE Festival (1966), Advance FGR-5

This album is the only recorded document featuring music that was exclusive to the ONCE Festivals, which ran in Ann Arbor between 1961 and 1968. The only electronic music on

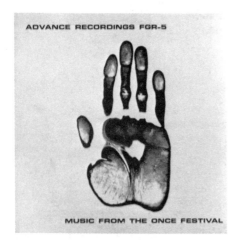

ADVANCE RECORDINGS FGR-5

MUSIC FROM THE ONCE FESTIVAL

this monophonic LP is that by Gordon Mumma. (A stereo remix of the same piece is available on his own album from Lovely Music VR 1091.) The collection of experiments found on this album serves as a fitting tribute to the remarkable performances that took place over the years of the festival. It was at ONCE that Ashley and Mumma first gained prominence, departing in 1968 when the ONCE group split to form the Sonic Arts Union.

AMM (Live electronic improvisation), MEV (*Spacecraft*).

Live Electronic Music Improvised (1968), Mainstream MS-5002

An important live recording of two influential electronic groups from the late 1960s. AMM members were Cornelius Cardew, Lou Gare, Christopher Hobbs, Eddie Prevost, and Keith Rowe. MEV members were Alan Bryant, Alvin Curran, Frederic Rzewski, Richard Teitelbaum, and Ivan Vandor. It was not easy to perform live in those days.

GORDON MUMMA (*Cybersonic Cantilevers*), JOEL CHADABE (*Echoes*), VLADIMIR USSACHEVSKY (*Conflict*), NOA AIN (*Used to Call Me Sadness*), ANN MCMILLAN (*Whale, Carrefours*).

New American Music, Volume 4 (1975), Folkways FTS 33904

Diverse collection featuring such things as interactive computer music with percussionist (Chadabe), live electroacoustic music (Mumma), voice plus electronics on tape (Ussachevsky), modified whale sounds (McMillan), and text-sound composition with violin accompaniment (Ain).

GODFREY WINHAM (*Two Pieces for Computer-Synthesized Sounds*), BARRY VERCOE (*Synapse for Viola and Computer*), HOFFMAN (*In Memoriam Patris*), JOEL GRESSEL (*Crossings, P-Vibes, Three Canons*).

Computer Generations (1976), CRI S-393

Recent compilation of computer music.

JAMES TENNEY (*Stochastic Quartet*) MAX MATHEWS (*Masquerades, Slider, Swan Song*), J. C. RISSET (*Computer Suite from Little Boy*), J. R. PIERCE (*Eight-Tone Canon*).

Voice of the Computer (1968), Decca 710180

Vintage computer music from Bell Labs in the mid-1960s.

BARTON MCLEAN (*Etunytude, The Last Ten Minutes*), KARL KORTE (*The Whistling Wind*), REED HOLMES (*Moire*).

Computer Music from the Outside In (1983), Folkways FSS 37 465

Demonstrations and performances of contemporary computer music.

LARRY AUSTIN (*Canadian Coastlines*), JOHN CELONA (*Music in Circular Motions*), CHARLES DODGE (*Any Resemblance*), STANLEY HAYNES (*Prisms*), BRUCE PENNYCOOK (*Speeches for Dr. Frankenstein*).

Computer Music (1983), Folkways FTS 37475

Excellent variety of contemporary computer music using a variety of digital systems.

Eleven

ELECTRONIC MUSIC
by
INDIVIDUAL ARTISTS
and
GROUPS

AMBOY DUKES

Journey to the Center of the Mind (1968), Mainstream 6112

One of the Motor City's first contributions to psychedelia. Four high school lads with little distinguishing talent except for the frantic and loud guitar work of lead motorhead, Ted Nugent. He was known for his encores in which he would place his guitar up against an amplifier, turn the volume all the way up, and walk off for a few minutes while the audience's teeth fell out. Their only hit single, "Journey to the Center of Your Mind" displayed polished feedback, distortion, and echo effects.

CHARLES AMIRKHANIAN

Lexical Music (1979), 1750 Arch S-1779

Text-sound composition using some ingenious tape machine set-ups and delay systems.

AMM

An Afflicted Man's Musica Box: "Commonwealth Institute" (1982),
United Dairies UD 012
AMMmusic (1966), Electra EUKS 7256
To Hear You Back Again (1974), Matchless MR3
It Had Been an Ordinary Day in Pueblo, Colorado (1979), Japo-
ECM 60031
The Crypt (1981), Matchless MR5

> Obscure recordings that document the music of AMM, the
> live improvisatory group from England which took electronic
> music on the road in 1966. Largely appealing to jazz circles,
> AMM made an important contribution to modern ap-
> proaches to instrumental improvisation of all kinds. Members
> included Cornelius Cardew, Lou Gare, Christopher Hobbs,
> Eddie Prevost, and Keith Rowe.

LAURIE ANDERSON

Big Science (1982), Warner Brothers BSK 3674
Mister Heartbreak (1984), Warner Brothers 25077-2

> New York musician, artist, and text-sound composer Laurie
> Anderson has been doodling for years with rock-jazz instru-
> mentations and words about the common life, armed with
> tape loops, synthesizers, and a vocoder. *Big Science* is an
> elegant combination of pop and avant-garde. Contains *O
> Superman*, her hypnotic mix of pulsing voice loops, vocod-
> erized lead vocals, Farfisa and Casio keyboards, flute, and
> sax. A cutting lyric about man's submission to social deco-
> rum. A classic, really.

JON APPLETON

Four Fantasies for Synclavier (1982), Folkways FTS 37461

> Jon Appleton was instrumental in the development of the
> synclavier, the first portable digital synthesizer. This album
> illustrates his virtuosity at the instrument and contains a va-
> riety of pieces that successfully mix the keyboard and non-
> keyboard attributes of synthesis that are embodied in the
> synclavier.

ROBERT ASHLEY

The Wolfman (1965), ESP 1009 or sterco S-1009
The Wolfman (1968), CP-E, Source Publications Source 4,

Vol. II No. 2, July 1968
In Sara, Mencken, Christ and Beethoven There Were Men and Women (1973), Cramps Records Nova Musicha N.3 CRSLP 6103
Private Parts (1977), Lovely Music LML 1001
Automatic Writing (1979), Lovely Music VR 1002
The Bar (1980), Lovely Music VR 4904
Music Word Fire and I Would Do It Again (1981), Lovely Music VR 4908

Robert Ashley has a prolific recording career. In addition to the albums listed here dedicated entirely to his work, many of his pieces are found on collections. Ashley's influence is vast, especially with the younger breed of composers and video artists reared with television.

Ashley turned to video work around 1970 at a time when most of his peers were either still tinkering with studio synthesizers or turning back to instrumental music after having experienced frustration with electronics. He is an arche-

(Courtesy Lovely Music, New York.)

type of the avant-garde artist, etching out an existence in New York and performing vigorously around the world to keep his work in top form. He is an unusual and gifted talent, managing to combine the most abstract and experimental tendencies of the avant-garde with strains of popular culture. He has accomplished this without losing respect for popular music and media arts. He is the living embodiment of Charles Ives in the modern day.

Ashley is adept at dipping into American culture and extracting genuine moments of art and energy for use in his own work. He does not deal in imitations. He calls himself a songwriter. The Source recording of *The Wolfman* features a performance by Gordon Mumma and Ashley. This is the famous theater piece in which Ashley uses the cavity of his mouth to modify feedback in the performance space while he delivers a nightclub act. The ESP disc features an earlier version of the piece by the Bob James Trio, a jazz outfit.

In Sara, Mencken, Christ is a text-sound work for voice and electronics. The version featured on the Cramps disc from Italy is the only remaining mix put together by Ashley and Paul DeMarinis. The original tapes were stolen from Ashley's car, so the only remaining material was a rough mix which Cramps decided to issue (a story not related in the liner notes to the album). The text is by John Barton Wolgamot. It features the rapid delivery of a text in a rather monotone fashion accompanied by indeterminate moments of electronic sound. A lovely piece of stream of consciousness. "Private Parts" was the first segment of Ashley's video opera *Perfect Lives Private Parts* to be issued on disc. It features the sound of tablas, the tinkling of a piano, and the droning of an electronic keyboard. Then the voice, somber and monotone, carries on a desperate monologue. A character develops and other personalities are introduced, rather like James Joyce in New York City. This record is much more forbidding than the other sections of the opera released later. *The Bar* is a zoom-out from the perception of the character and contains a kind of social stream of consciousness that is manifested by the jocular behavior of the various characters. *Music Word Fire and I Would Do It Again* is Ashley's soundtrack for *The Lessons*, a set of brief vignettes produced as backup material for the main opera itself. It is the most rhythmic and kinetic of the opera albums. The good humor that is expressed by the boogie-woogie chorus and the jumping percussion makes it most enjoyable. I have always wondered what kind of party I would have to throw in order to play this record.

Automatic Writing is altogether different from the opera works. It is an effective bromide for those who have had a steady dose of pulse and minimalist music. It is a quiet album featuring the amplified sounds of the vocal cavity (tongue, lips, breath, etc.) set against a distant Polymoog track by Ashley. The synthesizer spatters a pattern of rhythm, melodies, and chords. The spoken words lose all meaning because of the way they are amplified. Ashley complicates the sounds by providing sparse echo effects and playing voice sounds in reverse and simultaneously. In so doing, he strips the words of any significance and permits them to exist as pure sound events.

MARC BARRECA

Twilight (1980), Palace of Lights .05-1000

Pleasant synthesizer music blending jazz and classical structures with ambient effects.

BEACH BOYS

Smiley Smile (1967), Brother Records ST 9001
Surf's Up (1971), Reprise S-6453

The odd and simple *Smiley Smile* album, released the same year as the Beatles' *Sgt. Pepper*, was the antithesis of most psychedelic rock being produced at the time. For this release, the Beach Boys turned to the basic vocal harmonies that had made them famous but used the studio to layer and edit the material into a bizarre mixture of songs of childlike innocence. Only "Good Vibrations," the first single taken from the album, gained much attention, and it remains one of the finest examples of studio tape composition in rock music. It featured what was probably one of Robert Moog's transistorized theremins during the chorus lines. The remainder of the LP contains many other interesting, though less grandiose, experiments by the Beach Boys.

The title track from the album *Surf's Up* was actually composed during the *Smiley Smile* days but not released on an album until 1971. It is perhaps the group's best, and most complex, vocal work. The album was also noteworthy for its use of synthesizers and tape effects, particularly in the processing of voices and the use of vocal tracks played in reverse to harmonize with normal tracks.

THE BEATLES

Rubber Soul (1965), Capitol ST 2442
Revolver (1966), Capitol ST 2576
Sgt. Pepper's Lonely Hearts Club Band (1967), Capitol SMAS 2653
Magical Mystery Tour (1967), Capitol SMAL 2835
The Beatles (1968), Capitol SWBO 101
Abbey Road (1969), Apple SO 383

The Beatles did for rock music what Cage and Stockhausen did for the avant-garde: they opened up the world of music to any and all possible sounds. They tinkered with odd instrumentation, used ambient sounds and noise as part of many of their songs, played with tape editing tricks, and established the power of the recording studio for rock music. With *Rubber Soul* the Beatles stopped performing live and devoted the remaining years of the group to studio work. *Rubber Soul* is noteworthy for its unusual instrumentations,

(Courtesy of Capitol Records.)

the clarity and separation of the stereo effects due to multitracking, and Paul's first use of fuzz bass in the song "Think
For Yourself."

Some of their experiments with tape recorders began
quite by accident. In early 1966, John Lennon was attempting
to play a session tape they had just recorded for the song
"Rain" but got the tape threaded improperly in the machine,
and it began to play in reverse. Delighted with the results,
he mixed in a line of the song played backward in the final
release of the single. Later the same year while working on
Revolver, the Beatles collaborated on an unusual piece called
"Tomorrow Never Knows." This was a starkly experimental
piece for them and prominently featured tapes played backward combined with George's sitar music and lyrics derived
from *The Tibetan Book of the Dead*.

"Tomorrow Never Knows" introduced the era of psychedelic music, but it was the album *Sgt. Pepper's Lonely
Hearts Club Band* in 1967 that turned the entire industry
inward toward the power of the recording studio. The album
cover, incidentally, includes a photograph of Karlheinz
Stockhausen in that cavalcade of famous faces surrounding
the Beatles. The music of *Sgt. Pepper* was an intriguing blend
of rock and roll, ballads, Indian ragas, psychedelia, and 1940s
pop. The kaleidoscopic nature of the album ran one song
into another with amazing ease, often using sound effects or
brief musical bridges to form transitions. Every second of
available sound was used with dramatic effect to propel the
record forward. Sound effects were used generously on *Sgt.
Pepper*. Crowd sounds, an alarm clock, barnyard animals,
and other effects all found their way onto various tracks.

One of the Beatles' best examples of special tape effects
appears in the song "For the Benefit of Mr. Kite." This bit
of tape work is reminiscent of the chance operations performed by Cage in the early 1950s. The group was attempting
to simulate the sound of circus music. In addition to using
electric organs and harmonicas, it took a recording of a circus
steam calliope, cut the tape into small pieces, and then ran-
domly spliced the tape together with no regard for whether
it was in the correct order or would play in forward or reverse.
The result is the haunting, surreal calliope that graces the
middle and concluding sections of the song.

The Beatles also featured many unusual experiments
with instrumental sounds on *Sgt. Pepper*. In addition to their

usual complement of organs, pianos, and guitars, the album featured the harp, kazoo, sitar, harpsichord, harmonium, string quartet, horn, saxophone, and full orchestra. Ringo's drums became the focal point of many songs ("Lovely Rita" and "A Day in the Life") with their unusual de-tuned sound, later imitated by many rock drummers. Orchestral sounds were used effectively throughout *Sgt. Pepper*, most notably during the two thundering crescendos found in "A Day in the Life." According to Beatles expert J. P. Russell, author of *The Beatles on Record*, the orchestra featured forty-one pieces and was layered four times on tape, slightly out of phase, to create the desired depth of the sound. The idea to use these massive crescendos of rising pitches was a bold one for the Beatles and reflected an influence from a more classical spirit of avant-garde experimentation.

With *Magical Mystery Tour* and *The Beatles* (usually known as the White Album), the group continued to experiment on a grand scale with sound and electronics. John Lennon became interested in collage effects and began to include strange mélanges of sound on some of the Beatles' songs. "I Am the Walrus" is one of these and is perhaps one of the most truly experimental songs ever to become a hit. In addition to the droning of strings, the chanting of background voices, and the abstract, apocalyptic lyrics of Lennon, the song features layers of random radio sounds, snatches from old Beatles songs, recitations from Shakespeare, and sped-up voice tapes. Lennon only outdid this experimental extravagance with his collage piece "Revolution No. 9" (1968) on the White Album and the album *Unfinished Music No. 1—Two Virgins*, composed with Yoko Ono in 1968.

Although the Beatles really ended their career prior to the synthesizer age, George Harrison's interest in the Moog (which he first used on his 1968 solo frolic "Electronic Sound") brought this unusual studio device into the sessions for *Abbey Road*. The Moog played by George is most apparent in cuts like "Maxwell's Silver Hammer," where it is used for some delightful soloing; the opening cascading tone of "Here Comes the Sun"; the electronic crickets found at the end of "You Never Give Me Your Money"; and the powerful waves of white noise modulated to simulate wind sounds at the conclusion of "I Want You." The use of synthesizer was so restrained that its presence went virtually unnoticed by most who heard the album.

DAVID BEHRMAN

On the Other Ocean; Figure in a Clearing (1977), Lovely Music LML 1041

Behrman was a member of the Sonic Arts Union in the late 1960s and has worked closely with the likes of Ashley, Mumma, DeMarinis, and Lucier for many years. He was a producer for Columbia Records during the late 1960s and was responsible for some of the most important record releases of new music ever, including Terry Riley's first two discs and collections of electronic music on the Columbia and Odyssey labels.

Behrman's own work has often involved specially designed circuitry to allow for the interaction of performers and synthesizing equipment. This album presents two important pieces in which a microcomputer "hears" the pitches made by live musicians and responds with sounds of its own. Behrman's experiments in interactive computer music date from the mid-1970s and anticipated the growing interest in computer music, which continues to broaden as personal computers become more affordable.

LARS-GUNNAR BODIN

For Jon (Fragments of a Time to Come) (1978), Folkways FTS 33443

Modern Swedish electronic music, picking up in the tradition of Karl-Birger Blomdahl and others from the 1960s. Melodramatic music featuring exchanges between a choir and the Synclavier digital synthesizer. Preoccupied with cyborgs, space ships, and other science fiction themes, the piece is too ambitious for its own good.

DAVID BOWIE

Low (1977), RCA CPL1-2030
Heroes (1977), RCA AFL1-2522

While many of Bowie's records over the years have included determined attempts to mix electronics with rock, the work he did with Brian Eno on *Low* and *Heroes* represents his purest efforts along these lines. The sparse and simplistic instrumentations of *Low* were tinged with the kind of pulsing electronic robotics that later became the mainstay of the growing technorock movement. The second side of *Low* was presumptuous in its synthesizer doodling but represented an honest attempt on Bowie's part to breathe new life into his music. *Heroes* was a more fully developed album in its use of electronics and is the more successful of these two forays into experimental rock. *Low* possesses a quaint innocence, however, that an artist such as Bowie rarely reveals, and for that reason it is an excellent album for exploring the possibilities of electronics in rock. Following these sessions, Bowie has returned to his more familiar songwriting habits but has maintained a very high profile for the synthesizer in his work.

CABARET VOLTAIRE

Mix-Up (1979), Rough Trade 4
Live YMCA 27.10.79 (1979), Rough Trade 7
Voice of America (1980), Rough Trade 11
Red Mecca (1981), Rough Trade 27

Cabaret Voltaire is certainly one of the most prolific of recent experimental rock bands. Their name is taken from the cabaret where the dada movement was centered back in 1917. The patented CV sound consists of droning electronic percussion overridden by the monotone male vocal of Stephen Mallinder and the cutting guitar waves of Richard Kirk. The group liberally uses tapes for effects, often inserting snatches of dialogue from the radio or TV. Unlike Kraftwerk, the blend of sounds is not so pleasant at times. The music has bite and anger, however, reflecting the political views of the group. With *Red Mecca*, CV mellowed their sound somewhat by adding a real drummer and some horns. Extremist music, for those who like a little noise with their drones. The live Cabaret Voltaire LP presents a good example of the sound of one hand clapping.

JOHN CAGE

25-Year Retrospective Concert of the Music of John Cage (1958), Avakian
Variations IV: John Cage with David Tudor (1965), Part I, Everest 3132; Part 2, Everest 3230
Indeterminacy (1959), Folkways FT 3704
Cartridge Music (1962), Mainstream MS-5015
HPSCHD (1969), Nonesuch H-71224

Although John Cage is often associated with electronic music, not many of his works in this medium have been translated

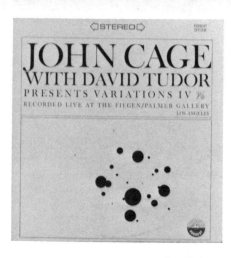

to disc. This is primarily because so much of the work is improvisational and was made successful through its interaction with live action and dancers. Most record companies have concentrated on releases of his piano and orchestral music, or text material. Luckily a few vintage discs are still available that display Cage's importance to the medium.

Early examples of his tape music include *Williams Mix* found on the Avakian disc and *Fontana Mix* on Turnabout (listed earlier under "Collections"). The live electronic music that Cage and Tudor performed in the early 1960s has been preserved on the Mainstream recording of *Cartridge Music* and the marvelous, enigmatic *Variations IV* recordings on Everest. The two *Variations IV* recordings capture the sounds of an early avant-garde happening organized by Cage and Tudor and performed at a gallery in Los Angeles in 1964. The Everest recordings of this mixed-media event are preceded by a polite disclaimer from a studio announcer who apologizes to the listener for the chaos that is to follow.

Indeterminacy on Folkways is a two-record gem. This performance captures on disc the collaboration that Cage and Tudor took on the road for many years during the 1960s and 1970s. It features Cage reading short anecdotes while Tudor provides electronic music accompaniment. The reading and the electronic effects are only related in as much as they are taking place at the same time in the same space. This landmark in text-sound composition also demonstrated that there was humor to be found in the avant-garde.

For a bit of computerized chaos, Nonesuch released *HPSCHD*, which is the music that accompanied a mixed-media event composed and organized in 1969 by Cage and Lejaren Hiller. *HPSCHD* is scored for harpsichords and computer-generated sound tapes. Hiller produced electronic sounds using Illiac II, a computerized sound synthesizer. The album package also contains a printout called *KNOBS* that was one of 10,000 "different numbered solutions" of a program that instructs the listener as to how to "perform" the playback of the LP by controlling the volume and tone controls of a stereo set. In addition to these recordings of his electronic music, there are many discs available featuring the piano, voice, percussion, and text work of John Cage.

WALTER (WENDY) CARLOS
Switched on Bach (1968), Columbia MS-7194
Switched on Brandenburgs CBS M2X-35895

(Courtesy of Lovely Music, New York.)

Sonic Seasonings, Columbia PG-31234
A Clockwork Orange, Columbia PC-31480
The Well-Tempered Synthesizer, Columbia MS-7286

> These renderings by Carlos of classical keyboard music are by far the best ever done in the electronic medium, if that's what you like.

ROBERT CEELY

Instrumental and Electronic Music (1975), Beep 1001

> Ceely worked in electronic music in the early 1960s, eventually settling down in New England to teach and work in the academic world. This album represents some of his best work, from pure tape composition done at the Milano studio in 1964 to more recent instrumental work.

JOEL CHADABE

Rhythms (1981), Lovely Music VR 1301

> Chadabe works with microcomputers to create interactive music combining the sounds of live musicians with that of computer synthesis. This album joins a percussionist with the computer and the result is a lively exchange of action that makes it difficult to distinguish who is initiating which sounds.

Marimbas, vibraphone, glass bowls, and log drums combine nicely with the computer, forming a kind of electronic gamelan orchestra.

DEVO

Q: Are We Not Men? (1978), Warner Brothers BSK 3239
Duty Now for the Future (1979), Warner Brothers K-3337
New Traditionalists (1982), Warner Brothers 3595

The first album by this group from mid-America was produced by Brian Eno. Its music is a blend of rock farce and social commentary, although it is most enjoyable when its members shut their mouths and stick to the music. The synthesizer is key to their sound, as are guitar and bass parts played with mechanical flair.

Devo gained popularity on the strength of a fine debut album and a robotic version of the Rolling Stones' classic "Satisfaction." In using a heavily electronic sound to depict their stories of a cold and brazen society, they unfortunately promulgate the notion that electronic music is both monotonous and threatening.

TOD DOCKSTADER

Luna Park; Traveling Music; Apocalypse (1966), Owl ORLP 6
Drone; Two Fragments from Apocalypse; Water Music (1966), Owl ORLP 7
Quartermass (1966), Owl ORLP 8

Organized sound work in the tradition of Varèse. Excellent music by a neophyte who used some pretty ordinary objects and equipment to create an impressive body of music during an outburst in 1966.

CHARLES DODGE

Synthesized Voices (1978), CRI 348

Readings of poetry that are digitized and then restructured via computer to modify vocal sounds.

DOME

Dome 2 (1980), Rough Trade Dome 2

Caustic electronic rock music from England. Represents the movement to marry abstract expressionism with conventional rock sounds. Somewhat successful; brooding and hard to fathom at times.

ROGER DOYLE

Rapid Eye Movements (1982), United Dairies UD 011

This album by Irish composer Roger Doyle features two electronic works that run through the entire grammar of studio techniques. Somewhat reminiscent of Stockhausen's *Hymnen*, the music is structured intuitively to form an effective discourse in sound. Doyle has been an active member of the European avant-garde since the early 1970s.

HERBERT EIMERT

Etude über Tongemische; Fünf Stücke; Glockenspiel, Deutsche Grammophon 16132

Purely electronic tone works from one of the leaders of the Cologne studios, composed between 1953 and 1956.

EMERSON, LAKE, AND PALMER

Emerson, Lake, and Palmer (1971), Cotillion SD 9040

Even though the Beatles actually used a Moog synthesizer on *Abbey Road* in 1969, it was Keith Emerson who brought the instrument to prominence in 1971 with the premiere album by ELP. During the 1960s, Emerson earned a reputation for wild stage antics with the Nice, a quaint art-rock group that featured electrified versions of many classical pieces. He was known to manhandle his Hammond organ by rolling it around the stage or knocking the reverb unit to produce rolls of electronic thunder. He began using one of Robert Moog's full studio synthesizers in 1971 and even managed to take it on the road for a while. It was not an easy task performing with this burdensome and temperamental device in a live setting, and Emerson required an assistant who could change patch-cord arrangements while he fiddled with other keyboards during his performances.

Emerson's first album to feature the Moog was this debut effort by ELP. The record features a set of classically rooted numbers with rock-music intervals. Emerson was trying very hard to squeak all kinds of unusual sounds out of his keyboards. In "Take a Pebble" he employs the old Henry Cowell technique of stroking the piano strings directly to accompany music played on the keys. The Moog does not appear until the final track of the LP. In the song "Lucky Man" it percolates for a while in the background and then rips open the seams of the music for a solo finale that astounded many. Emerson's flamboyance brought much attention to this instrument, and many thought it was the first time a Moog had been used on an album.

BRIAN ENO

Here Come the Warm Jets (1973), Island 9268
Fripp and Eno: No Pussyfooting (1973), Antilles AN7001
Taking Tiger Mountain by Strategy (1974), Island 9309
Another Green World (1975), Island 9351
Discreet Music (1975), Obscure No. 3
Before and After Science (1978), Island 9478
Music for Films (1978), Antilles AN-7070
Music for Airports (1979), Ambient
Possible Musics: Eno and Hassell (1980), Editions EG EGS 107
Ambient #2—The Plateau of Mirrors: Eno and Budd (1980), Editions EG
On Land (1982), Editions EG

After having come to prominence as the original synthesist and resident experimenter of Roxy Music in 1971, Eno split with the group in 1973 to pursue his personal music projects. One of these was the creation of his own record label, Obscure, for the release of serious works by experimental music composers. The Obscure project came and went, contributing a number of important recordings to the avant-garde catalog by people like Gavin Bryars, John Adams, Jan Steele, John Cage, Michael Nyman, and Harold Budd. In addition to this work, Eno began to refine his own approach to composition and to get involved with other artists, record production, and the development of his own catalog of works on his newest label, EG. Eno has been extremely prolific as a producer for rock musicians. Credits include work for Talking Heads, David Bowie, Devo, and Ultravox.

Eno is best known for his series of "ambient" compositions. Beginning with the "No Pussyfooting" collaboration with guitarist Robert Fripp in 1973, he formed a style that straddled the repetitive instrumental droning of minimalist music and the environmental soundscapes of Cage, Schaeffer and other experimental purists. *Music for Airports, On Land, Before and After Science*, and *Ambient #2* are fine

Brian Eno. (Courtesy of E. G. Records, Ltd.)

examples of this work. *Discreet Music* utilized tape delay to create slowly changing patterns of repeating sounds; it remains one of Eno's finest contributions to the serious avant-garde repertoire.

MICHAEL WILLIAM GILBERT

Moving Pictures (1978), Gibex 001
The Call (1980), Gibex 002
In the Dreamtime (1982), Palace of Lights .02-2000

Michael William Gilbert is a resourceful electronic-music composer from Massachusetts. His first album was a genuine masterpiece recalling the heyday of studio composition in the mid-1960s. *Moving Pictures* is an album of ethereal beauty, echoing Far Eastern folk music in combination with syn-

(Courtesy of E. G. Records, Ltd.)

thesizers, flutes, voice, and percussion. Gilbert's successive works move closer and closer to a combination of jazz and electronics. Striking, but his best moments remain those when he sheds the vogue and embraces electronics.

PHILIP GLASS

Music with Changing Parts (1971), Chatham Square 1001-2
Music in Similar Motion (1973), Chatham Square 1003
Music in 12 Parts, Parts 1 and 2 (1977), Caroline
North Star (1977), Virgin 2085
Einstein on the Beach (1979), Tomato 4-2901
Glassworks (1981), CBS FM-37265
The Photographer (1983), CBS FM-37849

Philip Glass emerged from the New York scene in the early 1970s with his ensemble of electric keyboards, woodwinds, and voices playing what has been popularly termed "mini-malist" music. Often likened to the work of Riley and Reich, Glass's focuses on the process of developing a piece rather than the end result. Rhythm is constant, changes are slow to occur, and the overall energy of the music is fairly steady. Not much happens in Glass's music, although I hesitate to say that about the work of his counterparts Riley and Reich, where large-scale alterations in form and structure often underlie the seemingly static quality of the music. Glass is somewhat more atmospheric that other minimalists, a state that comes across very well in concert situations but can often fall flat on disc.

The early Glass work depended on electronics to weave an unending flow of aural mantras. The power of electronics to sustain sound was key to the process of his work. His first discs on Chatham Square were nearly impossible to find outside of New York City, but thanks to a few larger record companies, his work is now readily available. Most of Glass's music is lengthy and requires great devotion on the part of the listener.

Einstein on the Beach is perhaps his magnum opus and represents the music he composed for an impressive opera libretto by Robert Wilson. The album is a four-disc set and lasts about three hours. It is one of those albums that a collector should own but that is rarely listened to in entirety. *North Star* is an anomaly in that it consists entirely of short works. Comparing these pieces to other Glass compositions is like comparing an epic poem to haiku. There is much to be said for economy.

GRATEFUL DEAD

Live Dead (1970), Warner Brothers 2-WAR S-1830

For some reason, someone decided to add some musique concrète between the live cuts on this album by the Grateful Dead. Most Deadheads had little tolerance for this strange intrusion into their music.

JIMI HENDRIX

Are You Experienced? (1967), Reprise 6261
Axis: Bold As Love (1968), Reprise 6281
Electric Ladyland (1968), Reprise 6307
Cry of Love (1971), Reprise S-2034
At the Monterey Pop Festival (1970), Reprise S-2029

Jimi Hendrix released the single "Purple Haze" in June 1967, the same month that *Sgt. Pepper's Lonely Hearts Club Band* debuted. No one was ready for this American-bred, London-altered guitar player who had spent his early years playing backup to such rhythm-and-blues greats as King Curtis, Curtis Knight and the Squires, and the Isley Brothers (he appeared on the single "Testify" in 1964). Hendrix was from Seattle, moved to Harlem and then Greenwich Village in

New York in 1964. There he began to get a full taste of modern jazz and the folk-rock of Bob Dylan. It was during some of Hendrix' outrageous performances at the Cafe Wha? in Greenwich Village that he was spotted by groups like the Rolling Stones and the Animals and a following began. Chas Chandler, a former member of the Animals, was entirely taken by Hendrix and persuaded him to fly to England to form a band. In October 1966 the Jimi Hendrix Experience was formed, with Englishmen Noel Redding on bass and Mitch Mitchell on drums. Their first release was "Hey, Joe" in May 1967, followed by the tour de force of the summer of 1967, "Purple Haze."

Hendrix was an artist of extraordinary creative power. The electric guitar became transformed in his hands. His

(Courtesy Warner Brothers Records.)

music not only contained skilled guitar riffs and surreal lyrics but blended vast sonic contours and electronic sounds into works of abstract beauty. He was not merely a rock performer but also truly an electronic-music composer. The guitar just happened to be his sound source. He set rhythm to electronic music and made it palatable to the masses.

The resources and sounds of Hendrix were both perplexing and unmistakable. He played an inverted Fender Stratocaster, which placed the controls at the top of the instrument so he could manipulate them more freely. He was a seasoned live performer long before he stepped into the studio to work with the Experience. His performances were legendary for his sensual antics with the guitar, for his playing of the instrument with his teeth or behind his back, and especially for his masterful control of feedback. His style was a blend of funk, blues, pop, jazz, and pure electronic strangeness. He understood how to pull the most unusual sounds out of his guitar, sounds that nobody else had ever heard before. Hendrix coaxed a variety of sounds from his Stratocaster through the extended use of sustain, adjusting his tone controls, tapping the bridge of the guitar, scraping the strings against a mike stand, and waving the instrument like a magic wand in the space around him. He worked with an amazing intuition for electronic sound and how to control it.

Hendrix used every gizmo and effects unit he could obtain, including some custom-made for him. His standard props included the Dalas-Arbiter Fuzz Face, Jen Cry Baby wah-wah, echo boxes, reverb, specially designed speakers, and a custom-made effects unit called the Octavia, which could boost treble sounds and change their harmonics. This was a powerful arsenal when used live or in the studio.

The official studio recordings of the Jimi Hendrix Experience number only three: *Are You Experienced?*, *Axis: Bold As Love*, and *Electric Ladyland*. Although dozens of other Hendrix recordings exist, including many live recordings, only these three feature his complete studio treatment of his music, presented as he intended it to be.

Hendrix worked as hard in the studio as the Beatles, using all available studio techniques. His use of phasing was most apparent on his second album, *Axis: Bold As Love*. In the song "If 6 Was 9," rather than just apply phasing to a novel passage, he used it for a good four minutes to alter the sounds of the guitar, voice, drums, and flute, that make up the instrumental track. In the delicate "Little Wing," he isolates a guitar solo at the end with gently embracing phasing to soften the sound. Finally, the cut "Bold As Love" finishes with one of the most fully orchestrated phasings ever committed to vinyl.

Hendrix used multitracking to great advantage. One of his techniques was to add multiple renderings of a passage, each slightly delayed. He also liked to use stereo to make sound wander back and forth from one speaker to the other.

All of the recordings of Hendrix are also rich with sounds presented in reverse. The title track of *Are You Experienced?* is one of the best examples. It opens with a guitar bit in reverse and persists throughout to blend deftly his normally presented guitar with the reversed parts. Snippets of reversed sound consistently appear in his music. Like other composers interested in tape composition, Hendrix also used the familiar techniques of tape-speed changes and tape echo. "Third Stone from the Sun," from his first album, is a fine example of speed adjustment to affect the sound of the voice and the guitar.

PIERRE HENRY

Orphée, Philips L00.564
Variations pour une porte et un soupir (1964), Philips 836 898
Le Voyage (1964), Philips 836 899
Dieu (1978), Philips 6510 019
Futuriste (1980), Philips 6510 020

Pierre Henry's contributions to electronic music span thirty years. *Orphée* is a classic example of his early musique concrète interpretations of familiar musical motifs and dates from the early 1950s. *Dieu* and *Futuriste* are recent ensemble works that combine musique concrète textures with live performance.

Variations pour une porte et un soupir and *Le voyage* were each released in America on the Mercury Limelight label in the late 1960s. *Variations* represents Henry's most resolute and important musique concrète work. Following this work, he went on to more expansive studio compositions, beginning with the haunting *Le voyage*. *Futuriste* is a fitting tribute to the Italian futurist movement (1915) that later inspired Schaeffer and Henry to explore a new music that included common noises as well as instrumental sounds.

KING CRIMSON

In the Court of the Crimson King (1969), Atlantic 8245
In the Wake of Poseiden (1970), Atlantic 8266
Lizard (1971), Atlantic 8278
Islands (1972), Atlantic 7212

> Robert Fripp and King Crimson became known for their use
> of mellotron and the unusual sounds produced by Fripp and
> his guitar. By the time *Islands* was released, the group had
> shifted from the sophomoric karma that characterized their
> earlier records to a more artsy attempt at jazz fusion. Fripp
> later became involved with Brian Eno, and I for one am
> afraid that the damage was nearly fatal. Through his asso-
> ciation with Eno he developed "Frippertronics," a tape loop
> system that allows him to play solo guitar to the accompan-
> iment of droning, undulating sounds on tape that repeat re-
> lentlessly. "Frippertronics" have taken the bite out of his
> sound; experimental music requires more than the endless
> repetition of a single idea. At least King Crimson provided
> emotions and energy, not to mention some spacey sounds
> and memorable songs.

RICHARD KOSTELANETZ

Invocations (1983), Folkways Records FRS 37902

> Sound poet and author Kostelanetz composed his text-sound
> work through the editing of the recorded voices of preachers,
> priests, and other religious spokespeople from around the
> world. An excellent example of text-sound composition using
> the tape medium to control the structure of a work.

KRAFTWERK

Kraftwerk 1 (1971), Philips 6305 058
Kraftwerk 2 (1972), Philips 6305 117
Kraftwerk (1973), Vertigo 6641 077
Autobahn (1974), Vertigo 2003
Radioactivity (1975), Capitol SW-11457
Trans Europe Express (1977), Capitol SW-11603
Man Machine (1978), Capitol SW-11728
Computer World (1981), Warner Brothers HS-3549

> The name of this German group means "powerplant" and
> represents their approach to electronic pop music, which
> combines catchy melodies with robotic voices and banally

poetic lyrics. Most remembered in America for the hit single "Autobahn" in 1974, the group was heavily influenced by a small faction of electronic groups from the early 1970s: Pink Floyd, Tangerine Dream, Ashra Temple, Soft Machine, and others. In marrying the minimalist tendencies of Terry Riley and Steve Reich with synthesizer technology, this four-man keyboard group from Dusseldorf has managed to produce a consistently pleasant set of albums of unpretentious innocence and style. Their sound has influenced numerous artists of late, particularly Devo.

KERRY LEIMER

Closed System Potentials (1980), Palace of Lights .03-1000
Land of Look Behind (1982), Palace of Lights .06-2000
Imposed Order (1983), Palace of Lights .17-2000.

Kerry Leimer, from Seattle, Washington, works mainly in synthesized ambient music, somewhat like Eno. It is a distilled blend, though, and is usually measured with more discretion than some of Eno's endless romps. *Land of Look Behind* gets uncharacteristically funky at times because it was written for the soundtrack to a film about Jamaica.

LOTHAR AND THE HAND PEOPLE

Lothar and the Hand People (1968), Capitol SM-2997
Space Hymn (1969), Capitol

This five-man band from Connecticut featured a theremin named Lothar. It was responsible for the space sounds that dominated their music. The second album was quite a bit more tame than the first. These are difficult discs to find but represent a creative effort by rock musicians to stretch the boundaries of their music beyond the usual limits of the audience.

ALVIN LUCIER

I Am Sitting in a Room (1981), Lovely Music VR 1013
Music for Solo Performer (1982), Lovely Music VR 1014

These two albums document some of the work done by Lucier in the period from 1964 to 1970. Each album contains a new performance of the works. *I Am Sitting in a Room* is a tape-recorder piece that regenerates a brief text passage over and over until the articulation becomes meaningless and is transformed into abstract sound. *Music for Solo Performer* was an early experiment with the use of amplified brain waves, the first attempt by a composer to use the brain wave as a source for a composition. Lucier's status as an experimenter of the highest order is also represented on album collections from the Sonic Arts Union (Mainstream MS-5010) and an album of vocal experiments called *Extended Voices* (Odyssey 32160156).

RICHARD MAXFIELD

Bacchanale; Piano Concert for David Tudor; Amazing Grace (1969), Advance FGR-8S

This seldom-recorded but influential artist was making electronic music at a time when Stockhausen, Cage, Feldman, and others were making waves. He served as an inspiration to the newer American composers of the early 1960s: La Monte Young, Terry Riley, Joe Byrd, and many others. His class at the New School in New York was the focal point of many avant-garde social circles. In contrast to the stoic mathematical approach of Stockhausen in the early 1960s and the relative chaos of Cage's chance work, Maxfield wrapped his work in a warm lyrical cloak of emotion and romanticism.

(Courtesy of Lovely Music, New York.)

MERZBOW

Material Action 2 (1982), Chaos 00001

> A performance duo in Japan that uses electronics to combine junk sounds, noise, and other distractions into a music of collage. The music is continuous, without pause.

ILHAN MIMAROGLU

Music Plus One for Violin Solo and Electromagnetic Tape (1970), Vox Turnabout TV-S 34429
Wings of the Delirious Demon (1972), Finnadar SR 9001
Face the Windmills, Turn Left (1974), Finnadar SR 9012
Tract, Folkways 33441
To Kill a Sunrise; La Ruche, Folkways 33951

> Mimaroglu, like Pierre Henry, can often urge dramatic sounds out of the most common everyday objects. *Wings of the Delirious Demon* is a modern work of musique concrète styled after Henry's famous *Variations on a Door and a Sigh*. It uses brief provocations of sound derived from such things as rubber bands, voices, viola, clarinet, and celesta. *Tract* is a text-sound work using electronics to alter various quotations from historical figures. *To Kill a Sunrise* and *La ruche* combine electronics with vocals, piano, cello, and harpsichord. Good contributions to the more serious side of electronic music. Highly kinetic, effective, melodramatic adventures.

AKIRA MIYOSHI

Ondine (1960), Time S-2058

> Vintage electronic music from the studios of the Japanese Broadcasting Corporation. *Ondine* combines singers with orchestra, ondes martenot, and tape composition.

MNEMONISTS

Some Attributes of a Living System (1980), Dys 02a
Horde (1981), Dys 03A
Biota (1982), Dys 07
Gyromancy (1984), Dys 10

> Mnemonists is a collective of artists and musicians from Colorado who record complicated and effective collages of electronic and instrumental sounds. Each disc is packaged with an array of art prints from group members. Powerful music for those who can get by without much rhythm.

MOODY BLUES

Days of Future Passed (1967), Deram 18012
In Search of the Lost Chord (1968), Deram 18017
On the Threshold of a Dream (1969), Deram 18025

The Moody Blues are best known for their unusual instrumentations and gimpy mysticism. The mellotron, as played by Mike Pinder, was responsible for the eerie orchestral sounds found at the core of their music. *Days of Future Passed*, released the same year as *Sgt. Pepper* and *Are You Experienced?*, combined the sound of a rock combo with that of a full orchestra in a way that had not been done before. The use of the mellotron (which plays tape recordings of orchestral instruments) proved to be the magic ingredient to make this venture successful. It was an achievement they were never able to match. Although their lyrics persistently wallowed in pop spiritualism, the music of the Moody Blues was always fresh and full of intrigue. They certainly wrote the book on the mellotron, an instrument that continues to retain some of its popularity in spite of the move toward totally electronic synthesizers.

MOTHER MALLARD'S PORTABLE MASTERPIECE CO.

Mother Mallard's Portable Masterpiece Co. (1973), Earthquack EQ0001
Like a Duck to Water (1976), Earthquack EQ0002

This was one of the early synthesizer groups to hit the concert road on the East Coast back in the early 1970s. Original members David Borden, Steve Drews, and Linda Fisher used a keyboard sound incorporating synthesizer and piano. Their self-produced albums were devoted to serious electronic music and were important contributions to the synthesizer movement in America as well as to the burgeoning movement toward independent record producing. There is a diversity of sounds and pieces on these albums, all with an improvisational feel that perched the group between contemporary classical and jazz. The group dabbled in everything from chance music to pulse music.

GORDON MUMMA

The Dresden Interleaf; Music from the Venezia Space Theatre; Megaton for William Burroughs, (1979), Lovely Music VR 1091

This is one of Mumma's few solo record albums, though many of his works can be found on other collections. This album contains a number of electronic works spanning Mumma's early career in the 1960s. All of the works represent the creative spirit of American studio composition during the 1960s. Mumma did not follow any particular school of thought regarding electronic music; he concentrated on creating experiences that were unique expressions of his beliefs and sensibilities. These works are rich with concrete sounds, purely electronic passages, environmental-type atmospheres, and spontaneous motion inspired by the spirit of the performance. This is an important testament to the studio work of one of America's most gifted experimental composers.

New Order

Blue Monday/The Beach (1983), Factory Records 10.
Power, Corruption and Lies (1983), Factory Records 12.

This four-man rock group began their career as Joy Division and changed their name after their lead singer killed himself. They re-emerged as New Order and tightened up their sound into an appealing combination of synthesizer rock and dance music. *Power, Corruption and Lies* was thought by many critics to be the best rock album of 1983. Engaging and skilled music using electronics but without losing the human touch.

(Courtesy of Lovely Music, New York.)

THE NICE

Thoughts of Emerlist Davjack (1968), Immediate
Nice (1969), Impulse Z1252020
Elegy (1971), Mercury 61324

> One of the first rock groups to feature keyboards as the center
> of attraction, this precursor to many progressive rock bands
> was the spotlight for Keith Emerson, a classically trained
> pianist. He played piano and organ with a fury and theatri-
> cality that totally overshadowed other members of the band.
> In fact, when the guitar player eventually left the group, they
> did not even replace him. The group's repertoire included
> rock interpretations of classical pieces, Dylan songs, and tunes
> from *West Side Story*. Emerson's own compositions were usu-
> ally no more than a combination of rock and classical clichés,
> but his wild stage antics gained him a strong following. Nice
> disbanded and Emerson became the focal point of Emerson,
> Lake, and Palmer in 1971. Upon leaving the Nice, Emerson
> spent some time with Robert Moog, learning how to use the
> latter's synthesizer. The synthesizer eventually became the
> embodiment of the ELP sound and so influenced a new school
> of progressive rock keyboardists.

NOCTURNAL EMISSIONS

Fruiting Body LP (1981), Sterile ION2
Drowning in a Sea of Bliss (1983), Sterile SR4

> Collage composition from England featuring some rather
> frightening sounds. Xenakis taken to extremes. Is music vi-
> olent? This can be at times.

YOKO ONO

Two Virgins (1968), Apple T-5001
Yoko Ono–Plastic Ono Band (1970), Apple SW 3373
Fly (1971), Apple SVBB 3380

> Yoko has taken a lot of abuse over the years. In these, the
> most experimental recordings she made with John Lennon,
> she at least succeeded in showing the Beatles' audience that
> other types of music really did exist. But for the most part
> Ono's works are naive ramblings using voice and tape echo.
> *Two Virgins* was made in a night with Lennon while the two
> experimented with tape collages. "Touch Me" from the *Yoko*

Ono–Plastic Ono Band LP is perhaps her tightest and weird-est rocker. Her vocal style, which combined singing with other odd yodelings, proved to be rather influential in later years as new-wave rocks acts began to produce similar stylings.

PÈRE UBU

The Modern Dance (1978), Blank 001
Dub Housing (1979), Chrysalis CHR 1207
The Art of Walking, Rough Trade US4
Song of the Bailing Man (1982), Rough Trade US21

Industrial-strength rock plus electronic noise, surprisingly spry and full of humor. Tapes, sound effects, distortion, deadpan voices, broadcast sounds, rarely used better with rock music.

PHILIP PERKINS

Neighborhood with a Sky (1982), Fun Music 1002

Perkins composed these tape pieces in the classic mold. He deals with fairly basic techniques—like amplitude modula-tion, reverb, and echo—to shape and form a luscious collec-tion of richly vibrant sounds. The ten tracks on the album contain ample variety. The opening works are traditional musique concrète and electroacoustical pieces. Perkins uses measured amounts of modulation, filtering, tape delay, and splicing to transform everyday sounds in powerful expres-sions in the tradition of Varèse.

PINK FLOYD

Piper at the Gates of Dawn (1967), Tower ST 5093
Saucerful of Secrets (1968), Tower ST 5131
Ummagumma (1969), Capitol STBB-388
Dark Side of the Moon (1973), Harvest SMAS 11163

Pink Floyd began making records in England in 1967. Their first LP, *Piper at the Gates of Dawn*, demonstrated their unusual penchant for composing long, sonorous guitar and organ "pieces" with dissonant harmonies, swirling effects, and erratic rhythms. "Interstellar Overdrive," featuring the incredible lead guitar work of original member Syn Barrett, truly rivaled Hendrix in originality and forcefulness. For the second album, *A Saucerful of Secrets*, the group produced the title track as a massive tape composition in the classic sense. This was truly an attempt by rock artists to take the sonics of the avant-garde and apply them to a more predictable, or classic, musical structure. This was not rock music.

The group received little acclaim until it changed its style to a more standard, lyrical approach. Its later albums, although rather tame when compared with its early work, continue to show a respect for the use of sound effects and noise as part of the music.

PROCOL HARUM

Procol Harum (1967), Deram DES 18008
Shine On Brightly (1968), AM 4151

Best known for the Hammond organ sound offered by original member Matthew Fisher on these early works, Procol Harum was an enigmatic group that flirted with popularity by wrapping its music with humor and sound effects and the abstract lyrics of Keith Reid. *Shine On Brightly* was both a brilliant concept album, which made wide use of electronic effects, and a poke at the Eastern-mysticism fad of the 1960s.

STEVE REICH

Violin Phase; It's Gonna Rain (1969), Columbia MS-7265
Four Organs (1973), Angel S-36059

Although Reich's early work often involved tape experiments (*Violin Phase; Come Out*), most of his recordings are of instrumental work for orchestral ensembles. The work represented on these two albums illustrates his methods for using phase processes to develop his works. *Four Organs* is particularly interesting for its staged overlapping of organ chords.

THE RESIDENTS

Meet the Residents (1974), Ralph Records 0677
The Residents Present the Third Reich 'n' Roll (1975), Ralph Records 1075
Duck Stab/Buster & Glenn (1978), Ralph Records 0278
Not Available (1978), Ralph Records 1174
Eskimo (1979), Ralph Records 7906
The Residents Commercial Album (1980), Ralph Records 8052
Mark of the Mole (1981), Ralph Records 8152
The Tunes of Two Cities (1982), Ralph Records 8202
Intermission (1982), Ralph Records 8252
Residue (1983), Ralph Records 8302

(Courtesy of CBS Records.)

This four-person group residing in the Bay Area has never revealed the identity of its members nor shown their faces. In concert they don bizarre head gear to disguise themselves. Their musical efforts launched Ralph Records as a successful independent record label. The music ranges from Zappa-esque parodies of pop-rock to brooding electronic atmosphere and orchestrations. A true original.

TERRY RILEY

A Rainbow in Curved Air (1969), Columbia MS-7315
Persian Surgery Dervishes (1974), Shandar 83502
Shri Camel (1980), CBS M 35164

Master of the minimal and originator of space music using droning organs and repetitive musical structures, Terry Riley deserves more credit for changing the state of mind in music in modern America than almost any other composer. The influence of his music, though only recorded on a few discs, has been wide and lasting. The modern frolics of Philip Glass and Steve Reich owe much to the ground originally broken by Riley in the mid-1960s when he began to perform his live concerts of multikeyboard electronics. The rock world has also been permanently affected, as evidenced by the mini-malist riffs used by such artists as the Who, Bowie, Fripp, Eno, and many others.

Riley's music is almost transcendental in nature. Although pulsing and repetitive in structure, the textures and feel of the music change continually to offer a warm experience somewhat akin to hearing the floating patterns of Bach's music. *A Rainbow in Curved Air* uses the combo organ in general use by rock groups to weave a beautiful set of meandering, never-ending melodic lines. *Persian Surgery Dervishes* does much the same. *Shri Camel*, a more recent album, explores unusual scales using an electric organ with just intonation. Here the emphasis is not so much on long process pieces but brief, concise musical statements using light harmonics. The music of Riley remains some of the most imitated music from the avant-garde.

DAVID ROSENBOOM

Collaboration in Performance (1978), 1750 Arch S-1774
Future Travel (1981), Street Records SRA-002

David Rosenboom has been known for his brain-wave music and other meditative sorts of noodling. On *Collaboration* he combines forces with Donald Buchla, inventor of the Buchla synthesizer. Together they have succeeded in producing a mildly spacey, somewhat minimalist venture using piano and electronics. The music makes use of one of Buchla's recent computer-assisted instruments, the 300 Series Electric Music Box, and successfully blends improvisation with computer-assisted sound control. *Future Travel* is a glossy space opera.

ERIC ROSS

Electronic Études; Songs for Synthesized Soprano (1982), Doria ER-103

Contemporary classical work by American Eric Ross combining synthesized sounds with other instruments like the piano, clarinet, and voice. Diverse instrumentations show there is still ground to be broken in this idiom. Ross also uses a modern theremin on this recording, a rarity nowadays.

KLAUS SCHULZE

Irrlicht (1971), Brain 0001.077
Cyborg (1972), Brain 0021.078
Picture Music (1973), Brain 0001.067

Blackdance (1974), Brain 0060.406
Timewind (1975), Brain 0001.075
Moondawn (1976), Brain 0001.088
Body Love (1976), Brain 0060.047
Body Love, Vol. 2 (1977), Brain 0060.097
Mirage (1978), Brain 0060.040
X (1978), Brain 0080.023
Dune (1979), Brain 0060.225
Mindphaser, Brain 0060.423
Dig It, Brain 0060.353
Live (1980), Brain 0080.048
Trancefer, Brain 06864636
Aphrica (1984), Inteam ID 20.001 (with Ernst Fuchs and Rainer Bloss)
Drive Inn (1984), Inteam ID 20.002. (with Rainer Bloss)
Angst (1984), Inteam ID 20.003

Klaus Schulze emerged as a prolific and influential synthesizer composer in the early 1970s after having done tenure in the German electronic groups Ash ra Tempel and Tangerine Dream. He has assembled a large inventory of electronic instruments and is noted for his ambitious solo albums and performances. His music, much like that of Tangerine Dream, is repetitive and harmonic, supported largely by the automatism of synthesizer sequencers and other control devices. Unlike his Teutonic counterparts, however, Klaus Schulze often wraps his harmonics in a shroud of mysterious special effects. This is the most interesting feature of his music, and places his work between the aesthetics of the elder avant-garde (e.g., Stockhausen) and new rock sounds. His tenth album, *X*, was notable for its use of synthesized orchestral sounds, making it sound more like contemporary classical than electronic.

SILVER APPLES

Silver Apples (1968), Kapp KS-3562
Contact (1969), Kapp KS-3584

This curious duo from New York City emerged in mid-1968. Calling themselves Silver Apples, Dan Taylor played dual drum sets and banjo, and a fellow named Simeon played an electronic contraption named after himself. The simeon was actually just a collection of nine audio oscillators with numerous manual controls. He divided them up so that "lead

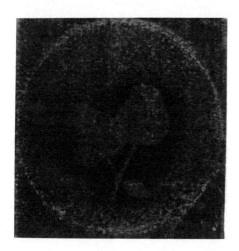

and rhythm oscillators" could be played with the hands, el-
bows and knees, and "bass oscillators" with feet. In addition,
both sang.

Silver Apples produced pulsing, whining music with
machinelike harmonies and simple melodies. They foreshadowed the use of sequencers with synthesizers and the music
of Tangerine Dream, Kraftwerk, Devo, and countless other
electrorock groups. One of their more intriguing tracks was
an adaptation of a Navajo Indian song called "Dancing Gods."
I do not know how they managed it, but Kapp records (normally a producer of albums by the likes of Jack Jones, Sergio
Franchi, and the Chad Mitchell Trio) released two albums
and a single by Silver Apples during 1968 and 1969. I think
I may be their only remaining fan.

LAURIE SPIEGEL

The Expanding Universe (1980), Philo 9003

Using computers (from Bell Labs) and synthesizers, Spiegel
creates highly focused electronic music that explores small
nuances of pitch, texture, and rhythm. She ignores process
as a means for predicting what will happen next in a work,
instead concentrating on expanding a momentary occurrence
such as a certain timbre or note sequence. Although using
computers, her music is warm and human.

SPK

Information Overload (1981), Side Effects Records
Leichenschrei (1982), Thermidor T-9
The Last Attempt at Paradise (1982), Fresh Tape 103

> Thoroughly upsetting electronic music from three lads from New Zealand. SPK stands for "systems planning korporation" or "surgical penis klinik," whichever you prefer. Dark, brooding music somewhat reminiscent of the movie *Apocalypse Now*. Not for the faint of heart.

KARLHEINZ STOCKHAUSEN

Studie I; Studie II (1960), Deutsche Grammophon 16133
Gesang der Jünglinge; Kontakte (1965), Deutsche Grammopon 138811
Mikrophonie I; Mikrophonie II (1966), Columbia MS-7355
Telemusik; Mixtur (1967), Deutsche Grammophon 137012
Prozession (1968), Candide CE 31001
Hymnen (1967), Deutsche Grammophon 139 421-22
Kurzwellen (1968), Deutsche Grammophon 2707045
Stockhausen-Beethoven, Opus 1970 (1970), Deutsche Grammophon 139 461
Mantra (1971), Deutsche Grammophon 2530208
Es; Aufwärts (1972), Deutsche Grammophon 2530 255
Kommunion; Intensität (1972), Deutsche Grammophon 2530 256

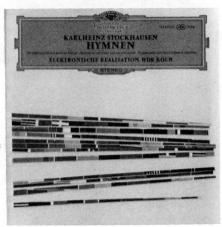

(Courtesy of Deutsche Grammophon Records, a division of PolyGram Classics, Inc.)

Ceylon; Bird of Passage (1975), Chrysalis CHR 1110
Sternklang (1977), Deutsche Grammophon 2707 123
Sirius (1980), Deutsche Grammophon 2707 122

Sometimes I feel that the only electronic music one needs to
listen to is Stockhausen. Then again, his fairly liberal style
is not to everyone's liking. This selection of albums covers a
wide range of Stockhausen's electronic music. *Gesang der
Jünglinge (Song of the Youths); Hymnen; Telemusik; Mixtur*;
and *Stockhausen-Beethoven, Opus 1970* represent fine examples of studio composition. For the combination of live
electronics with traditional instruments, *Mantra* (for piano
and ring modulators), *Mikrophonie II* (for choir, organ, ring
modulators, and microphone), and *Prozession* (for tam tam
viola, electronium, piano, and electronics) serve as good samples. For Stockhausen's fine art of improvisation with electronics, *Kurzwellen* (for shortwave radios and electronics) is
important, as are his "intuitive" works, *Es, Aufwärts, Kommunion*, and *Intensität*.

Song of the Youths and *Hymnen* are perhaps the best
studio compositions by any electronic composer. In their time,
they were considered innovative and original, two qualities
they still possess twenty years later. And the fine recordings
by Deutsche Grammophon ably preserve the beauty of the
two works.

Stockhausen is a master of the studio. From the early
days of the Cologne studio in 1951 through its development
in the 1960s and 1970s, he maintained the latest equipment
and had specially designed circuits made to provide effects
made to order (such as the regenerator used in *Hymnen* to
suspend any given tape sound indefinitely).

Finally, of those pieces that combine large orchestral
ensembles with electronics, *Sirius* and *Sternklang* are two
recent examples. *Studie I* and *Studie II* were Stockhausen's
very first purely electronic works, composed in the Cologne
studios in 1953.

One of the enigmas of Stockhausen is that every piece
he does seems to evolve from a unique process. He has been
obsessed with experimentation throughout his career, and
the unique approaches he takes to composition can be either
inspirational or irksome, depending on your point of view.
He is truly an obsessive-compulsive composer, but the most
important electronic-music composer to have emerged from
the avant-garde.

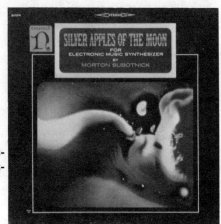

(Copyright 1967, Nonesuch Records. Used by permission. Illustration by Anthony Martin.)

MORTON SUBOTNICK

Silver Apples of the Moon (1967), Nonesuch H-71174
The Wild Bull (1968), Nonesuch H-71208
Sidewinder, Columbia M-30683
Four Butterflies, Columbia M-32741
A Sky of Cloudless Sulphur; After the Butterfly (1980), Nonesuch N-78001

Subotnick goes back to the formative years of the Bay Area avant-garde in the early 1960s. He was influential in the development of the Buchla synthesizer, which is used on most of his recordings. He is a composer in the classic sense, trying to use his electronic orchestra to create serious works of lasting beauty. Not one to conform to fashionable styles or movements in new music, Subotnick's work is always quite spectacular and fresh. The Buchla instrument itself is not designed for keyboard virtuosity but rather as a kind of sound palette for nonkeyboard composition. Subotnick has carried the art of studio composition to great heights.

His first two recordings on Nonesuch were somewhat special in that they were probably the first electronic pieces composed expressly for the record medium. *A Sky of Cloudless Sulphur* was perhaps the first digital recording of an electronic music piece. On the latter album, Subotnick returns to his early practice of combining live instrumentalists with

Talking Heads, a band whose recordings combine a sophisticated lyric with effective electronic treatments. (Courtesy Sire Records.)

electronics. *After the Butterfly* features cello, trombone, and clarinet amplified and shadowed by electronic "ghost" sounds that move from side to side in the stereo field. The result is one of those rarely successful marriages of electronics and conventional instruments, and demonstrates that Subotnick continues to be a composer of major impact.

TALKING HEADS

Talking Heads '77 (1977), Sire 6036
More Songs About Buildings and Food (1978), Sire K-6058
Fear of Music (1979), Sire K-6076
Remain in Light (1980), Sire K-6095
The Name of This Band Is Talking Heads (1982), Sire 2590
Speaking in Tongues (1983), Sire 1-23771

The first album by Talking Heads was sparse instrumentally but featured some daring intellectual acrobatics. The quirky voice of lead singer David Byrne became the group's instant trademark, and songs like "Psycho Killer," with its frantic, paranoid lyrics, made it easy to class the Heads with other up-and-coming new-wave acts. This was an art band, however, soon to be distinguished by its well-tempered experimental nature. Its abstract messages and arrangements soon gained the attention of Brian Eno. Eno was recruited to produce the second Talking Heads album, and he also contributed to the electronic effects.

The first joint album by Eno and the Talking Heads was *More Songs About Buildings and Food*, a cultivated blend of the cerebral and the emotional. The music ranges from a cover version of the Al Green soul ballad "Take Me to the River," to the countrified slide guitar of "The Big Country," to the driving rock of songs like "With Our Love" and "Found a Job." The lyrics are intelligent, reflective, and downright surreal at times in their harsh descriptiveness. And there has seldom been a more calculated use of effects on a rock album, largely prerecorded snatches of synthesizer, voice, and guitar sounds. These are woven into the texture of the songs to complement the changing chords and rhythms.

The instruments are often filtered and processed to gain special nuances. The drums during "Warning Sign," for example, seem to be clipped on one hand using an envelope generator and then made more resonant using reverb, an unusual technique that totally alters the normal attack characteristics of drums. Later Talking Heads albums, done with and without Eno, have persisted in this adept blend of rock and abstract electronics.

Speaking in Tongues is their best outing since *More Songs About Buildings and Food*. Freed from Eno's indulgence in African rhythms, the Heads returned to their native mixture of superb vocals and formative song structures. Outside of the Talking Heads, Byrne and Eno produced the glib *My Life in the Bush of Ghosts* in 1981, an album of tape collage work using broadcast media as input.

TANGERINE DREAM

Electronic Meditation (1970), Ohr OMM556004
Alpha Centauri (1971), Ohr OMM556012
Zeit (1972), Ohr OMM256021
Atem (1972), Ohr OMM566031
Phaedra (1974), Virgin 2010
Rubycon (1975), Virgin 2025
Ricochet (1976), Virgin 2044
Stratosfear (1976), Virgin 2068
Cyclone (1978), Virgin 2097
Force Machine (1978), Virgin 2111
Thief (1981), Elektra-Asylum 5E-521

Tangerine Dream was formed in Germany in 1967 by Edgar Froese and Christoph Franke. Originally conceived as an improvisational rock band, it released its first album, *Elec-*

(Courtesy of JEM Records and Virgin Records.)

tronic Meditation, in 1970. Soon joined by Peter Baumann, the group took on an entirely keyboard-oriented sound laced with drums and distorted guitar. The group is known for its repetitious synthesizer rhythms and spacey sound.

The keyboard sound of Tangerine Dream has been highly influential. Its use of sequencers to create the rhythm and harmonics of its music is a tidy idea borrowed from minimalist composers like Riley, Reich, and Glass. Its middle period (*Phaedra; Rubycon*) embodied the use of string synthesizers to produce lush, cosmic, electronic orchestrations. The group's music has tended to remain the same over the years, however, which lessens its impact on today's music as other, more adventurous artists experiment with the union of rock and electronics. One special niche it has developed is that of the movie soundtrack, one of the more successful of these being for the American film *Thief* (1981).

THROBBING GRISTLE

Second Annual Report (1978), Industrial LTM 1002
D.O.A (1979), Industrial LTM 1036
Twenty Jazz Funk Greats (1979), Industrial
Greatest Hits (1979), Rough Trade US23

This engagingly named rock group played electronic pranks on the punksters for a good three years. Behind the ugly

David Tudor
RAINFOREST IV

(Courtesy of Edition Block.)

facade was a bright group of musicians interested in exploiting pop myths and lacing their rollicking music with obtuse, sometimes rather noisy, sounds. Bright moments include the *Jazz Greats* album as well as the *Greatest Hits* package. At its best, the Throbbing Gristle represented happy chaos.

ISAO TOMITA

Snowflakes Are Dancing (1974), RCA ARL1-0488
Pictures at an Exhibition (1975), RCA ARL1-0838
Firebird (1976), RCA ARL1-1312
The Planets (1976), RCA ARL1-1919
Kosmos (1978), RCA ARL1-2616
Bermuda Triangle (1979), RCA ARL1-2885
Bolero (1980), RCA ARL1-3412

Whereas Carlos is unsurpassed in electronic interpretations of classical keyboard music, Tomita is the master of electronic symphonic works.

DAVID TUDOR

Rainforest IV (1980), Block Gramavision GR-EB 1

Although Tudor's work is often found on collections of Cage's music and others, his solo albums are rare. This recording of one of his electroacoustic pieces documents a performance in Berlin. The piece dates from 1973 and involves the use of sound-generating devices in an environment that the performers move through to activate the sounds. The original "Rainforest" piece was commissioned by the Merce Cunningham Dance Company, with whom Tudor has often worked.

UNITED STATES OF AMERICA

United States of America (1968), Columbia CS-9614

In 1967, Joe Byrd formed an unusual rock ensemble known as the United States of America. Byrd was a young composer with roots in the avant-garde, having worked with La Monte Young and Terry Riley and having cut his teeth on classic electronic music, studying with Richard Maxfield in New York. He and La Monte Young gave their first concerts in the Bank Street loft of Yoko Ono, who was then active as an organizer of happenings.

Byrd formed a "rock" group that then consisted of himself on synthesizer, Dorothy Moskowitz on vocals, Craig Woodson on tabla and electronic and African drums, Gordon Marron on electric violin, and Rand Forbes on fretless bass. This was an esoteric group of musicians, and their music was a hybrid of rock that tried to employ some of the finer points of the avant-garde. The sound was a blend of electronics and voice, often using ring modulation to alter the sound of the lead singer. They were by nature uncompromising and soon disbanded after having recorded an unsuccessful album. It is now a collector's item. The music of the United States of America was surprisingly prophetic in its use of synthesizer and electronic percussion.

EDGARD VARÈSE

The Varèse Album, Columbia MG 31078
Offrandes; Intégrales; Octandre; Ecuatorial (1972), Nonesuch H-71269

A number of good collections such as these are available of the music of the grandfather of the avant-garde. *Poème électronique* from *The Varèse Album* is the classic work of musique concrète that was used in the Philips Pavilion of the Brussels World's Fair in 1958. *Deserts*, from the same album, was one of Varèse's most ambitious combinations of orchestra and tape, and perhaps the best attempt of its kind by any composer. *Ecuatorial*, found on the Nonesuch disc, is notable for its use of two ondes martenots. Composed in 1934, *Ecu-*

atorial is a marvelous example of the music that was composed for the kind of electronic instruments that were played live in the early days.

WHA HA HA

Wha Ha Ha (1984), Re Records RR 17

This extraordinary record contains a selection of music originally released in 1981 on three Japanese albums by the group Wha Ha Ha. Electronics are used heavily in a pop and rock format to ape the style and superficial nature of Western pop music. Pop/rock/jazz/comedy fusion.

RUTH WHITE

Seven Trumps from the Tarot Cards (1968), Mercury Limelight LS 86058
Flowers of Evil (1969) Mercury Limelight LS 86066
Short Circuits (1971), Angel S-36042

Remarkably original work produced in the private studio of independent composer Ruth White, one of the early users of Moog equipment. Inspired studio composition by someone who worked largely outside the circles of the avant-garde.

CHARLES WUORINEN

Time's Encomium (1970), Nonesuch 71225

This piece, composed at the Columbia-Princeton Electronic Music Center, won the 1970 Pulitzer Prize for music, a rare occurrence for an electronic work. Because he used the RCA music synthesizer, the piece is a twelve-tone work using the equal-tempered scale. Wuorinen's chief contribution in this piece was the freedom with which he varied the temporal scale and rhythm of the music with the ease and complex control that is intrinsic to the medium.

IANNIS XENAKIS

Electro-Acoustic Music (1969), Nonesuch H-71246

This is a recording of brilliant electroacoustic music using natural sounds that have been modified electronically. A collection of deep, brooding works, darkened mysteriously by the abstract, nonmusical nature of the sounds. Composed between 1957 and 1968, using the Paris studios of O.R.T.F. Includes a version of *Orient-Occident* (1959–1960) an extended ending that was completed in 1968.

(Used by permission of Frank
Zappa.)

YES

Yes Album (1971), Atlantic 19131
Fragile (1971), Atlantic 19132
Close to the Edge (1972), Atlantic 19133

Skilled and flashy musicianship was the trademark of this
group. Electronics were frequently used as a backdrop to the
rock combo. *Close to the Edge* is a well-developed blend of
rock and electronic music. Later work is repetitious and tedious, although no less skilled.

FRANK ZAPPA AND THE MOTHERS OF INVENTION

Freak Out! (1966), Verve V6-5005-2X
Absolutely Free (1967), Verve V-V6-5013
Lumpy Gravy (1967), Verve V6-8741
We're Only in It for the Money (1967), Verve V6-5045X
Uncle Meat (1969), Bizarre 2Ms-2024
Weasels Ripped My Flesh (1970), Bizarre MS-2028
Waka-Jawaka (1972), Bizarre 2094

In 1966, when his group first became popular, Frank Zappa
was already an admirer of "serious" contemporary music
composers. He knew the work of Varèse, Webern, and Stockhausen, and sought to issue a kind of controlled use of unusual sounds in the context of a rock group. He should be

credited as being perhaps the earliest composer to attempt this in a serious way. He should also be credited with producing an early rock concept album, *Freak Out*, in 1966, almost a full year prior to the Beatles' *Sgt. Pepper*. This album was characterized by odd rhythmic signatures, the addition of orchestral musicians to the rock ensemble, and a wide use of tape effects, including speed changes, echo, and multi-tracking. The final side of *Freak Out* features a twelve-minute cut called "The Return of the Son of Monster Magnet," which is pure musique concrète in the classic sense. In 1967, Frank Zappa produced the *Lumpy Gravy* album, consisting of one ambitious piece of music using amplified symphonic instruments, rock instruments, percussion, and chorus. The entire project was edited like a tape piece in a jocular style not unlike Varèse's. Zappa's work has always been tainted by his tedious sense of humor and has since lost some of its original intrepidness. Even so, he should probably be thought of as the Erik Satie of rock music, and a true original.

Twelve

ANCIENT INSTRUMENTS and RARE RECORDINGS

Even though the modern era of electronic music is only

about thirty-five years old, recordings of classic pieces in

the experimental form are increasingly difficult to come

by. Any recording of electronic music made prior to 1970

will have increasingly collectible value over the coming

years. Most releases of electronic music do not remain in

print very long because they do not sell well in comparison with popular music. Following are some notes regarding a number of collectible items as well as some recordings of "ancient" electronic musical instruments—those that predate the synthesizer era.

RECORDINGS OF SYNTHESIZER PRECURSORS

As the years roll by, it becomes increasingly difficult to locate recorded examples of some of the older electronic musical instruments like the ondes martenot and theremin. Not many recordings were made to begin with, and many of those that were made have long since been deleted from record company catalogs. Following are some discs to look for, a few of which are still available:

ANDRE JOLIVET

Concerto for Ondes Martenot and Orchestra, Westminster XWN-18360 (out of print).

OLIVIER MESSIAEN

Trois petites liturgies de la présence divine, Music Guild S-142 (out of print). This music uses the ondes martenot.
Turangalîla-Symphonie (1949), RCA Victor 2-VIC LSC-7051. Both Messiaen discs use ondes martenot. The second is still in print.

ERIC ROSS

Electronic Études (Op. 18); Songs for Synthesized Soprano (Op. 19) (1982), Doria Records ER-103. This album features the playing of a modern, solid-state theremin in "Floreal" and "Chorale."

MIKLOS ROZSA

Music from Films for Piano and Orchestra, Angel SZ-37757. The *Spellbound* Concerto from the 1945 Hitchcock film *Spellbound*, which featured dream sequences designed by Salvador Dali, includes the eerie sounds of the theremin.

EDGARD VARÈSE

Ecuatorial and other works. Nonesuch H-71269. *Ecuatorial* features two ondes martenots. Although it was originally scored in 1934 for two theremins, the piece has always been performed using the ondes martenot.
Collection: *Les Ondes Martenot*. Works by MESSIAEN, MILHAUD,

JOLIVET, TESSIER. Ades POL 391, 21.007-2. Music using ondes martenot and performed by MFA (Musique Française d'Aujourd'hui).

Collection: *Music for Ondes Martenot.* Works by MESSIAEN (*Fête des belles eaux*, for a sextet of ondes martenot, from 1937); Milhaud (*Suite for Martenot and Piano*, from 1933); Jacques Charpentier (*Lalita*, for ondes Martenot and percussion). Musical Heritage Society MHS-821. This splendid record is still in print and is available from the Musical Heritage Society, 1710 Highway 35, Ocean, NJ 07712. It features the virtuoso ondes martenot playing of Jeanne Loriod, who studied with Maurice Martenot.

CLASSICS OF ELECTRONIC MUSIC

During the 1950s and 1960s, a wide variety of recordings were issued around the world featuring important works of electronic music. In the mid-1950s, the United Nations Educational, Scientific, and Cultural Organization (UNESCO) sponsored the release of two albums featuring the pioneering work being done in musique concrète at the Paris studios of Pierre Shaeffer. This set contained all of the important compositions from his earliest experiments, many of which were composed using disc recorders rather than tape recorders. Some of the pieces are still available on current releases (especially on the European Philips label); they were originally released by Ducretet-Thompson of Paris, with British copies distributed by London Records. The value of these recordings to an electronic-music enthusiast are without question. This set of recordings was referred to briefly in my preceding list of musique concrète albums; following is a complete listing of the contents of the records:

Panorama de la musique concrète no. 1. Works by ARTHUYS (*Boite à musique*), SCHAEFFER and HENRY (*Bidule en ut*), SCHAEFFER (*Étude au piano II, dite étude noire; Étude aux chemins de fer; Étude aux tourniquets; Étude pathétique, dite étude aux casseroles; Variations sur une flûte mexicaine*), HENRY (*Batterie fugace; Concerto des Ambiguïtés; Le voile d'Orphée; Musique sans titre* (parts 5 and 6); *Tam-tam III*). Ducretet-Thompson 320 C 100 and London DTL 93090 (out of print).

Panorama de la musique concrète no. 2. Works by SCHAEFFER and HENRY (*Symphonie pour un homme seul*), SCHAEFFER (*L'oiseau RAI*), HENRY (*Antiphonie; Astrologie; Tam-tam IV*; Vocalise), PHILIPPOT (*Étude I*). Ducretet-Thompson 320 C 102 and London DTL 93121 (out of print).

Another series of records worth scouting down is the Limelight series issued in the United States by Mercury records in the late 1960s. Many of these recordings were drawn from the large body of electronic music that Philips released in Europe in the early 1960s. They included vintage samples of musique concrète from France, as well as some of the more sophisticated extensions of that genre by people like Pierre Henry. Also included were some marvelous domestic releases by Ruth White, two albums of experimental percussion music from the Percussions of Strasbourg, electronic music from the Netherlands and other European nations, and some interesting releases of ragas and other Eastern music. The Limelight releases of electronic music have all been highlighted in the preceding discography, where you can find a listing of the pieces and the LP numbers. These, too, are out of print, but worth searching out.

Finally, I would like to recommend the series of records produced on the Time and Mainstream labels between 1962 and 1973. These were perhaps the most important and adventuresome recordings of experimental music issued during that time, and contain an amazing assortment of works both electronic and instrumental. The entire series was produced by avant-garde composer Earle Brown and began on the Time label but switched (with the same packaging) to the Mainstream designation. As for electronic music, the records ranged from a release of *Cartridge Music* in 1962, to *Live Electronic Improvised* (with MEV and AMM) in the mid-1960s and the Sonic Arts Union in the late-1960s. Brown also managed to include numerous recordings by avant-garde Japanese composers, a movement in music that was unknown in the West at the time. Some of these albums have been listed in the discography; some were released both on Time and Mainstream, with the Time recordings having separate mono and stereo issues. For collectors and enthusiasts, following is a list of the albums showing their contents and respective identification numbers:

CAGE (*Amores*), CAGE and HARRISON (*Double Music*), ROLDAN (*Two Ritmicas*), HARRISON (*Canticle No. 1*), RUSSELL (*Three Dance Movements; Three Cuban Pieces*), COWELL (*Ostinato Pianissimo*)

Concert Percussion for Orchestra, Time S/8000 (stereo), Time 58000 (mono), Mainstream MS/5011

STOCKHAUSEN (*Zyklus; Refrain*), KAGEL (*Transición II*)

Karlheinz Stockhausen/Mauricio Kagel, Time S/8001 (stereo), Time 58001 (mono), Mainstream MS/5003

NONO (*Polifonica; Monodia; Ritmica*), MADERNA (*Serenata No. 2*), BERIO (*Differences*)

Works for Chamber Orchestra, Time S/8002 (stereo), Time 58002 (mono), Mainstream MS/5004

CAGE (*Aria with Fontana Mix*), BERIO (*Circles*), BUSOTTI (*Frammento*)

Berio-Cummings-Busotti-Cage, Time S/8003 (stereo), Time 58003 (mono), Mainstream MS/5005

MAYUZUMI (*Nirvana Symphonie*)

Nirvana Symphonie, Time S/8004 (stereo), Time 58004 (mono)

IVES (*Concord Sonata*) performed by Aloys Kontarsky on piano.

Concord Sonata, Time S/8005 (stereo), Time 58005 (mono), Mainstream MS/5013

KELEMEN (*Études contrapuntiques*), CASTIGLIONI (*Tropi*), FELLEGARA (*Serenata*), YUN (*Musik* for seven instruments)

Kelemen-Castiglioni-Fellegara-Yun, Time S/8006 (stereo), Time 58006 mono

FELDMAN (*Durations*), BROWN (*Music for Violin, Cello, and Piano; Music for Cello and Piano; Hodograph I*)

Feldman-Brown, Time S/8007 (stereo), Time 58007 (mono), Mainstream MS/5007

EVANGELISTI (*Proporzioni*), BERIO (*Sequenza*), MATSUDAIRA (*Somaksah*), CASTIGLIONI (*Gymel*), MESSIAEN (*Merles noir*), MADERNA (*Honeyreves*)

Music for Flute (and Piano), Time S/8008 (stereo), Time 58008 (mono), Mainstream MS/5014

MIYOSHI (*Ondine*), conducted by Tadashi Mori.

Ondine, Time S/2058 (stereo), Time 52058 (mono)

Works by XENAKIS, REYNOLDS, TAKAHASHI, and BROWN, performed by Yuji Takahashi.

New Music for Piano(s), Mainstream MS/5000

Works by P. M. DAVIES, BIRTWISTLE, BEDFORD, and ORTON, performed by the Pierrot Players.

New Music from London, Mainstream MS/5001

Featuring the groups AMM and MEV (*Spacecraft*).

Live Electronic Music Improvised, Mainstream MS/5002

XENAKIS (*Achoripsis*), CLEMENTI (*Triplum*), NILSSON (*Frequenzen; Szene III*), SCHOENBERG (*Drei kleine Stücke*), KOTONSKI (*Canto*), TAKAHASHI (*Six Stoicheia*)

New Music for Chamber Orchestra, Mainstream MS/5008

BOULEZ (*Livre pour quartuor: I, II, V*), SCELSI (*Quartetto d'archi no. 4*), BROWN (*String Quartet 1965*)

New Music for String Quartet, Mainstream MS/5009

ASHLEY (*Purposeful Lady Slow Afternoon*), LUCIER (*Vespers*), BEHRMAN (*Runthrough*), MUMMA (*Hornpipe*)

Sonic Arts Union, Mainstream MS/5010

CAGE (*Cartridge Music*), WOLFF (*Duo for Violinist and Pianist; Summer* for string quartet; *Duet II* for horn and piano)

John Cage-Christian Wolff, Mainstream MS/5015

CAGE (*Six Melodies for Violin and Keyboard*), CRUMB (*Four Nocturnes for Violin and Piano: Night Music II*), YUN (*Gasa*), WUORINEN (*The Long and the Short*). Played by Paul Zukofsky (violin) and Gilbert Kalish (piano).

New Music for Violin and Piano, Mainstream MS/5016

6

GLOSSARY
OF TECHNICAL
AND MUSICAL
TERMS

This glossary contains definitions of technical terms associated with electronic music, as well as many fundamental concepts associated with musical composition. It is thought that this combination of the technical and the musical will be of special assistance to newcomers of both electronic music and composition.

Additive Synthesis   The combining of two or more audio waveforms to create a more complex sound. This may be done to add harmonics to a fundamental tone or to create a dissonant mixture rich in special effects and overtones.

AM   See *Amplitude modulation.*

Amplitude   The loudness of a sound. In electronic music, the maximum value of a waveform from the center of its periodic cycle, which is a function of amounts of AC voltage.

Amplitude Modulation   The use of a control voltage to alter (or modulate) the loudness of an audio signal. This control voltage may come from another audio generator or voltage-controlled amplifier to affect the attack and decay characteristics of a waveform.

Analog System   In an analog instrument sounds are represented in the form of continuously variable physical quantities (waves of electric current). Traditional electronic musical instruments and synthesizers (circa 1900 to the present) use analog techniques. Newer, microprocessor-based systems employ digital synthesis.

Analog-to-Digital Conversion   A conversion of analog quantities, represented by electrical-current patterns, to a digital bit sequence for storage and manipulation in a computer. This technique is used to "digitize" sounds from analog synthesizers, microphones, and electromagnetically amplified instruments (guitars, pianos, etc.).

Atonality   In musical composition, the absence of a tonal center (key). This permits notes of the chromatic, twelve-tone scale to be used independently of one another. Traditional concepts of harmony and dissonance do not apply. The term is often used to describe twelve-tone or serialist music.

Attack   See *Envelope.*

Band-Pass Filter   An electronic filter that allows only those sounds between specified high- and low-frequency cutoff points to be heard. A common component of synthesizers.

Band-Reject Filter   An electronic filter that allows only those sounds above or below specified high- and low-frequency cutoff points to be heard. A common component of synthesizers.

Beat Frequencies   In amplitude modulation, the audio signal that is the result of the mixing of two or more waveforms of near-equal frequencies. The resulting tone is equal in frequency to the differences between the two original signals and will contain periodic beats or frequencies generally characterized by a smooth wavering effect. This is basic to the theremin. The process used to create beat frequencies is *heterodyning.*

Chance Operations   Techniques employed to add elements of randomness to a musical composition. These elements occur independent of the disposition or control of the composer. The use of chance operations was formally pioneered by John Cage, who uses coin-tossing methods derived from the *I Ching* (Chinese *Book of Changes*) to contribute to the composition of his music.

Chromatic Scale   The conventional musical scale of Western music, employing twelve semitones per octave. In this scale, chords, intervals, and progressions of notes in the diatonic scale of a single key are altered by adding notes not found in that key.

Chord   A combination of notes sounded simultaneously, generally no fewer than three.

Computer Music   Music created with the aid of a computer. Types of computer music include (1) that in which the computer helps compose written music for performance by traditional, nonelectronic instruments; (2) that which is composed using a computer and is generated directly by the system through the digital-to-analog conversion of stored information into amplified sound; (3) that generated by an analog synthesizer with the computer providing control-voltage inputs and instructions; (4) the analog-to-digital conversion of sounds coming from analog sources such as synthesizers, microphones, and magnetic pickups, which are manipulated using a computer and then presented through the digital-to-analog conversion of the "digitized" sound; and (5) the interaction of musicians and computers that are programmed to respond to audio input in a real-time setting.

Control Input   An input port on a synthesizer that will accept a control voltage to activate and modulate such components as oscillators, amplifiers, and filters. This is usually a port for a patch cord, although some preset synthesizers may employ dials or slide controls to vary the amount of input.

Control Signal   The small amount of direct current (DC) voltage that is applied to the control input of a voltage-controlled component of a synthesizer (oscillator, amplifier, filter, etc.).

Counterpoint   The use of simultaneous independent melodic lines in a piece of music.

Crescendo   A gradual increase in the loudness of a piece of music.

Decay   See *Envelope*.

Diapason   In a pipe organ, the name given to certain fundamental organ sounds (or stops) that form the foundation of the instrument's character.

Diatonic Scale   A scale using only those notes confined to a single key, and not using naturals, sharps, and flats belonging to another key (as in the chromatic scale).

Digital System   In a computer system, the representation of all quantities of information as a sequence of "on" or "off" electrical pulses or bit patterns. A digital music system is one that employs a computer to store information related to the content or control of a piece of music. This digital information can then be converted to analog signals to generate sounds or control the generation of sounds using an analog voltage-controlled synthesizer.

Digital-to-Analog Conversion   The conversion of digital information stored in a computer system to analog signals. These analog signals may be used to create music directly through a loudspeaker system or to provide control voltages to activate the sound-generating components of an analog synthesizer.

Dissonance   In conventional music, a nonstandard harmonic combination. It may carry an unsettling effect that is in need of being resolved through a more harmonious chord. (Not to be confused with "atonality," which is a system of composition that altogether avoids key centers and chord structures.) Also known as *discord*.

Duration   The length of time that a sound can be heard. The total duration of a sound relates to the attack, sustain, and decay characteristics of a sound. See also *Envelope*.

Echo   The periodic repetition of the same sound with an accompanying decay pattern that decreases the loudness of the sound with each repetition. This effect is commonly achieved through the use of tape recorders with separate record and playback heads. (Not to be confused with "reverberation," which adds depth and resonance to a sound without adding repetition.)

Electroacoustic Music   Music that treats ambient sounds with electronic devices and control. This may be as simple as tape composition using everyday sound sources or may actually modify and change sounds in real-time using various forms of modulation, filtering, and amplification. This differs from purely electronic music, which uses only electronically generated sounds.

Envelope   The attack, sustain, and decay characteristics of a sound. This is a function of amplitude related to the way a sound begins, continues, and ends. "Attack" is the time it takes for a sound to reach maximum loudness. "Decay" refers to the time it takes for a sound to end after having reached maximum loudness. Electronic musical devices offer voltage control over the envelope characteristics of sounds.

Envelope Generator   The component of a synthesizer that sets DC control voltages to regulate the attack, sustain, and decay characteristics of sounds (voltages) produced through oscillators, filters, and amplifiers.

Feedback   In amplified music, the reaction of the system—usually in the form of a sustained whining sound—when a portion of the output is fed back to the input. This can happen when a microphone is placed near a speaker so that it picks up the amplification of the sound it is feeding into the system.

Filter   An electronic processing device that can selectively pass certain frequency bands of a sound. See also *Band-pass filter; Band-reject filter; High-pass filter*; and *Low-pass filter*.

Flanging   See *Phasing*.

FM   See *Frequency modulation*.

Frequency   The pitch of a sound, determined by the number of vibrations produced per second by the sounding body.

Frequency Modulation   In electronic music, the controlling of a signal (such as an oscillator) in order to alter the frequency or pitch of another signal. A variance in the pitch of the control signal will vary the pitch of the output signal in a corresponding amount.

Frequency Spectrum   The audible frequency range of human hearing, which is approximately 20 Hz to 20,000 Hz (*Hz* being a designation for the number of vibrations per second).

Fundamental   The primary note of a chord. In musical acoustics, the lowest frequency component of a sound, to which are added higher partials or overtones. The fundamental tone is generally the loudest component of the sound, and the overtones add color to define the timbre of the sound. Also called the *first harmonic*.

Glissando   A continuous gliding through pitches either up or down the scale.

Harmonics   Numerous frequencies are present in a pitched tone. The *fundamental frequency* is either the lowest or the dominant (loudest) frequency present in the note. Additional frequencies above the fundamental are called *overtones* or *harmonics*. The nature of harmonics in a tone will vary from instrument to instrument and account for the tone color or timbre which distinguishes the sound of one instrument from another. The fundamental frequency or any of the harmonics are called partials of the tone. In electronic music synthesizers, the composer can exercise finite control over the partials of a tone in order to alter its timbral characteristics.

Hertz (Hz)   Designation for the number of cycles per second of a periodic frequency.

Heterodyning   In electronic music, a method for mixing multiple signals of near-equal frequencies that results in a cancellation of the given tones and the creation of beat frequencies or wavering (tremolo) effects. The sound-generating method used in the theremin. A form of *amplitude modulation*.

High-Pass Filter   An electronic filter that only permits frequencies above a specified cutoff point to be heard. A common component of synthesizers.

Imitation   Repetition of a melodic sequence in more than one instrumental voice. The different parts are not presented simultaneously but overlap in time (i.e., one begins before the first is through).

Indeterminacy   A technique for creating music in which the results of a performance are unforeseen and independent of the composition process. A performance of such a work will never occur the same way twice. This approach was pioneered by John Cage, who created the term *indeterminacy* to refer to the creation of his own music.

Interval   The difference in pitch between two notes, also thought of as the distance between notes in a scale.

Inversion   The transposition or turning upside-down of melodies, chords, intervals, themes, or other parts of a piece of music.

Key   A grouping of tones and chords according to their relation to a certain central tone, the "tonic." The name of the key is that of the tonic. Keys adhere to the major or minor scales.

Keyboard Controller   A piano-type keyboard used to activate voltage controls to produce sounds in an electronic-music synthesizer.

Low-Pass Filter   An electronic filter that permits only frequencies below a specified cutoff point to be heard. A common component of synthesizers.

Magnetic Pickup   An electromagnetic device that can detect the oscillations of a vibrating metal element and translate the action into electric current to produce audible frequencies through amplification. Used with electric guitars, pianos, and other instruments.

Major Scale   A scale consisting of the major intervals of the diatonic scale.

Microtone   An interval smaller than the semitone (half-tone). The quarter-tone scale is an example, although any scale may be devised that divides the audible spectrum into smaller components.

Minor Scale   A scale consisting of the minor intervals of the diatonic scale.

Mixer   An audio device for combining or mixing sounds from multiple sources.

Mode   An ordering of the notes of a musical scale in which the difference between modes is not pitch-related (as with different keys) but is defined by the order of tones within a mode. Major and minor modes are two examples.

Modulation   The modification of an electronic sound source through the action of other electronic sources. Frequency modulation and amplitude modulation are two examples. The sound to be modified may be electrical in origin (as from an oscillator) or may be a conversion of an acoustic sound into an electrical signal through the use of a microphone or other pickup.

Monophonic   Capable of playing only one note at a time. Such instruments are used primarily for playing melodies.

Musique Concrète Classic tape-composition techniques as defined by Pierre Schaeffer around 1950. In this genre of electronic music, the only sound sources are recordings of ambient sounds that are then restructured and altered through the physical and electronic manipulation of the material. Musique concrète originated in 1948 through Schaeffer and his work at the studios of Paris radio. He used disc recording and playback to work with sounds prior to the availability of tape recorders in 1950. With the tape recorder, musique concrète techniques were extended to the tape medium. By the mid-1950s, as composers began to combine ambient sounds with electronic sounds, classic musique concrète evolved into the general approach known as tape composition.

Oscillator An electronic device for generating an audio waveform.

Ostinato A persistently repeated melodic, rhythmic, harmonic, or bass series in a piece of music. One of the favorite devices of the minimalist composers.

Overtones See *Harmonics*.

Partial See *Harmonics*.

Pentatonic Scale An ancient musical scale composed of five notes. Equivalent to the five black keys of the piano beginning with F sharp.

Phasing An audio effect created by simultaneously playing an identical passage on two tape recorders while slightly speeding one machine up to go out of synchronization with the other. At the point where synchronization is lost, an unusual "whooshing" sound is produced. Also called *flanging*.

Pink Noise A random noise signal (static) in which all frequencies above 1,000 Hz have been filtered out. Pink noise can be filtered and modulated for electronic-music purposes.

Polyphony In music, the use of multiple parts (i.e., melodies) at the same time. In electronic music, a polyphonic instrument is one that can play more than one note on the keyboard simultaneously (as opposed to "monophonic" systems).

Polyrhythm The use of several different rhythms simultaneously.

Polytonality The use of more than one kay in a piece of music simultaneously.

Presets In an electronic musical instrument, predetermined sounds that can be selected through simple control-panel switches rather than through the manual use of patch cords. A simplified approach to selecting desired voices for an instrument, especially helpful with live-performance instruments.

Progression The advance of the melody or chord structure from one unit to the next.

Reverberation An electronic effect used to add depth and resonance to a sound, typically generated by running an audio signal through a spring device that adds a slight delay to the sound of the original signal. (Not to be confused with "echo," which is the periodic repetition of a sound in a fixed decaying pattern.)

Ring Modulation A form of amplitude modulation in which one input signal is modulated by another to produce a resulting signal that consists of sidebands equal to the sum and difference between the two frequencies. In ring modulation, neither of the original signals is retained as part of the output.

Scale Any defined series of ascending musical notes, such as twelve tones of the chromatic scale. Scales may consist of any mathematically divided series of tones of any intervals.

Sequencer A device for generating a repeatable series of control voltages for the triggering of tonal or percussive sounds in a synthesizer. Sequencers may be analog or digital in design.

Serialism A system of composition that is derived from Schoenberg's twelve-tone atonality and that is concerned with the individual development of specific notes and sequences independent of key and mode considerations. In serial composition, all sound parameters (pitch, volume, duration, envelope, and timbre) are closely controlled for each note. The electronic medium offers a great degree of control over sound and has thus become the vehicle for many serialist composers.

Subsonic   Below the range of human hearing (frequencies under 20 Hz).

Subtractive Synthesis   The modification of electronic sounds through the rejection or filtering of given overtones or frequency ranges.

Synthesizer   A self-contained instrument designed for the generation, modification, amplification, mixing, and presentation of electronic sounds.

Tape Composition   The use of tape recorders and tape-editing techniques for the manipulation of recorded sounds to make music. Originally called musique concrète, it initially involved only the use of ambient, nonelectronic sound sources. The term *tape composition* is broader in scope and includes the manipulation of any recorded sounds, whether electronic or nonelectronic in origin.

Tape Delay   A method for recording sounds in real time and replaying them after regularly spaced intervals. This is done using a single loop of tape that is threaded through the record head of one tape machine and the playback head of another. The distance between the two heads of the two machines determines the length of the delay that will occur.

Tape Loop   A single piece of magnetic tape, spliced end to end. Loops are used to repeat sound patterns over and over upon playback or in tape-delay configurations in real time.

Tape Reversal   The inverting of a recorded tape so that sounds can be played in reverse. A common technique for manipulating sound in tape composition.

Timbre   The quality or nature of a sound, sometimes known as *tone color* in music. Timbre is a sound parameter that is considered independent of pitch and may be illustrated by comparing the sound of the same note played on different instruments (i.e., a piano or a violin playing middle C).

Tremolo   A rapid variation in the amplitude of a single pitch. (Not to be confused with "vibrato," which is a rapid variation in pitch.)

Twelve-Tone Music   A method of composition originated by Arnold Schoenberg in which all twelve notes of the chromatic scale are treated equally and the use of major and minor tonalities is disregarded. In twelve-tone composition, a piece is organized primarily by the patterns of notes rather than by harmonic progression. Has been extended into serialism. Both techniques are often used by experimental music composers. Also called *atonality*.

Ultrasonic   Above the range of human hearing (frequencies over 20,000 Hz).

Variable-Speed Tape Recorder   A tape recorder that is equipped with a clutch mechanism to allow for the continuous adjustment of record or playback speed over a given range. Such machines are used in tape composition to modify sound material that has been recorded.

VCA   See *Voltage-controlled amplifier*.

VCF   See *Voltage-controlled filter*.

VCO   See *Voltage-controlled oscillator*.

Vibrato   A rapid fluctuation in the pitch of a note. (Not to be confused with "tremolo," which is a rapid variance in loudness.)

Vocoder   An electronic-music device designed to modulate the sound of the human voice. This is done via microphone input of vocal sounds and analyzer-modifier electronics that filter or add sidebands to the processed sound.

Voltage Control   In electronic music synthesizers, the use of DC voltages to activate and regulate the generation of sound. Voltage-controlled synthesizers (originating with the Moog in 1965–1966) use oscillators, filters, amplifiers, and other components that can be systemically controlled in this way.

Voltage-Controlled Amplifier   An amplifier component of a synthesizer that can be controlled with voltage inputs.

Voltage-Controlled Filter   A filtering component of a synthesizer that can be controlled with voltage inputs.

Voltage-Controlled Oscillator   An oscillator component of a synthesizer that can be controlled with voltage inputs.

Waveforms   In electronic music, the basic shapes or types of audio signals used for composition. These include sine, pulse, sawtooth, and triangular. Each is characterized by different timbral qualities.

White Noise   A random electronic noise signal (static) containing all audible frequencies. White noise can be filtered and modulated for composition purposes.

Whole-Tone Scale   A musical scale that contains no semitones (half notes). As a result, it only contains six notes of the normal twelve-note scale.

7

INFORMATION
SOURCES

Thirteen

MAIL ORDER RECORD RETAILERS

The following services specialize in selling records and tapes of experimental music. The type of material available from each source ranges from the very experimental to new rock. All of these outfits sell recordings through the mail. Some of these sources are specialty distributors handling many record labels; some are actually independent record companies that sell through the mail as well as through record stores. Most of these outlets have catalogs you can obtain.

Aeon Records, Inc.
604 Princeton
Fort Collins, Colorado 80525
Telephone: (303) 484-0963

> Distributor of contemporary instrumental and electronic music. Many small labels and interesting finds. Home base for Mnemonists, the electronic music collective.

Breakthru' Records (SCANAM MUSIC)
2 Lincoln Square
New York, New York 10023

> European jazz, electronic, instrumental, and progressive rock. Many Scandinavian selections. Artists like Zamla, Pekka Pohjola, Ensemble Oriental.

CRI (Composer's Recordings, Inc.)
170 West 74th Street
New York, New York 10023
Telephone: (212) 873-1250

> They bill themselves as the "oldest and largest record company specializing in contemporary music." CRI is an independent record company with a devotion to the American classical and contemporary classical scene. They often work on a joint basis with composers to sponsor recordings of their work. Operating since the 1950s, they have a vast catalog ranging from the conservative to the ultramodern.

Cross Country
P.O. Box 50416 Dept. 1109
Washington, D.C. 20004

> Distributor of domestic and import postrock, blues, cutouts, and publications.

Electronical Dreams (CLIVE LITTLEWOOD)
Silverton Villa, Higher Bugle
St. Austell
Cornwall PL26 8PY England

> Sells selected albums and cassettes of European electrorock and space music. Not a huge listing, but some very special things that are not available elsewhere. Also willing to swap or search for items.

Euro-Collectibles Enterprises (DAVID H. DELLAPELLE)
P.O. Box 513
DeKalb, Illinois 60115

> European progressive rock and electronic, including artists such as Can, Tangerine Dream, Ash Ra Tempel, Syd Barrett, and items from such countries as Czechoslovakia, Italy, Poland, and Hungary.

Eurock Distribution (ARCHIE PATTERSON)
P.O. Box 13718
Portland, OR 97213

> Distributor of European postrock and experimental music
> from around the world. A large selection of cassettes, and
> some unusual items from Japan. Publishes *Eurock*, a mag-
> azine covering the European electrorock scene.

Folkways Records
43 West 61st Street
New York, New York 10023

> Folkways is a veteran record company that specializes in the
> unusual, the instructional, and the esoteric. They have a pi-
> oneering catalog containing many selections of electronic mu-
> sic, ethnic music, folk music, and blues. They deal with music
> that the large commercial record companies ignore. Excellent
> listings of experimental music.

German News Company, Inc.
218 East 86th Street
New York, New York 10028
Telephone: (212) 288-5500

> Distributor of European imports of contemporary classical,
> mainstream classical, plus jazz on ECM. They handle Wergo,
> EMI, RCA, and many more labels.

Innersleeve
Box 844
Pembroke, Massachusetts 02359

> Distributor of electronic, experimental, rock, and the bi-
> zarre. A nice catalog of many diverse offerings. Many re-
> cordings of Eno, Ultravox, Tangerine Dream, and the Res-
> idents.

Lovely Music, Ltd.
325 Spring Street
New York, New York 10013
Telephone: (212) 243-6153

> Lovely Music is the record label for many of America's best
> known experimental composers, including Robert Ashley,
> Gordon Mumma, Alvin Lucier, Pauline Oliveros, and David

Behrman. Perhaps the most progressive and prolific record company handling the avant-garde.

Lotus Records
23 High Street
Newcastle-Under-Lyme
Staffs, England

Distributor of experimental music recordings, particularly of European origin. Also handles electronic rock recordings.

Micrart Group (P. BONNE)
Industriepark Noord 10 2700
SINT-NIKLAAS Belgium

A formidable collection of cassette releases from western Europe including the groups Autumn, Linear Movement, Micrart, Use, Twilight Ritual, HSR, and Autumn Ense. Meditative music, or in their own words, "neo-platonic light metaphysics."

New Music Distribution Service
500 Broadway
New York, New York 10012
Telephone: (212) 925-2121

Sells domestic and import albums of jazz, contemporary experimental, electronic, and postrock music. One of the largest catalogs in existence, and a very successful operation. Some very hard-to-find labels like Advance as well as the Jazz Composer's Orchestra (their sister organization). Independent labels are their business. Retail store too.

Opus One
Box 604
Greenville, Maine 04441

Opus One is an American record company that has been releasing interesting albums of contemporary music since 1966. Their catalog includes albums by artists such as John Adams, Bulent Arel, Ruth Anderson, Joel Chadabe, John Cage, Lou Harrison, Frederic Rzewski, and Elliot Schwartz. Contact them for their catalog.

Paradox Music Mailorder
20445 Gramercy Place, P.O. Box 2896

Torrance, California 90509
Telephone: (213) 320-1331

Distributes domestic and import postrock and experimental music. Specializing in European electrorock (Tangerine Dream, etc.). Unusual selection, good catalog. Many foreign pressings (Japan, Europe, etc.).

Pop 'n' Roll Family
Arrendegatan 67
58331 Linkoping, Sweden

Distributor of European electrorock music, especially of obscure Swedish groups. Albums and cassettes. In their own words, "Swedish not-commercial weird experimental music, industrial alternative sound for yer mind and body—high quality muzik!" Agreed.

P.P.D.
P.O. Box 30044
Chicago, Illinois 60630

Distributes a wide selection of jazz and avant-garde labels, including Folkways, Dys, CRI, Avant, and Giorno Poetry Systems. A good monthly catalog and update sheet.

Recommended Records
583 Wandsworth Road
London SW8, England

Distributor of unusual rock selections, old and new, particularly of European origin. Founded by Chris Cutler of Henry Cow. If you know him, you have an idea what they handle. A fine update sheet and catalog, although irregular. This trend-setting distributor also produces records under this name as well.

Records International
P.O. Box 1140
Goleta, California 93116-1140

An intriguing emphasis on hard-to-find contemporary classical music and some classics, mainly of western European origin. Records found on such labels as the Donemus Composer's Voice series (contemporary Dutch music), Erato (France), Centre Culturel de Valprivas (France), Hyperion

(England), RCA (Mexico), Deutsche Harmonia Mundi (West Germany), and Finlandia (Finland) make this catalog stand out. They choose their selections with loving care and support their sales with a monthly catalog with loads of descriptive detail.

Stephen Roberts
9003 Old Whipps Mill Road
Louisville, Kentucky 40222

Sells mainstream and new rock, new and used recordings. Very nice selection in a thirty-page catalog. Tends to have some of the more esoteric stuff. LP's and singles. Exceptional prices. Many imports.

Round-Up Records
P.O. Box 147
East Cambridge, Massachusetts 02141

Distributes contemporary classical, rock, and jazz. Labels include 1750 Arch and Rough Trade.

School Kids Records
523 East Liberty Street
Ann Arbor, Michigan 48104
Telephone: (313) 994-8031

This retail store deals in all types of music and offers the most extensive catalog of Japanese pressings of Western music we have ever seen. The first edition of the catalog was 217 pages of listings and covered jazz, rock, soundtracks, blues, reggae, country, and folk recordings. Many releases that are no longer handled in the United States. Very impressive. The catalog is $10. Album prices range from $3.99 to $1,100. Their wholesale branch is called East Side.

Seidboard World Enterprises
75 Bleecker Street
New York, New York 10012

Distributors of domestic and import rock, electronic, avant rock, experimental, and other. Good selection of hard-to-find European material and a special catalog for collectors.

Small Wonder Records
P.O. Box 23

Sudbury, Suffolk CO10 OTF, England
Telephone: (0787) 76206

> Distributes new rock and what is left of hardcore. An impressive selection in twenty-page catalog. Singles and albums, plus some fanzines. Reportedly provide very quick service.

1750 Arch Records
1750 Arch Street
Berkeley, California 94709

> 1750 Arch is one of the more important American record companies that deals almost exclusively with contemporary classical and experimental music. This independent outfit has a reputation for releasing high quality pressings of interesting new music, complete with copious and helpful liner notes. It accepts mail-orders directly, or you may order material through some of the other distributors listed in this directory.

Systematic Record Distribution
Berkeley Industrial Court, Space 1
729 Heinz Avenue
Berkeley, California 94710
Telephone: (415) 845-3352

> Distributes domestic and import rock, postrock, and contemporary music. A marvelous catalog of material ranging from hardcore (what is left of it) to the experimental. One of the best.

Wayside Music
P.O. Box 6517
Wheaton, Maryland 20906

> Sells domestic and import avant-garde, rock, postrock, and other new music. Large selection of hard-to-find cutouts. Very diversified selection and inexpensive prices. One of the veterans in this genre, and consistently one of the finest. Write for their catalog; you will be amazed.

Fourteen

PERIODICALS

Artist/Musiker
Droste Verlag GmbH
Abt. Ed. Lintz Verlag
Pressehaus am Martin-Luther-Platz
Postfach 11 22
D-4000 Dusseldorf 1, West Germany

CLEM (Contact List of Electronic Musicians)
Alex Douglas
P.O. Box 86010
North Vancouver, British Columbia V7L 4J5, Canada

> This newsletter is really a directory of people to contact in
> the world of electronic music. A marvelous and valuable
> resource.

Computer Music Journal
P.O. Box E
Menlo Park, California 94025

Keyboard Magazine
20085 Stevens Creek
Cupertino, California 95014

Ear Magazine East
New Wilderness Foundation
325 Spring Street
New York, New York 10013

> A highly diverse and artistic tabloid covering the avant-garde, primarily of New York activities and artists.

Electronics and Music Maker
Maplin Publications
242 London Road
Westcliff-on-Sea
Essex, England

Eurock
Archie Patterson
P.O. Box 13718
Portland, Oregon 97213

> A highly informative magazine covering the European technorock scene.

High Fidelity
ABC Leisure Magazines
825 7th Avenue
New York, New York 10019

> The all-American magazine of audio equipment does not include as many record reviews as it used to on new music, but there are still a few lurking in there sometimes.

Music Maker
Delta Magazines bv
Postbus 16
NL-6500 AA Nijmegen, Holland

Music World
Central House
42 Rayne Road
Braintree, Essex CM7 7QP, England

New Music Chicago
Box 10742
Chicago, Illinois 60610-0742

> A newsletter designed to keep people up to date on avant-garde concerts and events in Illinois. Published by a not-for-profit cooperative of artists.

Perspectives of New Music
Bard College
Annandale, New York 12504

> The long-lived journal on new music. Intelligent, academic.

Recordings of Experimental Music
104 Fern Avenue
Collingswood, New Jersey 08108

> This is my own magazine. We review disc and cassette releases of experimental music, and publish interviews (e.g., Cage, Ashley), and discographies.

Stereo Review
Ziff Davis Publishing Co.
One Park Avenue
New York, New York 10016

> Another American standard that is heavy on record reviews of the classics and rock, but little experimental.

Village Voice
842 Broadway
New York, NY 10003

> Even outsiders will like reading this tabloid about activities in New York. Many good reviews and news concerning experimental music events.

A number of interesting publications concerning electronic and experimental music have come and gone over the years, but they are still available in well-stocked music libraries, and I urge you to seek them out.

Source: Music of the Avant-Garde. 9 issues, 1967–1971. *Source* often included recordings as part of its packaging, including one issue featuring "The Wolfman," by Robert Ashley.

Die Reihe. 8 issues, 1955–1962. The title means "The Row." Jointly produced by Herbert Eimert and Karlheinz Stockhausen, this journal featured many technical articles on early electronic-music techniques and aesthetics, as well as writings on serial music (from which the title of the journal is derived). English translations of the journal were done between 1958 and 1968 and made available in America through the Theodore Presser music publishing company of Bryn Mawr, Pennsylvania.

Electronic Music Review. 7 issues, 1967–1969. A flexible and ambitious journal that featured articles on technique and equipment, as well as a first publication of Hugh Davies' massive compilation of all electronic musical works, which has since been made available through MIT Press as the *International Electronic Music Catalog*.

Fifteen

SELECTED BIBLIOGRAPHY

Apollonio, Umbro (editor), Futurist Manifestos, Viking Press, New York. 1973.

Austin, William W., *Music in the 20th Century*. Norton, New York. 1966.

Backus, John, *The Acoustical Foundations of Music*. Norton, New York. 1969.

Bacon, Tony, editor, *Rock Hardware*. Harmony Books, New York, and Quill, London. 1981.

Barbour, J. Murray, "Music and Electricity," *Papers of the American Musicological Society*, December 29–30, 1937.

Basart, Ann Phillips, *Serial Music: A Classified Bibliography of Writings in Twelve-Tone and Electronic Music*. University of California Press, Berkeley. 1961.

Cage, John, *Silence*. Wesleyan University Press, Middletown, Conn., and Columbia University Press, New York. 1961.

———, *A Year from Monday*. Wesleyan University Press, Middletown, Conn. 1967.

———, *Notations*. Something Else Press, New York. 1969. A compilation of experimental music scores, edited with Alison Knowles.

————, *M: Writings '67–'72*. Wesleyan University Press, Middletown, Conn. 1973.

Chamberlin, Hall, *Musical Applications of Microprocessors*. Hayden, Rochelle Park, N.J. 1980.

Cott, Jonathan, *Stockhausen—Conversations with the Composer*. Simon and Schuster, New York. 1973.

Cross, Lowell, *A Bibliography of Electronic Music*. University of Toronto Press, Toronto. 1966.

————, "Electronic Music: 1948–1953," *Perspectives of New Music*, Fall/Winter 1968.

Crowhurst, Norman, *Electronic Musical Instruments*. Tab Books, Blue Ridge Summit, Pa. 1977.

Davies, Hugh, *International Electronic Music Catalog*. MIT Press, Cambridge, Mass. 1968.

Deutsch, Herbert A., *Synthesis*. Alfred, New York. 1976.

Douglas, Alan, *The Electronic Musical Instrument Manual*. Tab Books, Blue Ridge Summit, Pa. 1976.

Ewen, David, *Composers of Tomorrow's Music*. Dodd Mead, New York. 1971.

Griffiths, Paul, *A Guide to Electronic Music*. Thames and Hudson, London. 1980.

Henderson, David, *'Scuse Me While I Kiss the Sky: The Life of Jimi Hendrix*. Bantam/Doubleday, New York. 1981.

Holmes, Thomas B., "John Cage Interview," *Recordings of Experimental Music*, Vol. 3, no. 3, December 1981.

Holmes, Thomas B., "Robert Ashley Interview," Recordings of Experimental Music, Vol. 4, no. 2, November 1983.

Horn, Delton T., *Electronic Music Synthesizers*. Tab Books, Blue Ridge Summit, Pa. 1980.

Kirby, Michael, *Futurist Performance*. Dutton, New York. 1971.

Kostelanetz, Richard, *John Cage*. Praeger, New York. 1970.

Logan, Nick, and Woffinden, Bob, *The Illustrated Encyclopedia of Rock*. Harmony Books, New York, and Salamander Books, London. 1977.

Luening, Otto, *The Odyssey of an American Composer*. Scribners, New York. 1980.

Machlis, Joseph, *Introduction to Contemporary Music*. Norton, New York. 1961.

Mackay, Andy, *Electronic Music: The Instruments, Music and Musicians*. Control Data, Minneapolis, and Harrow House, London. 1981.

Mathews, Max V., *The Technology of Computer Music*. MIT Press, Cambridge, Mass. 1969.

Miessner, Benjamin F., "Electronic Music and Instruments," *Proceedings of the Institute of Radio Engineers*. Vol. 24, no. 11, November 1936.

Myers, Rollo H., editor, *Twentieth-Century Music*. Orion, New York. 1968.

Nyman, Michael, *Experimental Music: Cage and Beyond*. Schirmer, New York. Rev. ed. 1981.

Rhea, Thomas L., "The Evolution of Electronic Musical Instruments in the United States," Ph.D. thesis, George Peabody College for Teachers, Nashville, Tenn. 1972.

Roxon, Lillian, *Rock Encyclopedia*. Grosset and Dunlap, New York. 1969.

Russell, J. P., *The Beatles on Record*. Scribners, New York. 1982.

Schafer, R. Murray, *The Tuning of the World*. Knopf, New York. 1977.

Schwartz, Elliot, *Electronic Music: A Listener's Guide*. Praeger, New York. 1975.

Stockhausen, Karlheinz, "Electronic and Instrumental Music," *Die Reihe*. Vol. 5., 1959.

Strange, Allen, *Electronic Music: Systems, Techniques and Controls*. Brown, New York. 1972.

Stuckenschmidt, H. H., *Twentieth-Century Music*. McGraw-Hill, New York. 1969.

Tjepkema, Sandra L. *A Bibliography of Computer Music*. University of Iowa Press, Iowa City. 1981.

Trythall, Gilbert, *Principles and Practice of Electronic Music*. Grosset and Dunlap, New York. 1973.

Whitney, John, *Digital Harmony: On the Complementarity of Music and Visual Art*. Byte, Peterborough, N.H. 1980.

York, William, *Who's Who in Rock Music*. Scribners, New York. 1982.

Sixteen

EQUIPMENT SUPPLIERS

Arp Instruments, Inc.
45 Hartwell Avenue
Lexington, Massachusetts 02173
  Synthesizers.

Bode Sound Company
1344 Abington Place
N. Tonawanda, New York 14120
  Synthesizer effects units.

Casio, Inc.
15 Gardner Road
Fairfield, New Jersey 07006
  Electronic keyboards and synthesizers.

Crumar/Music Technology, Inc.
105 Fifth Avenue.
Garden City Park, New York
11040
  Electric pianos and keyboard
instruments.

EMS/EMSA
269 Locust Street
Northampton, Massachusetts
01060
  Synthesizers.

Fairlight Instruments USA
11426 Santa Monica Boulevard
West Los Angeles, California
90025
  Digital synthesizers.

Fender
CBS Musical Instruments
1300 East Valencia Drive
Fullerton, California 92634
  Electric pianos and guitars.

Gibson
Norlin Music, Inc.
7373 North Cicero Avenue
Lincolnwood, Illinois 60646
  Electric guitars

Hammond Organ Company
4200 West Diversey
Chicago, Illinois 60639
   Electric organs.

Korg/Unicord
89 Frost Street
Westbury, New York 11590
   Synthesizers.

Linn Electronics Inc.
18720 Oxnard St.
Tarzana, California 91356
   Electronic percussion devices.

Mellotron
36 Main Street
Port Washington, New York 11050
   Distributors of the Mellotron
in the U.S.

Moog Music, Inc.
2500 Walden Avenue
Buffalo, New York 14225
   Synthesizers.

MXR
Musical Products Group
740 Driving Park Avenue
Rochester, New York 14613
   Effects units.

New England Digital Corp.
Box 546
White River Junction, Vermont
05001
   Manufacturers of the Syncla-
vier.

Novatron
Streetly Electronics
388 Aldridge Road
Streetly, Sutton, Coldfield
West Midlands B742DT, England
   Manufacturers of the mello-
tron.

Oberheim Electronics, Inc.
1455 19th Street
Santa Monica, California 90404
   Synthesizers.

Octave-plateau Electronics Inc.
51 Main Street
Yonkers, New York 10701
   Manufacturers of the Voyerra
polyphonic synthesizer.

PAIA Electronics, Inc.
1020 West Wilshire Boulevard
Oklahoma City, Oklahoma 73116
   Makers of synthesizer kits.

PPG
1638 W. Washington Boulevard
Venice, California 90291
   Manufacturers of the PPG Music Computer System, a digital
synthesizer.

Revox/Studer Revox America, Inc.
1819 Broadway
Nashville, Tennessee 37203
   Tape recorders.

Rhodes
CBS Musical Instruments
1300 East Valencia Drive
Fullerton, California 92634
   Electric pianos.

Roland Corporation U.S.
7200 Dominion Circle Avenue
Los Angeles, California 90040
   Synthesizers.

Seiko Musical Products
Kaman Music Distributors
P.O. Box 507
Bloomfield, Connecticut 06002
   Digital synthesizers.

Sequential Circuits, Inc.
3051 North First Street
San Jose, California 95134
   Synthesizers.

Siel Music Technology Inc.
105 5th Avenue
Garden City Park, New York
11040
   Synthesizers.

Syntauri Corporation
3506 Waverly Street
Palo Alto, California 94306
   Digital synthesizers for microcomputers.

Teac Corporation of America
7733 Telegraph Road
Montebello, California 90640
   Tape recorders.

360 Systems
18730 Oxnard Street #215
Tarzana, California 91356
   Synthesizers.

Wersi USA
P.O. Box 5318
Lancaster, Pennsylvania 17601
   Synthesizers.

Wurlitzer Company
403 East Gurler Road
De Kalb, Illinois 60115
   Electric organs and pianos.

**Yamaha International
Corporation**
P.O. Box 6600
Buena Park, California 90622
   Synthesizers and keyboards.

Index